A SLAVE

in the

WHITE HOUSE

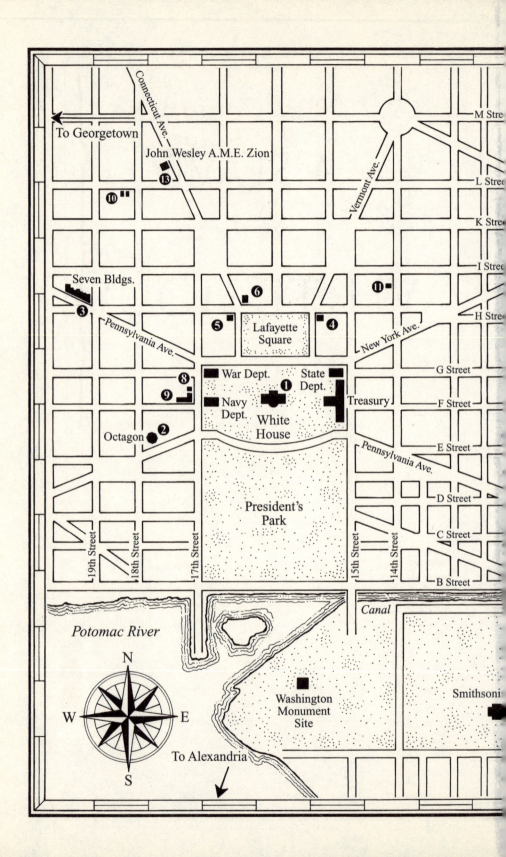

To Georgetown

Connecticut Ave.

M Stre

Vermont Ave.

L Stre

K Stre

I Stre

John Wesley A.M.E. Zion

13

10

Seven Bldgs.

6

H Stre

3

Pennsylvania Ave.

5

Lafayette Square

4

11

New York Ave.

G Street

War Dept.

State Dept.

1

Treasury

F Street

8

Navy Dept.

White House

9

Octagon **2**

Pennsylvania Ave.

E Street

D Street

President's Park

C Street

19th Street

18th Street

17th Street

15th Street

14th Street

B Street

Potomac River

Canal

N

W E

S

Washington Monument Site

Smithsoni

To Alexandria

Paul Jennings's Washington

❶- White House
❷- Octagon
❸- Seven Buildings
❹- Dolley Madison house
❺- John Gadsby house
❻- Daniel Webster house 1841–1844
❼- Daniel Webster house 1845–1852
❽- Sarah Smith house
❾- Winder Building, pension office,
   PJ's workplace 1851–1854
❿- PJ's houses, his home from
   1854–1860 & 1867–1874
⓫- PJ's address 1860–1867
⓬- Patent Office Building, pension office,
   PJ's workplace 1854–1867
⓭- Church where PJ married in 1870

Scale of Miles

0   1/4   1/2

w York Ave.

9th Street

7th Street

5th Street

4th Street

3rd Street

2nd Street

1st Street

North Capitol Street

Louisiana Ave.

Indiana Ave.

Center
Market

Pennsylvania Ave.

Canal

U.S. Capitol

Maryland Ave.

To Wharves

To Navy Yard

A SLAVE

in the

WHITE HOUSE

PAUL JENNINGS AND THE MADISONS

Elizabeth Dowling Taylor

with

Foreword by Annette Gordon-Reed

and

A Colored Man's Reminiscences of James Madison
by Paul Jennings

palgrave
macmillan

A SLAVE IN THE WHITE HOUSE
Copyright © Elizabeth Dowling Taylor, 2012, 2013, 2014.

This 2014 edition printed for Barnes & Noble, Inc.

First published in hardcover in 2012 by PALGRAVE
MACMILLAN® in the United States—a division of St. Martin's
Press LLC, 175 Fifth Avenue, New York, NY 10010.

Palgrave® and Macmillan® are registered trademarks in the United
States, the United Kingdom, Europe and other countries.

ISBN 978-1-137-27973-6

Library of Congress Cataloging-in-Publication Data
is available from the Library of Congress.

A catalogue record of the book is available from the British Library.

Design by Letra Libre, Inc.

10 9 8 7 6 5 4 3 2 1

Printed in the United States of America.

This book is dedicated to

Luke Taylor,

my son and inspiration.

I AM A PROUD AMERICAN
14 February 1960

I have every reason to be proud of being an American. My ancestors contributed so much to make this country what it is today. They fought to give America its freedom, even gave their lives. They have done the same in every war since. Thus, they have helped to preserve America. They nursed it in its infancy and for two centuries sweated and suffered as slaves to lay the foundation of its great wealth. Today, we find ourselves on the threshold of a new era ushering in the type of freedom for all for which my fore-parents sacrificed so much.

—*C. Herbert Marshall, M.D.*

Dr. Herbert Marshall was the great-grandson of Paul Jennings. His statement for "I Am a Proud American" Day was published in the *Negro History Bulletin,* organ of the Association for the Study of Negro Life and History, in 1960. It is reproduced here with the kind permission of the Association for the Study of African American Life and History (www.asalh.org).

CONTENTS

◆

Eight pages of photographs appear between pages 134 and 135.

ACKNOWLEDGMENTS

IT IS A PLEASURE TO ACKNOWLEDGE THOSE COL-leagues and friends who generously gave of their time and expertise in reviewing part or all of the manuscript: Catherine Allgor, Andrew Burstein, Bruce Carveth, Breena Clark, Amy Larrabee Cotz, William Freehling, Ralph Ketcham, David Mattern, Drew McCoy, Matthew Reeves, Mary Kay Ricks, Leni Sorensen, Lucia Stanton, John Taylor, and Marsha Williamson. I have benefited immeasurably from their comments. Any errors of fact or interpretation that remain are mine alone.

The research that the book is based on was facilitated by support from a number of institutions. At the Montpelier Foundation, I extend my appreciation to president Michael Quinn, board members Elinor Farquhar, Greg May, Hunter Rawlings, and Roger Wilkins, and staff members Thomas Chapman, Christian Cotz, and Peggy Vaughn. At the National Trust for Historic Preservation, I am especially grateful to Max van Balgooy, and at the White House Historical Association, to Neil Horstman and John Riley. I also thank White House curator William Allman. Other individuals who supported this work with information, discussion, or encouragement include Will Harris, Lee Langston-Harrison, Deborah Lee, David Levering Lewis, Betty Monkman, Peter Onuf, Carla Peterson, Kym Rice, Holly Shulman, Susan Stahlberg, Karen Williams, and Michael R. Winston.

Many long days searching archives at various research facilities were rewarded by fellowship among researchers, and I particularly recognize Barbara Bates, Mary Belcher, Susan Borchardt, John Sharp, Doreen Stevens, and Beverly Veness. I acknowledge, too, the kind assistance from staff members Jeffrey Flannery and Julie Miller at the Library of Congress, Robert Ellis at the National Archives and Records Administration, William Branch and Ali Rahmann at the District of Columbia Archives, and Yvonne Carignan at the Historical Society of Washington, DC.

Over the final six months of writing this book, I was generously supported by a fellowship through the Virginia Foundation for the Humanities at the University of Virginia. I am grateful to Margaret Jordan, Mary Alexander, and all the donors who made the fellowship possible, and to the foundation's president, Robert Vaughn.

Thanks to my literary agent, Michelle Tessler, and to Palgrave Macmillan assistant editor Isobel Scott for steering me through the publication process. I am very grateful to Annette Gordon-Reed for the thoughtful foreword that opens the book and to Rick Britton for the original maps and other graphics that illustrate it.

Last, I thank from the heart two families—my own and the Jennings family—for the steadfast support and encouragement that has sustained me through this long labor of love. Forever indebted, I am fondly yours.

FOREWORD

ANONYMITY IS THE USUAL FATE OF THE MILLIONS OF people who were enslaved in America during the seventeenth, eighteenth, and nineteenth centuries. With no access to legalized marriage and family life, no right to make contracts or enter into business relationships, American slaves rarely entered the public record of their own accord. Instead, they more often entered as property: the subject of sales, division of estates, and, in extreme cases, when they were participants in criminal cases. They do, of course, appear in private documents. The family letters of slave owners refer to the enslaved, very often those who served in the household and were closely involved in the day-to-day life of the masters and mistresses and their children. The business of slavery also required compiling lists of the names and configurations of families as slave owners kept track of the human beings over whom they exercised power. While the family letters of slave owners and their inventories of their human property can sometimes give us clues and starting points for considering the lives of the enslaved, they do not begin to get at the complexity of lives lived in bondage. For the most part, the feelings, thoughts, and yearnings of the enslaved will remain hidden under the blanket oppression of the slave system. Their own assessments of the people who enslaved them and other whites are also extremely rare. Every now and then a few people, because of circumstances and fortuitous timing, were able to escape the shroud of anonymity. Paul Jennings was just such a person.

The circumstances: Paul Jennings was born in 1799 at Montpelier, the Virginia plantation of James Madison. Madison had been on the national scene for over a decade as a legislator in the state and national governments and as one of the principal shapers of the United States Constitution. Jennings was mixed race; his mother was of African and Indian ancestry, his father an Englishman. It was not the rule, but it was frequently the case that mixed-raced enslaved people served within the household at Virginia plantations. They were maids to the mistresses of plantations, child companions/"minders" to the white children of the owners, and valets to the masters of the house. This type of proximity is often characterized as a form of privilege. But the story told in the pages of this book shows that it was a mixed privilege at best. Proximity to slave owners meant being more directly subject to their needs, both whimsical and serious. Also, when members of the family traveled, their enslaved servants had to travel with them, whether they wanted to or not.

As readers will see, the Madisons' travels had a profound effect on the course of Jennings's life. First and foremost, he moved beyond the confines of the plantation where he was born to experience the ways and mores of another more complicated society. When James Madison went to Washington as President in 1809, Jennings went along to serve in the White House. In that still-underdeveloped capital, he saw free blacks, a sight that undoubtedly helped shape his view of the world and, perhaps, put the seed in his mind that he too would one day become a free man. He was also able to observe not only two of the most well-known figures in American history: the Madisons at the height of their power and influence; he saw dignitaries foreign and domestic who called on the First Couple. It must be remembered that he viewed these proceedings as an enslaved man with all the limitations of that status. There is little doubt, however, that his observations gave him valuable insights into the workings of the world and how he might improve his place in it.

As for timing, Jennings was in the White House at a crucial period in American history. What some called "Mr. Madison's War"—the War of 1812—provided an occasion for Jennings to show his courage and heroism and to test his mettle. When the Madisons' days in the White House were over, Jennings had reached maturity, and he became the former President's valet at Montpelier. This position put him in even more intimate and daily contact with the man called the Father of the American Constitution. The totality of his experiences with the Madisons ultimately would enable him to do something that had never been done before: produce a White House memoir that included an intimate look at the life of a president and, then, former president. That memoir, discussed in these pages, stands as a singular document in the history of slavery and the early American republic.

James Madison's death in 1836 and Dolley Madison's return to Washington in 1837 brought Jennings back to the city where he had spent his formative years. Readers will note evidence of tension between the flamboyant former First Lady and the man who had served in her household from boyhood. Jennings's final period in the Madison household is a stark reminder of the true predicament of the so-called privileged house slave, showing what it really meant for human beings to be treated as property. In the end, proximity to the master or mistress of the household did not translate into respect or affection, particularly when the interests of the enslaved person bumped against the economic interests of the people who owned them.

Although the circumstances surrounding the end of his time in the Madison household were stressful (and make for sobering reading about the character of Dolley Madison), Jennings, who was well known in Washington, ultimately became a free man because of his connections to the political world—specifically to Daniel Webster. Jennings's dealings with the great orator represented a startling turnabout in the life of a man who had spent all of his forty-eight years in slavery. Through a combination of luck and personal determination, Jennings was able to begin his life anew.

Jennings made the most of his time as a free man, becoming a pillar of the community and a property owner, working for the U.S.

government, and doing what he could to help others along the way. It would be wrong simply to read his story as one of triumph. Jennings's progress through life showcases the oppression at the heart of the American slave system. Jennings was an intelligent man forced to live in the service of others. He developed his talents and character in spite of the society into which he was born. It is proper to highlight his achievements, but it is also important to consider how much further he could have gone if slavery and white supremacy had not blighted his existence. His is a life to marvel at, but one that invites deep and clear-eyed consideration of America's past.

Annette Gordon-Reed

AUTHOR'S NOTE

"Throughout history, the powers of single black men flash, here and there, like falling stars, and die sometimes before the world has rightly gauged their brightness."

—W. E. B. Du Bois

IN 1865 A SLIM VOLUME TITLED *A Colored Man's Reminiscences of James Madison* was published. It offered an intriguing viewpoint from a former slave who had a shared history with James and Dolley Madison. The person identified in the title as "a colored man" was Paul Jennings, who was born as property on James Madison's Virginia plantation, Montpelier, in 1799 and died bequeathing valuable property in Northwest Washington, DC, to two sons in 1874. Early in the *Reminiscences,* Jennings recalled, "When Mr. Madison was chosen President, we came on and moved into the White House." The "we" included Jennings because he was selected from among Montpelier's approximately one hundred slaves for the household staff of the President's mansion. Jennings's opportunity to go to Washington placed him at the scene of tumultuous current events.

As one of a limited number of slave memoirs, *A Colored Man's Reminiscences of James Madison* is a precious document. It has added significance as the first White House memoir. While it has been cited by scholars over the years and the text can be found on the Internet, it is not widely known, and it has never been published in a new edition since the 1865 original. The only dedicated treatment of Jennings in the historical literature is a 1983 article in the journal *White House History.*[1]

As the title implies, the *Reminiscences* concentrates not on the author and his life but, typical for the time, on the "Great Man." Certainly, one of the reasons Jennings matters is because of his association with James and Dolley Madison. What counts, however, are not insider anecdotes about newsmakers with whom Jennings interacted as a servant, but rather what his sustained contact with these history-making personages might have taught him, as well as what is revealed about the character of the Madisons when the focus is their relationship with a given household slave. Wishing that Jennings had included more of his personal story in the *Reminiscences,* I began to research it myself. I located a variety of primary sources that allowed me to piece together Jennings's own biography; uncovered the circumstances behind the original publication of the *Reminiscences;* and made contact with living descendants of three of Jennings's children, who shared their family histories. The interpretive biography of Paul Jennings presented here is followed by the full text of *A Colored Man's Reminiscences of James Madison.*

It is a striking contradiction that Founding Fathers George Washington, Thomas Jefferson, and James Madison were slave owners, even during their service as Presidents of a new republic devoted to upholding individual liberties. Mount Vernon, Monticello, and Montpelier were lorded over by the general who won the War for Independence, the author of the Declaration of Independence, and the architect of the Constitution and Bill of Rights, respectively. As slaveholders these men were not remarkable. Slave life at their Presidential plantations was typical for the time and place. On the other hand, there was a lot about Paul Jennings's particular experience that was exceptional because of his association with James Madison, though it might have been inconsequential without Jennings's intellectual ability and emotional grounding. Serving as Madison's factotum, he was poised and motivated to take advantage as opportunities came up. Paul Jennings's story is an extraordinary journey from slavery to freedom within the highest circles of ideas and power. It is the story of his complicated relationship with James Madison; of his even more complicated relationship with the widowed Dolley Madison, who broke her promise to free him; and of the role of Senator Daniel Webster, who lent Jennings his purchase price. It is the story of Jennings's efforts to help seventy-seven still-enslaved men, women, and children reach freedom in the greatest-scale-ever-attempted slave escape. And it is the story of a vital antebellum African-American community in the nation's new capital that included the families of ex-slaves of Presidents Washington, Jefferson, and Madison.

Far too often in the past, the history of slavery and the stories of African Americans have been ignored, marginalized, or misrepresented. Slaves were not nameless, faceless groups of sullen or, alternatively, nonsensically happy people walking to the fields or big house each morning and back to their cabins at night with no real sphere of action or imagination. One key to appreciating our true African-American heritage is to examine personal journeys. Slaves were individuals with their own unique traits, talents, responses, and desires; they were members of families and households. They tried, like all people, whatever their circumstances, to infuse meaning and gratification into their lives. When slaves were queried by whites, there were candor issues. The Montpelier slaves seemed "happy and contented" to the visitor who reported, "They will tell you that Mr. Madison was the best man they ever saw, and speak to you of Mrs. M. as one of the kindest and most excellent of mistresses."[2] The search for historical truth is a complex and tentative exploration, and those in power tend to control the prevailing interpretation.

The process of correcting the American Master Narrative is ongoing. Those researching African-American history need to consider how writers before them used or privileged certain sources while giving others short shrift or discrediting them altogether. There was a time when slave narratives had to be "certified" by "upstanding" whites to be considered legitimate, though the testimonies of slave owners never required a similar vetting process. Even today some consider any product from an abolitionist's pen suspect or caution against modern or revisionist interpretations. To tease out answers and insights concerning Jennings's family, associates, experiences, and challenges, I consulted a wide variety of sources. In addition to seeking primary documents from courthouses and archives, I scrutinized period publications (including so-called abolitionist newspapers) and sought out diaries and narratives of Jennings's African-American contemporaries, even as I studied the canon of letters and memoirs from the Madisons and their associates.

As I worked up the Jennings family genealogy, I attempted to identify and contact living descendants. Of the three children mentioned in Paul Jennings's will, I had leads to reach descendants of daughter Frances and son John, but none for son Franklin. Finally solving Franklin's line to the living generations led me to the keeper of the Jennings family oral history, Paul Jennings's great-granddaughter, Sylvia Jennings Alexander. Mrs. Alexander lived with her daughter Mary in a spacious house in the Virginia countryside. I drove there for the first time on a Sunday afternoon in June 2008. Mary, with whom I had set up my date, answered the door, then left me in the living room while she went for her mother. Before she did, she pointed out Paul Jennings's daguerreotype on the wall. I was thrilled by it. I always assumed that should I be lucky enough to find a photograph of Jennings it would portray him in old age: I would look into the face but not really be able to sense the vital man. But here he was in his prime: fierce, light-colored eyes set in a handsome face that showed a formidable bearing and revealed at once his mixed ethnic heritage. Mrs. Alexander came in using a walker, and she and Mary sat together on a couch with their ancestor's likeness behind them. Mrs. Alexander had blue eyes and skin that was notably smooth, given her 93 years. She was definitely on top of her game when it came to recalling family history, and she was a gifted storyteller. She would take on the speaking voice of "Grandpa

Frank" in telling certain tales. Her stories went right back to Paul Jennings's time. She was steeped in the family traditions, having spent many of her early years in the home of her grandfather, who lived to be ninety. To interview, in 2008, a slave descendant who can contribute historical content that goes "back to slavery days" is definitely exceptional. Sylvia Jennings Alexander has been a rich source of knowledge in my quest to learn about Paul Jennings.

I have a great appreciation for oral history. Is it always accurate? Of course not—but neither are written sources. As researchers, we listen, we respect, we include, then we go on with the investigation. The liabilities are worth the benefits. This kind of intelligence is unique; there is no equivalent in the "records," especially with African-American history, suppressed as it was. Mrs. Alexander's description of how Paul Jennings acquired the skills to read and write meshed perfectly with what I had been discovering about him in other ways. I asked her how her grandfather referred to his father, and she answered "Pap." Ah! That helped confirm the legitimacy of a source, problematic because it had been written as a dramatization, where Jennings was referred to as Pap.[3] You don't find that in the archives. I returned to the Alexander home many times. I became familiar with all the family photographs on the walls; the heavy family Bible was taken down from a high shelf for my inspection; I was shown Franklin Jennings's Civil War swords.

I shared what I had discovered about Paul Jennings with his descendants. One of them informed me that her twenty-something son claimed that learning about his ancestor through my research was "a life-changing experience—I did not know black people did things like that then." Every schoolchild knows about the accomplishments of James Madison, but the story of Paul Jennings's deliberate and courageous pursuit of that most American of promises, the right to rise, offers fresh perspectives and sensibilities to all Americans.

CHAPTER ONE

"Raised and Nurtured"

On or about 28 February 1801, Montpelier, the Madison plantation in Orange County, Virginia

The old master died in the dullness of February. On their way to the burial in the family graveyard, the house servants passed by the slave graveyard where most of them expected to be buried some day. It was cold and they walked on, passing between the fallow tobacco fields to the east and the original homestead to the west. The Madison family graveyard was located in the backyard of this first home site, the main dwelling long burned to the ground and supplanted by the Georgian mansion whence they had started their third-mile informal procession. Once the household was circled around the open grave, the house servants raised expectant eyes to the new master of Montpelier, James Madison Jr., standing next to his mother, Nelly. There was this day at Montpelier another mother and son present. The mother's name is unknown. The name of the toddler at her skirts was Paul Jennings.

From the traditions shared by elders of the earlier enslaved generations, Paul Jennings's mother would have been aware of the history of the Montpelier plantation and especially of the stories connected with the fate of the first master, father of the man being buried. Ambrose Madison had acquired the land that was to become the nucleus of the Montpelier plantation through the brokerage of his father-in-law, James Taylor. Taylor was one of the Knights of the Golden Horseshoe, the expedition led by Governor Alexander Spotswood in 1716 of some of the first men of European background to cross Virginia's Blue Ridge Mountains. Taylor appreciated that a certain swath of land in the foothills, land that would become part of Orange County, was rich for farming, and he patented 8,500 acres for himself and helped the husbands of two of his daughters acquire 4,675 acres together in 1723. His daughter Frances had married Ambrose Madison, and the couple was living in Caroline County, fifty-five miles to the east, when they sent a gang of slaves and an overseer to the property to "perfect" the patent by commencing agriculture and construction, required in order to receive full title. Not until spring of 1732 did Ambrose, Frances, and their three children, the eldest and only son named James, move to the new plantation, accompanied by the rest of their enslaved people and hauling all their household goods. Ambrose would not see the year out. Court documents reveal that he was poisoned by slaves, two men named Pompey and Turk and a woman named Dido. There was much speculation as to how and why this happened, none of which could be voiced above a trusted whisper. Ambrose was thus the first Madison buried in the family cemetery. The slave cemetery that flanked the original house on the other side and farther out may have already received the first slave laid to rest.[1]

Frances, widowed at thirty-two with three small children, never remarried, which was atypical for the day. One mitigating factor may have been the company and support of extended family in the area. Taylor families held a number of estates in Orange County. The kin connections that Frances had with the Taylor elite were echoed by those among the enslaved individuals belonging to Taylors. The woman whom Paul Jennings eventually would marry was born into slavery on the plantation of Erasmus Taylor, Frances's brother.[2] But that union was two decades in the future, unknown of course to the little boy and his mother that winter day; she perhaps holding his hand but hoping not to transmit her anxiety over what might happen next, for the death of a slave master was always a time of tension for "his people." They would have little control over decisions about their futures, including the fates of their nearest family members.

PAUL JENNINGS HAD A CLOSE RELATIONSHIP WITH his mother, not an anchor every slave could count on. In his surviving letters, he referred to her as "mother" or "my mother," never revealing a name; she lived well into her son's middle age. The preface of *A Colored Man's Reminiscences of James Madison* states that Jennings was born a slave on James Madison's plantation in 1799. Both Paul Jennings and James Madison had their roots at Montpelier, but only Jennings was born there; in 1751 Madison's mother had chosen to give birth to her first child at her mother's home in Virginia's Northern Neck. Jennings's mother was a Madison slave, the granddaughter of an Indian; his father was a white merchant named Benjamin or William Jennings. What role, if any, did his father play on the plantation or in the local community? Was he passing through, an itinerant merchant perhaps, or did he have a sustained relationship with Paul's mother? If he was more to Paul than the paternal progenitor from whence his surname and half his genetic makeup were derived, there is no hint of it in the historical record.[3] It must have been his mother who told Paul about the Native American ancestry they shared.

The move by James Madison Sr., his wife Nelly, and their growing family to the new brick dwelling took place in the early 1760s. Their son James reported that he helped move the lighter pieces of furniture from the old to the new house—his token contribution. All of the real work, including building the house, was done by slaves. James Madison Sr. increased his status with this fine Georgian home as well as with the purchase of more land and of more slaves to add to the ten men, five women, and fourteen children listed in the inventory of his father, Ambrose. By the mid-1780s, he was a major slaveholder in the area; by the time he died, the Montpelier enslaved population had increased to 108 people. Of that number, about half were of prime working age; the others were assigned to chores for the very old or, infants aside, very young. The enslaved laborers not only worked in the mansion and in tobacco and corn fields but in various enterprises, including a blacksmith shop, a brandy distillery, and saw and flour mills, profitable ventures turning out goods for neighbors as well as for Montpelier itself. A true entrepreneur, James Madison Sr. also diversified his sources of income by hiring out slaves with specialized skills, such as carpentry and blacksmithing.[4]

All this involuntary labor gave the future President the freedom to pursue his intellectual interests and subsequent public service inclinations. Thus it was on a summer day in 1769 that eighteen-year-old James Madison set out on an intellectual adventure to Princeton, New Jersey: he was to attend the college there. A slave just his age named Sawney accompanied him: he was to attend the young master. Most Montpelier slaves never traveled more than five miles from their plantation home, within the distance to the county seat, Orange Court House, or to any of a dozen neighboring farms.[5] This applied to most of the slaves, but Paul Jennings would later be one in a series of exceptions like Sawney who traveled to new and fascinating places with James Madison. If a horse went lame, if a message needed to be delivered ahead, such attendants would be called into action. Their days were taken up seeing to the master's quotidian needs. Their waiting presence, while constant, was seemingly invisible to the elite class and is rarely noted in period documents. Sawney probably slept on a pallet by Madison's bed or in the passage outside his room at the college's Nassau Hall. *His* Princeton experience was never recorded.

Back at Montpelier, Sawney worked a tobacco quarter, while James Jr., who could choose his occupation, dithered over what career to pursue after completing his studies. He was tutoring his younger siblings some but mostly moping over missing the intellectual stimulation of college life when a current event captured his attention. Baptist ministers in a neighboring county were being persecuted, even jailed, for their religious practice, illegal in Virginia where the books asserted that Anglicanism was the state faith. Madison had embraced the tenets of the intellectual movement of the day—the Enlightenment—which included religious liberty or freedom of conscience. Here was an issue that a young man of learning could wrap his head around and devote some energy to. In the banner year of 1776, Madison became delegate from Orange County to the Virginia Convention: he had found his calling in politics and never looked back. There in the capital of Williamsburg he also found a like-minded, lifelong ally and friend, Thomas Jefferson. Jefferson, newly arrived from drafting the Declaration of Independence in Philadelphia, had been itching to return to "my country," meaning Virginia, to help form its first state constitution. His ears perked up in assent when he heard about how a new colleague, eight years his junior, who happened to be from the county next to his own, spoke up in defense of free and full exercise of religion in the Virginia Constitution's Declaration of Rights.[6]

What about Madison's philosophy or actions related to the right to freedom itself, freedom of person? The Enlightenment championed reason first and foremost, and Enlightenment philosophers reasoned that human beings had a natural right to liberty. Madison, the oldest of seven siblings, was traditionally in line to inherit his father's home plantation, but could he justify owning property that included people? His friend Jefferson offered a possible way out. Jefferson had come up with a scheme to entice some of his closest friends and associates to move near Monticello in Albemarle County, where they could establish a "society to our taste." He had even eyed a particular piece of land with his friend Madison in mind. "A little farm of 140 as. adjoining me, and within two miles, all of good land, tho' old, with a small indifferent house on it, the whole worth not more than £250," described Jefferson in February 1784, coaxing, "Such a one might be a farm of experiment and support a little table and household." Madison responded the next month, the letter written the day he turned thirty-three: "I feel the attractions of the particular situation you point out to me; I cannot altogether renounce the prospect; still less can I as yet embrace it." He added, "A few more years may prepare me for giving such a destiny to my future life." Madison was slowly but seriously mulling over this opportunity (or a similar situation outside of Virginia altogether) as an avenue to avoid slavery's stain. A letter a year later to friend and colleague Edmund Randolph reflects his thinking: "My wish is if possible to provide a decent and independent subsistence to depend as little as possible . . . on the labour of slaves." But between this date in mid-1785 and that of his father's will two years later, Madison came to a decision. Despite the "strongest bias of my mind," he accepted a future as master of the Montpelier plantation. By the terms of his father's will, he would receive a handsome allotment of land, including the home estate and the laborers to work it. By striking coincidence, the date on the will of James Madison Sr. was 17 September 1787. His son was not home the day that sealed his fate as his father's heir to the slavery system. He was in Philadelphia signing what would turn out to be the world's greatest achievement in self-sovereignty, or the right of people to govern themselves, the United States Constitution. By 1790, all hesitations were behind him, and he was taking a leadership role in managing the plantation, as evidenced by his authorship of a surviving document dated November of that year and headed "Instructions for the Montpelier Overseer and Laborers." Implying that he was now first in command, he instructed the overseer to "apply to my father on all occasions where application would be made to me if present."[7]

James Madison would, indeed, depend on the labor of Montpelier slaves until his death a half century later. That the position of Paul Jennings's mother was house servant is indicated by her son's role working in the Madison household from a young age. Positions within the plantation big house were often hereditary, and not only was Paul selected to be part of the Madison White House domestic staff at age ten, but from his own reminiscences, it is clear he was making observations from the vantage point of the master's household even earlier. He noted, "While Mr. Jefferson was President, he and Mr. Madison (then his Secretary of State) were extremely intimate; in fact, two brothers could not have been more so. Mr. Jefferson always stopped at Mr. Madison's, in going and returning from Washington." Paul must have been in the master's house to observe this dynamic, which continued throughout the Jefferson administration from 1801 to 1809. Later, when it was the young master's turn to be old master, housemaid Sukey and her young son Ben were in the mansion together. Benjamin Stewart recalled being "post-boy" and carrying Madison's favorite chair between his study and the garden. This is probably how Paul started— a boy under his mother's feet in the big house enlisted as errand runner. Though the only references to his mother in Jennings's letters are passing, one does provide further evidence that she was a house slave. In an April 1844 letter that Jennings wrote from Montpelier to Dolley Madison in Washington, he noted that "mother is well sends her love to you." Such a message would be unlikely unless she was a house servant well known to Dolley.[8]

Jennings accurately described the relationship between Madison and Jefferson. Jefferson actually learned he would be President while stopping at Montpelier during the last week in November 1800 on his way to Washington. At least that was the expectation at the moment Madison handed him a letter with the news that the opposition party that they cofounded—the Republicans—had been put over the top in expected election results. As it turned out, Jefferson faced a prolonged complication when, by the system then in place, his presumed running mate, Aaron Burr, and he were tied in electoral college votes. The log-jam was not resolved by the House of Representatives until February 1801, at which point Jefferson officially invited Madison to be Secretary of State. But Madison had news of the domestic sort to deal with as February closed. He wrote Jefferson that he had planned to be in Washington shortly after 4 March, inauguration day, but that "a melancholy occurrence has arrested this intention. My father's health . . . became sensibly worse, and yesterday morning rather suddenly, tho' very gently the flame of life went out."[9]

Not until after he filed his father's will at the courthouse in Orange on 27 April did Madison gather his immediate household and head to Washington. Arriving on 1 May, he took the oath of office as Secretary of State the next day. The family lived with widower Jefferson in the President's house until their town house was ready at the end of the month. Three geographical and population centers were contained in the ten square miles that delimited Washington, the District of Columbia, at this date. Two of those were the established towns of Alexandria and Georgetown; the third, Washington City itself, the national seat of government beginning in November 1800, was brand new, meaning it existed mostly only in plan, on paper. Its inchoate condition when James and Dolley reached it was described by a member of the first legislative session, Connecticut Congressman John Cotton Smith: "One wing of the capitol only had been erected, which along with the President's house, a mile distant from it . . . were shining objects in dismal contrast with the scene around them . . . Pennsylvania [Avenue] leading, as laid down on paper, from the Capitol to the Presidential mansion, was then nearly the whole distance a deep morass, covered with alder bushes." There were dwelling houses only here and there amid intervening stretches of shrub- and tree-studded land, much of it marshy. Among the few habitations Smith pinpointed was the one where the Madison family took up residence: "Between the President's house and Georgetown a block of houses had been erected, which then bore . . . the name of the *six buildings*."

"In short," Congressman Smith concluded, "it was a 'new settlement.'"[10] Dolley Madison would make her mark as the nation's foremost hostess in the nascent capital. This was possible because Washington was a blank canvas; there was no prevailing society on a par with that in the previous national capital of Philadelphia.

DOLLEY MET JAMES MADISON IN PHILADELPHIA, which had been her home since she was a young teenager, and her father had moved the family from rural Virginia to the "City of Brotherly Love" to pursue a career in commerce. A change in occupation was necessary because John Payne had determined that he was duty-bound as a good Quaker to free his slaves. This he did in 1782 outright and all at once, as a new Virginia law then allowed. This meant easing his conscience but giving up his livelihood as a planter. He became a starch merchant to support his family in Philadelphia, but the business venture did not work out as he had hoped, and he went bankrupt. This the Quakers did not abide and expelled John Payne or, to use their phrase, "read him out of meeting." The family tradition is that this so depressed him that he "never raised his head or left his room until he was carried to his last resting place." Dolley's mother was forced to support the family by taking in boarders. John Payne died a broken man in 1792, two years after his daughter married Quaker lawyer John Todd. The Todds' married life evaporated in 1793 when a yellow fever epidemic swept through Philadelphia and carried off a tenth of the population, including Dolley's husband and infant son. She herself barely survived the pestilence that took her "dear husband and little babe to the silent grave" on the same day. She had a remaining son to care for, one-and-a-half-year-old John Payne Todd, known as Payne.[11]

The boardinghouse Dolley's mother ran served members of Congress, including Senator Aaron Burr. Madison arranged for Burr to introduce him to Dolley Payne Todd. Before he was smitten by the

pretty widow, his colleagues had given him up, at forty-three, for a
confirmed bachelor married to his work. He had realized the promise
as a statesman that one political observer had discerned back in the
1784 Virginia Assembly and reported to Benjamin Franklin, describing Madison as "a rising young man" of whom much was expected. His
role in the Constitutional Convention had been masterful and would
lead to the epithet "Father of the Constitution" bestowed on him by
admiring contemporaries.[12]

Dolley, who turned twenty-six the month she and Madison had
their first date, was familiar with his merit. In asking her to chaperone
their meeting, Dolley gushed to her best friend, "Aaron Burr says that
the great little Madison has asked him to bring him to see me this evening." The modifier "little" was an apparent reference to Madison's less
than stately height. When Dolley Payne Todd married James Madison
in September 1794, only eleven months had passed since her husband
and infant died and only four since she met her husband-to-be. It was
clear, at least to her best friend, that she was not as infatuated as her
bridegroom. She wrote this intimate of a "soothing" union for herself
and "a generous and tender protector" for her son, while he, according
to another of Dolley's friends who claimed Madison's approval to plead
his case to his intended, carried a flame that "burns to such an excess
that he will be shortly consumed" (as recorded in an extant letter he
would surely wish had just as soon never survived).[13]

The minute Dolley married out of her faith, she was read out of
meeting by the Quakers. This did not seem to bother her at all. She
fancied jewelry and fashion; she even took up the habit of using tobacco snuff. Certainly during the War of 1812 she proved to be no
pacifist. Moreover, she never voiced a known murmur of conscience
at marrying a slave owner or presiding as mistress over a plantation
of a hundred slaves. Though she left no paper trail on the subject,
one might reflect on how her father selling his slaves and seeming to
come out the loser for it influenced her attitudes and behaviors regarding slavery and sacrifice. Dolley's niece Mary Cutts recorded that John

Payne "was called a fanatic" for giving freedom to his slaves.[14] Had Dolley decided that her father's nagging conscience would have been better off silenced?

BY THE TIME JAMES AND DOLLEY RELOCATED from Philadelphia to Virginia and had four rooms added to his father's house, she was deeply in love with her husband. Theirs was to be a supremely successful union on both a personal and public level, prevailing for forty-two years. When they moved to Montpelier in 1797, Dolley had Payne, now five, in tow of course. Dolley's sister Anna Payne, or "sister-daughter" as she called her, her junior by eleven years, completed the family unit. The foursome lived with James Sr. and Nelly (only their youngest child, Frances, was still at home), who continued to occupy the original part of the house, while the new rooms, two over two, were added to the formerly exterior north wall. Though there was still finishing work to do, the "vortex of housebuilding" was largely completed when Madison informed his friend and political associate James Monroe on 30 January 1799, "We have now been near six weeks settled in our new domicil."[15]

Thus Paul Jennings was born as the younger Madisons set up housekeeping in their part of the mansion, now a kind of duplex or row house for the two generations. The domestic slaves lived in cabins in the yard immediately to the south of the mansion. Baby Paul and his mother might have lived in a duplex, too—at least this was the form that the south yard slave dwellings took later—in a household that included additional kin or connections. Paul Jennings's birth year of 1799 started with snow on 3 January, the fifth snow of the season already, but by the first day of April the apricot blossoms were opening and the seasonal shift in work on the plantation was under way.[16]

Madison's return to Virginia in the late 1790s signaled a true hands-on management of Montpelier's five thousand acres and five-score people.

Though tobacco continued to be cultivated, wheat was now the major crop. Raising cash crops (a misnomer for some harvests) was just one of many occupations and activities that planters and their enslaved people tended to. Even given the livestock, gardens, orchards, and mills, farms like Montpelier never reached full self-sufficiency. Some commodities, such as salted fish, coffee, salt, and sugar, were purchased from merchants in Fredericksburg or other cities. Locally, county farmers bought and bartered produce and game among themselves. Francis Taylor, a nephew of Madison's grandmother, left a diary with scores of such transactions recorded. For 1799, he entered on 1 April: "intended to send soon to Madisons mill for cyder &c." On 25 September of that year he described the errands of two Montpelier slaves, Tyre and Sam. He noted that James Madison Jr. "sent Tyre to whom I delivered 3 Gammons, 2 Shoulders, & 1 Midling 86 lb Bacon—Tyre carried a Basket Peaches home . . . Col J Madison sen'r sent some pairs by Sam & got two baskets Peaches." Taylor caught up with the younger Madison for payment some days after; on the evening of 6 October, he received "a Doubloon pound sterling 4.11.3 in part for bacon" from him when they ran across one another socially.[17]

For the elite, and thus for their personal servants as well, the rhythms of plantation life included constant rounds of visiting. James Monroe had responded to Jefferson's call to move to Albemarle County to be part of the "society to our taste," and he and his wife were frequent visitors to Montpelier. Indeed, they were the first to be invited to James and Dolley's new abode after the addition was complete. It is apparent from Francis Taylor's diary that Madison participated in the more local visiting pattern, too. Some of his social activity at this time was no doubt for the benefit of establishing his wife, Dolley, among his Orange kin and connections. The night after Madison mixed business and pleasure with Francis Taylor, he was out again, this time to dinner at the home of Robert Taylor. At this 7 October dinner the year that Paul Jennings was born, several of the principals who would play into his future were present. Along with James and Dolley were the host's mother, Jane Moore Taylor, and sister Jane, with her husband, Charles P. Howard.

Jane Moore Taylor was the widow of Erasmus Taylor, the youngest brother of James Madison Jr.'s grandmother, Frances Taylor Madison. After Frances's husband Ambrose died, her brother served as overseer for one of the Montpelier farms. This was a short-lived occupation as Erasmus Taylor would soon acquire his own estate and slaves to attend to. His property, Greenfield, just to the north of Orange Court House, was inherited from his father, James Taylor, who had split up his original patent of 8,500 acres. In his own will, Erasmus divided his slaves among his sons and sons-in-law. One of the latter was Charles Howard, who had married Erasmus's youngest daughter, Jane. Born into slavery at Greenfield about 1798 and destined to go with the parcel of slaves that Charles Howard received was a girl named Fanny, who would one day become Paul Jennings's wife.[18]

News that two local citizens had been acquitted of the murder of a slave had just been announced from the courthouse in Orange on 5 October. At Robert Taylor's dinner two nights later, this must have been a topic of conversation, both at the dining room table and among the slaves behind the scenes. The courts throughout Virginia facilitated and sustained the race-based institution of chattel slavery. It was a self-perpetuating system since status followed from the mother: an enslaved woman's "future increase forever" belonged to her owner. Slaves could not testify against whites in court. They could not carry weapons. They could not gather without permission or travel from one plantation to another without a pass. Their marriages were not recognized by law.

James Madison was a third-generation slave owner. Paul Jennings was among the third and fourth generations of African Americans to call Montpelier home and Orange their community. The elite and the enslaved together created a unique society, the two interdependent elements evolving in response to one another. The layering and intertwining of connections, genetic and otherwise, was especially pronounced in Orange because so many gentry families, along with the enslaved families they held, came from the same counties to the east to settle the new county in the 1730s and 1740s. Not only did men and women often find mates within this cluster of a couple dozen families, but custom called for gifts of slaves to celebrate a new marriage among the master class, which increased and extended the ties among their enslaved people (as it also sometimes broke them). Legal limitations and social indignities at the hands of the white-controlled culture made the bonds among African Americans all the more vital to their sense of well-being. When Paul Jennings looked back at Montpelier long after he had left it, it was (if even among other characterizations) as the place where he had been "raised and nurtured."[19]

At least once during this same 1799–1800 period, James and Dolley had a remarkable dinner visitor at Montpelier, namely one Christopher McPherson, a free African American who was not intimidated by interactions with presidents. McPherson was a mulatto born into slavery in the nearby county of Louisa who achieved free status and steady occupation as a clerk. He wrote to the sitting President, John Adams, on 29 January 1800: "Mr. Jefferson by letter introduced me to Mr. Maddison—I sat at Table Even[in]g & morn[in]g with Mr. M his Lady & Company & enjoyed a full share of the Convers[ation]." He was at Montpelier again in April 1800, working contacts in high places by offering his services as carrier of books and letters between Jefferson and Madison. Madison not only invited McPherson to meals but lent him a horse when none was to be hired. McPherson wrote to thank Madison for this kindness and, ever primed to cultivate his connection, added that he would "watch for an opportunity to convince you how sensible I am of it." McPherson must have reminded Madison of the free black farmer whose circumstances astounded him and his traveling companion Jefferson during their trip to northern New York in 1791. At that time Madison took note: "[A free Negro] possesses a good farm of about 250 acres which he cultivates with 6 white hirelings . . . and by his industry & good management turns to good account. He is intelligent; reads writes & understands accounts, and is dextrous in his affairs."[20] It is not known whether such encounters influenced Madison's opinion of the abilities of people of African descent, or if he read them only as exceptions to the rule. One thing is certain: the enslaved domestics serving the meals at which McPherson was a guest would have been flabbergasted. The servants' hall in the cellar, the nearest thing to a private space where house slaves could catch a break and share news, must have been buzzing.

One Montpelier dining room servant not present when McPherson came calling who would have been fascinated by this particular visitor was Anthony. Anthony had run away years before. Twice. The first time, in 1786, he had been retrieved after James Madison Sr. placed a newspaper ad: "Run away . . . a Mulatto Slave, named Anthony, about 17 years old, low, but well made, had a very light hair and grey eyes . . . he has been used to house business, and as a waiting servant. Ten Dollars Reward will be given, if he be secured so that I get him again."[21] Anthony apparently found the lure of freedom irresistible, regardless of the risk and the reality that if successful—which he was with a second run—flight meant leaving behind one's connections and community forever. Each slave found his own way to resist or accommodate himself to the circumstances of being enslaved; usually it was some combination, and the forms of resistance chosen were short of running away. Possibilities included feigning illness, slowing down work, "losing" tools, pilfering, and even, as we have seen, poisoning the master.

◆

THOUGH MADISON HAD LEFT THE U.S. CONGRESS in March 1797 and would remain out of office until he took a seat in the Virginia State Assembly (now in Richmond) in December 1799, he never ceased behind-the-scenes activity. He wrote the Virginia Resolutions in 1798 at Montpelier, as he had his classic statement on religious freedom in 1785 and a system for self-government (that led to the Virginia Plan) in 1786. The Virginia Resolutions was yet another appeal against tyranny that Madison drafted at the place where he lived with scores of slaves. This treatise was part of an effort he and Jefferson waged against the Adams administration's Alien and Sedition Acts, encroachments against individual rights that, along with other issues, led to the two men activating the opposition party. "The Revolution of 1800" Jefferson called the Republicans' success in wresting power from the Federalists. For Madison and his wife, it was the start of sixteen years in the executive branch in the new federal city.

Madison's youngest sibling, Frances, had married in January 1801, the month before their father died, so when James and Dolley, along with Payne and Anna, went up to Washington that spring, Nelly was home alone. The senior and junior Madisons had always maintained not only separate parts of the house but parallel households in terms of meals, schedules, and provisions, and this did not change with James Sr.'s death. As Mary Cutts described, "[Mr. Madison's] mother still lived and retaining the use of all the original part of the house . . . kept up the ancient style, and the use of the servants, who had grown old in her service."22 In her early widowhood, during the periods when her son and daughter-in-law were in Washington, Nelly's was the only white face except for a few overseers' among about one hundred black ones on the plantation.

The plantation residents, white and black, were there to greet the Secretary of State upon his initial return to Montpelier on the first day of August. Now firmly established as a high official in the national government in Washington and plantation monarch in Orange County, Virginia, he was no longer James Madison Jr.: he had dropped the suffix.

This was not a quick visit. The family would remain on the plantation until October. President Jefferson's retreat from Washington was only slightly shorter. He left the city two days after the Madisons and presumably stopped at Montpelier on the way to Monticello as it is certain he did on his way back to Washington in the middle of September. This was the start of a tradition initiated by Jefferson of vacating the city of Washington each August for approximately two months.

Not only was the city dreadfully hot then, it was potentially dangerous because malarial disease-carrying mosquitoes proliferated in the city's swampy regions. Jefferson called it the "sickly season" and advised his Cabinet members to seek a healthier climate, as he would do by going home to the higher ground of his Piedmont plantation. "We all have property to take care of," as Jefferson justified it to his Secretary of State, and "we have health to take care of, which at this season cannot be preserved at Washington."[23] First President Jefferson, then President Madison, for two terms each, conducted the nation's business for two months from his home study, without the aid of an entourage or even a clerk. This proto–"Summer White House" led directly to the tradition still familiar in Washington today. Though the swampland is filled in and the retreat length is closer to two weeks and there is definitely an entourage, it is still unbearably hot in August when the President seeks a vacation destination, and many government officials and city workers follow suit.

During these breaks for the period from 1801 to 1809, President Jefferson and his Secretary of State communicated regularly by way of a post-rider carrying mail back and forth, with the letters between them sometimes in secret code; occasionally Madison would ride over to the President's home for face-to-face consultation. Monticello and Montpelier were twenty-eight miles apart. Jefferson measured it on a contrivance he "fastened upon the axle-tree of [his] sulky and would tell the number of miles gone over by the wheels." Both homes sat in the Southwest Mountains, which ran in a more pronounced southwest slant than the Blue Ridge Mountains to the west. Both homes had grand porticoes and extensive views of the majestic Blue Ridge. It is perhaps not altogether a coincidence that two of the country's greatest Founders grew up in sight of the ridge that marked the western frontier. The Blue Ridge Mountains represented hope in the unseen, in the newness, the vastness of America. "We have it in our power to begin the world over again," Thomas Paine wrote, and Madison and Jefferson believed.[24] America was a place where an experiment in self-government might be conceived and even work. During the late summer retreat of 1803, the President and Secretary of State reflected more than a little on the West and its promise. They had just concluded the Louisiana Purchase, more than doubling the size of the country.

Four years later, when a visitor from England visited both statesmen, the annual tradition was well established. Augustus John Foster, secretary to British Minister Anthony Merry, was familiar with the habit of the Jefferson and Madison households withdrawing every August for two months "in order to avoid the bad air of the city of Washington." He followed their lead and left the overheated city for a trip to Virginia in August 1807. When subsequently he set down his recollections of exploring their plantations, he noted that Madison and Jefferson "were notorious for their democratic tendencies . . . yet in their own houses were they surrounded with slaves." A later visitor from England to Montpelier, Harriet Martineau, made a more general comment on the area: "Rural life in the south was . . . all shaded with the presence of slavery."[25]

The Madisons themselves reached Montpelier "a little before sunset" on 7 August, a fortnight before Foster arrived. A week later there was a flood to deal with on the plantation, though the even-tempered Madison wrote calmly enough to Jefferson of the excessive rains: "In thirty six hours there fell upwards of 8 inches at least. How much more is uncertain, the vessel measuring it, running over each morning when examined. All the mills in this neighborhood have lost their dams. I learn that my little one, which I am about to visit, is among the sufferers." Jefferson commiserated, "About one half of my mill dam is gone," but went on to extend the annual invitation to visit Monticello: "We are flattering ourselves with the hope of a visit from Mrs. Madison and yourself some time this season." His friend replied: "Mrs. M and myself always include a visit to Monticello among the pleasures of the autumnal retreat from Washington; and we are not without hopes that the present season will not be an exception. It is far from certain however that we may not be disappointed; many circumstances uniting to render my continued presence here peculiarly requisite."[26]

Augustus Foster, meanwhile, had left Washington on 17 August. When he was fifteen miles from Montpelier, he crossed the Rapidan River at a ford and, with night upon him, took refuge in the home of a Scotsman. Foster's host served mint juleps first thing in the morning, telling him it was a Virginia custom to drink one before breakfast. Traveling the remaining miles to Montpelier, Foster observed cycles of wood, pasture, corn and tobacco fields, and plantation house, and passed through Orange Court House, which he described as a little village of about a dozen houses. From there, he noted a choice in taking a three-mile horse road or a five-mile carriage road to Montpelier.

He found Madison's estate surrounded by forest. Foster remembered great numbers of wild turkeys and enormous chestnut trees in the woods. He must have also seen the many impressive tulip trees at Montpelier, as he did at Monticello later that month, describing Jefferson's creative use of them as temporary columns. Monticello's west portico, Foster noticed, "was not quite completed, and the pediment had, in the meanwhile to be supported on the stems of four tulip trees, which are really, when well grown, as beautiful as the fluted shafts of Corinthian pillars."

As for the brick portico at Montpelier, Foster described it as "of the plainest and most massive order of architecture, but which Palladio gives as a specimen of the Tuscan." Madison employed no architect, Foster noted, but rather superintended construction himself, "which he had executed by the hands of common workmen to whom he prescribed the proportions to be observed." The result was a rare example of a domestic two-story portico: "forty-seven feet wide, and together with its pediments it is as high as the house, viz., forty feet." Foster described the sweeping view from the portico of "the [Blue] Ridge and of a well wooded plain that lies in front of it from whence the ascent is so gradual that the house scarcely appears to be upon an elevation." He recalled that though Madison spoke of one day laying out an English park, such a pleasure ground "would in fact be very expensive, and all hands are absolutely wanted for the plantation."[27]

The enslaved hands that Foster observed at Montpelier made it hum with activity. Like other large plantations, Montpelier was divided into a number of farms, and Foster spent most of his approximately five-day visit at the home quarter, the farm where the family mansion was seated. Though Foster wrote that "Tobacco and Indian corn are the principal produce of his lands," Madison raised wheat as well. Grain culture did not wear the soil out like tobacco did, as planters had learned from hard experience, nor was it as labor-intensive. Madison was a scientific farmer interested in every advancement in equipment and technique. His workmen constructed plows based on the latest model, practiced crop rotation, and experimented with soil additives. Once introduced to America, merino sheep grazed among the cows and oxen at Montpelier. A visitor who came during the last autumnal retreat of Madison's presidency reported that merinos were cross-bred with the old stock of sheep and that the wool from the resultant flock "is highly prized and brings a good price." The same visitor noted, "I went today to one of the farms of the President to see a wheat thrashing machine; it is composed of two parts, one of which receives the sheaves fed into it by Negroes as fast as the stripping process allows, while the other, made up of large cogwheels which turn the wooden cylinder which acts on the first machine, is driven by four horses."[28] By midsummer each year, the wheat harvest was completed. Bringing the crop in was an all-hands effort. The number of individuals owned by Madison from the time that his father's slaves were distributed among his widow and children until his own retirement from public service in 1817 rose not by purchase but by natural increase, reaching a population equilibrium at about one hundred people.

One of the enslaved men, Moses, who by the terms of Madison Sr.'s will was allowed to choose his next master from among the heirs and had elected to remain at the home farm with James Jr., ran the blacksmithing operation. Highly skilled, Moses directed the work of

several black men under him. This shop was one of several home industries noted by Foster: "When at a distance from any town it is necessary [the tradesmen] should be able to do all kind of handiwork; and,
accordingly, at Montpellier I found a forge, a turner's shop, a carpenter,
and wheelwright. All articles too that were wanted for farming or the
use of the house were made on the spot." A later visitor commented
similarly: "They work a saw and grist mill for the plantation and neighborhood, and employ a carpenter, blacksmith, shoemaker, weaver, &c.
So that the cloth and shoes of the servants, the bread they eat and the
planks that protect them from the weather, are all manufactured on the
plantation. Such an establishment is, therefore, a little kingdom of itself." Among the agricultural workers, Sawney, who had accompanied
Madison to college back in 1769, had responsibility for a tobacco quarter that bore his name. His initial was even included on the tobacco
mark for the crop grown at Sawney's quarter.

Moses and Sawney filled foreman positions on the plantation, but
the white overseers hired by Madison were a notch above in the hierarchy. The overseer for the home quarter at the time of Foster's visit
was compensated with "£60 Virginia currency or £48 sterling per an-
num, and was furnished with lodging and everything he or his family
could want." In the memo to overseers that Madison wrote in 1790,
he included among the practical instructions a directive "to treat the
Negroes with all the humanity & kindness consistent with their necessary subordination and work." As Foster noted, since "he was obliged
to be often absent from home, he was under the necessity of trusting
to his overseer a great deal."[29] But even when under Madison's day-to-
day management, slave life at Montpelier was typical for the time and
place. James Madison was an exceptional statesman, a political philosopher without peer, but a garden-variety slaveholder. He followed the
basic patterns and norms for slaves' living conditions and treatment
that had long been established on Virginia plantations and like most
owners respected the customary "rights"—such as Sundays off—that
enslaved people had come to consider their due. An Englishman who

visited both Montpelier and Monticello reported that he heard about instances of serious mistreatment of slaves in the region, "but public opinion prevents individuals from proceeding to great severities. The whip is employed to make them labor; I was told it was necessary, but saw no instances of its being used." This same visitor quoted Thomas Jefferson as claiming, "Any planter who treated his negroes cruelly would be shunned by his neighbors."[30]

Slaves worked a six-day week, dawn to dusk, with a break at midday. This meant about a nine-hour workday in the winter but as long as fourteen hours in the heat of the summer. Enslaved people worked in the main house and its domestic dependencies, such as kitchen, dairy, and smokehouse; in home industries such as blacksmithing, carpentry, and weaving; and as field laborers. Women worked right alongside men in the fields (with consideration given to pregnant women and nursing mothers). Cooks, maids, waiters, and other house servants had some advantages, receiving occasional cast-off items from the big house and extra clothes to add to the standard two outfits per year, one for summer and one (plus blanket) for winter. But they tended to be on call twenty-four hours a day, and being under the constant eye of the master was taxing. Field slaves were exposed to outdoor conditions during a brutally long day, but the night was their own.

After work, families regrouped in their cabins. Foster wrote, "The Negro Habitations are separate from the Dwelling House both here and all over Virginia, and they form a kind of village as each Negro family would like if they were allowed it, to live in a House by themselves." There was a series of slave quarters at Montpelier. The enslaved domestics lived in the south yard next to the mansion while other families lived nearer to the fields they worked. The slave master had come to appreciate that allowing family households to prevail was good management all round. As historian Lucia Stanton, writing of Jefferson, summarized it, "He could foster family ties through benevolent intercession, he could exploit them to control behavior, or ignore them in the interests of efficient management."[31]

References to food rations for Montpelier slaves include cornmeal, bacon or other pork, salted fish, vegetables, fruit, and milk. Though one Montpelier visitor noted, "Each family raise their own pigs and poultry, eat meat twice a day, and have meal, vegetables, milk and fruit without restriction," a peck of Indian cornmeal and one to two pounds of meat per week were standard. Occasionally, especially during stretches of arduous work, whiskey or beer was allotted. Madison Sr.'s records reveal that women in childbirth were allowed whiskey. His son customarily distributed whiskey during the long days of bringing in the wheat harvest. One Montpelier guest described how "Mr. Madison had undertaken to substitute Beer in the room of whiskey as a beverage for his slaves in Harvest time." While the two men were riding about the plantation together, they stopped at a wheat field and Madison asked a gray-headed laborer what he thought of the change. "O! ver fine—vere fine masser—but I tink a glass of whiskey vere good to make it wholesome" came the response. The guest reported that Madison was amused by this rejoinder and "often made merry with it afterwards."[32]

Montpelier slaves had "the privilege of attending church every Sabbath, and sometimes on the week day nights," according to one visitor account. Besides Sundays, slaves were traditionally granted a few holidays over the course of the year, most notably several days running at Christmas. In their off time, some slaves caught up on sleep or relaxed with kith and kin. Others, perhaps more enterprising, made brooms or baskets that could be sold or bartered. Most slaves kept poultry yards and vegetable gardens to supplement their food rations. Some, like Sawney, sold their products to the master's family. "He had his house and ground, where he raised his favorite vegetables, cabbages and sweet potatoes, as well as chickens and eggs, to be sold to 'Miss Dolley,'" niece Mary Cutts remembered.

The living conditions for Montpelier slaves were not greatly different from those of free poor to middling people, which classification would include most free Virginians at this time, making a bare living out of subsistence farming. Madison was part of the *very* top elite with brick mansions, thousands of acres, and scores of slaves. One visitor to Montpelier who started his pilgrimage from the Shenandoah Valley on the far side of the Blue Ridge observed that only after he crossed the mountain did he see tobacco plantations with "large, noble houses . . . with the 'negro quarters' not far from them." This contrasted with what he had observed on the valley side, where "there are few negroes, the farms are small, the houses appear to be those of substantial yeoman but nothing more, and there is a general aspect of equality in fortunes."[33] It was not so much the difference in living standards but rather the lack of basic freedom of action and opportunity for advancement that defined the deep and profound discrepancy between enslaved and most free Virginians.

◆

BY THE TIME JAMES MADISON'S TWO TERMS as Secretary of State were drawing to a close, Paul Jennings was in his tenth year and well acquainted with where he stood in the pecking order. Likewise, Payne Todd, seven years older than Jennings, who was Todd's playmate *and* servant while both were young, knew he occupied a high rung in the plantation hierarchy. Payne had been a toddler, aged two, when his mother remarried after just a few months' courtship. The year before that, when the yellow fever epidemic hit Philadelphia, he had lost his paternal grandparents, his father, and his baby brother in quick succession. It was no doubt this tragic episode that led Dolley to give in to precious Payne's every whim. Anyway, as a foreign visitor to the region noted of slave owners' offspring, "Having so many to wait on them the white children are very much indulged." All indications are that as stepfather James Madison extended not only his protection and resources but paternal warmth to Payne. Madison used his connections to arrange for Payne to attend St. Mary's College in Baltimore, a new school for Catholic and Protestant boys. In a letter dated the last day of October 1805, Madison, referring to the school, informed his wife, "A berth seems at last to be secured for our son."[34]

Paul Jennings had none of Payne's advantages, but he managed to learn to read and write, rare for a slave during a period when it was common for free poor people to substitute a mark for a signature because they were unable to write their own names. Paul was educated, according to Jennings family tradition, with "the little master" or "the white boy," who sat and participated in the class while Paul stood and observed. The white boy might have been Payne Todd, who despite his outside schooling was often at Montpelier and may have required remedial tutoring, or he might have been among Madison's many nephews. Madison employed a private tutor for his brother William's son Robert, who lived at the White House for six months in 1812–13. There is no way to know whether Paul learned to read and write before going to Washington in 1809. His earliest known letters were written while he was still enslaved but well after his adolescence. However, given the facility with which children acquire language skills, it is likely that Jennings picked up his literary abilities while still a youth. One Virginia-raised slave named Almira told a foreign visitor that she was unable to read and, at fourteen, "'Spect I am too large to learn now." Jennings's own children, raised in slavery on the farm of a separate master, never learned to read and write with the exception of the youngest, who became free at about age twelve. The likely picture that emerges is of a young Paul absorbing language skills by "standing in" on lessons offered to one or more boys of the Madison extended family. Listening in, secondhand learning: this is perhaps the first instance of Jennings taking advantage of his circumstances.

"When Mr. Madison was chosen President, we came on and moved into the White House," Jennings stated early in the *Reminiscences*.[35] Jefferson, for his part, was relieved to turn the reins of power over to Madison. The embargo strategy that they had devised for dealing with impressments of American sailors on the seas and other national indignities at England's hands was a disaster. After ten years of observing and being observed in the big house, Paul was chosen for the White House, too; he was to be part of the domestic staff. What did

Paul's mother think of his selection? Like all the Montpelier slaves, she would have been familiar with what happened to Billey Gardner, son of Betty and Old Anthony, another intelligent boy selected for special duty with James Madison but one who never came home.

History would not know William Gardner by any name but Billey if he was identified only through Madison's records. Masters rarely used their slaves' family names, which led to the myth that slaves did not have last names. More recent research in sources other than owners' ledgers and letters show that most enslaved people certainly did have enduring family names. For examples of masters rarely deigning to use them, however, one need look no further than to slave-owning presidents. The Jennings surname is one of only three or four for Montpelier slaves that can be pulled from the Madison records. Even then, a resistance to using the surname often led to awkward phrasing, such as "my man servant Paul, sometimes called Paul Jennings." Likewise, George Washington referred to his enslaved valet "calling himself William Lee" while he, Washington, persisted with "Billy"; and Thomas Jefferson names Christopher McPherson in writing to Madison, only to immediately modify the name with "better known as mr. Ross's man Kitt."[36] The reluctance of slave owners to acknowledge the last names of slaves, and to promote diminutives besides, was a way of marginalizing slaves' individuality and pinning their identity to the master's.

William Gardner had accompanied James Madison to Philadelphia in early 1780 and served as his factotum for the nearly four years that he was delegate to the Continental Congress. When it was time for the two of them to return home in the fall of 1783, Madison wrote his father, "I have judged it most prudent not to force Billey back to Virginia. . . . I am persuaded his mind is too thoroughly tainted to be a fit companion for fellow slaves in Virginia." Gardner's mind was apparently "tainted" with ideas. He had caught the contagion of liberty making the rounds in Philadelphia in the 1780s. Before heading back to Montpelier, Madison sold Gardner, knowing he would be free by Pennsylvania's Emancipation Act in seven years' time. Once free,

Gardner became a merchant's agent in Philadelphia, handling business for the Madisons, Thomas Jefferson, and others. He married a woman named Henrietta who took in laundry, with Jefferson among her customers, too.

The lack of freedom for Montpelier's enslaved residents even as he was advocating for the cause of individual rights was an irony that Madison was well aware of and expressed tellingly in the letter to his father wherein he admitted that he could not blame Gardner "merely for coveting that liberty for which we have paid the price of so much blood, and have proclaimed so often to be the right & worthy the pursuit, of every human being." Madison's selling Gardner in Philadelphia to preclude his sharing his light of knowledge with his kin and friends on the plantation was consistent with Madison's own understanding of the connection between liberty and learning. Here was the political philosopher following through on what he knew: "A people who mean to be their own governors must arm themselves with the power that knowledge gives."[37] And Madison knew the corollary was true: if you would keep a people unfree, then you must keep them ignorant. From his point of view, it surely was "prudent" not to reintroduce Gardner to the Montpelier enslaved community.

Gardner lost his home and his mother and father lost their son, and the best Madison did to make any of this up was to sell the young man in Philadelphia instead of to the Deep South, where slave prices were much higher but where Gardner's future would hold little prospect of freedom. In the letter to his father, Madison wrote that he had "taken measures for [Billey's] final separation from me," but there is no mention of Gardner's separation from his home or family. However, Madison communicated Gardner's sad demise twelve years later for his father to pass on to the parents: "Let old Anthony and Betty know that their son Billey is no more." On a voyage to New Orleans, Gardner had became ill and, hovering at the rail, accidentally fell into the sea or, as Madison rather poetically described it, "tumbled in a fainty fit overboard & never rose."[38]

Did William Gardner's story affect the way the Montpelier enslaved people thought about their future ambitions and behavior? Did it alter the degree to which some took risks or pushed the envelope? Paul's mother might wonder if she wanted to see her son go off with Madison to the larger world if it meant that he might never return. As the wagon for Washington was being packed, she might have consoled herself with the thought of Sawney. Though Billey Gardner did not come home after his experience with Madison, Sawney did. Afterward, Sawney worked in the field but with a fair amount of autonomy and responsibility, and continued to interact directly with the master's family. In the end he was a slave, not free like Billey, but he was not forever alienated from his home and family.

The slave family differed from others in that parents were not able to bequeath the profits and products of their labor to their children; instead these fruits were passed on to the children of their white owners. All that enslaved parents could pass on was their experience and wisdom, and much of that concerned how to maneuver as nimbly as possible in a white man's world, how to dissemble, how to keep one's own counsel. Paul had that knowledge and a mother's love as he packed his own few things for Washington.

When Jennings noted that upon Madison becoming President, "we came on and moved into the White House," he was identifying with the master's household; whom else among the Montpelier enslaved community did the "we" include? One additional Montpelier slave known to have been in residence at the White House was Sukey, who served as house servant and Dolley's personal maid. Sukey, the nickname for the Madison slave named Susan, was Paul's contemporary but has been erroneously identified in some sources as his eventual wife. The sensibilities of the prevailing culture did not preclude children as young as ten or twelve, as Paul and Sukey were, from being servants out on their own. In Dolley Madison's 1841 will, for example, she bequeaths to each of three female relations "one negro girl of ten or twelve," which would mean separation—in this case permanently—

of the girls from their mothers. Childhood ran out early for enslaved children.

As Paul and Sukey were carried from the plantation, the small caravan winding its way to Washington probably included the wagon made a year and a half earlier that Augustus Foster remembered: "I saw a very well constructed Waggon that had just been completed."[39] The blacksmith, carpenter, and wheelwright whom Foster observed at Montpelier would all have been employed in producing this vehicle. The trip to Washington took a full three days if they were lucky and if early spring winds had dried out the roads. They faced rivers without bridges and endless stretches without inns. For all that might have caught the eye of Paul and Sukey as they rumbled along, they would have been totally unaware of the moment they actually entered the federal city. The approach to Washington was *so* unremarkable that a number of travelers in period accounts remarked on the need to be told that they had crossed the city limits.[40]

CHAPTER TWO

Presidential Household

31 May 1809, The first of Dolley Madison's
White House "Drawing Rooms"

It was a rainy Wednesday. Paul Jennings in his footman's livery likely had the initial duty that evening of meeting guests at the north entrance with an umbrella—there was no portico then to protect ladies and gentlemen from the elements upon arrival at the White House. Tonight was the first of what would become Dolley Madison's legendary "Drawing Rooms," with the presidential mansion open for the reception of everyone who was properly introduced. More gentlemen than ladies attended this premiere night, as would be expected in a town populated with many government men in residence without their families, though at least one lady "had to be content with only hearing the music" because "It was raining and our carriage could not get near the door."[1]

The stage was set, thanks to a fruitful collaboration between Dolley and the dramatic Benjamin Latrobe, Surveyor of Public Buildings and all-round design genius. The largest of the three rooms given over to the event was the oval drawing room in the center of the house (its future blazing red décor still in the planning stages). It adjoined Dolley's sunflower yellow sitting room, which in turn led to the state dining room in the southwest corner of the house. Doors between the rooms allowed the company to flow among them.

Dolley was ready for opening night and for what would be a remarkable performance, not just for the evening but for her entire run as First Lady (as the role was eventually named). But Dolley was not an actress, or if she was, then a transformative one, for the consensus would be that she was genuine and welcomed intimacy and spontaneity. The levees of the first two administrations had been set and precise in their presentation. Even the word "levee" harkened back to the formal stiffness of those earlier assemblages. On the other hand, Dolley's style was not as casual as third president Jefferson's often-criticized pell-mell approach. Anyway, as one congressman put it, it was "a subject of congratulation" to have a president with a wife again. As the weeks went by, the designation "Drawing Room" was all a lady or gentleman need say ("D. Room" in a note would do) for reference to Dolley's Wednesday gatherings in the presidential mansion to be understood.[2]

Had more ladies been present, Dolley still would have stood apart, not because she was seated on a platform, as Martha Washington had been at her courtly receptions, but because of the charming intertwining of her personality and visual impact. Her teenage maid Sukey helped her to dress. We do not know what she wore on this first occasion, but Jennings himself later recalled some of her ensembles—fabrics of purple velvet and white satin, always with "turbans of the finest materials and trimmed to match," as were her shoes.

President Madison, happy to leave the limelight to his wife, was attired as usual "in the old style" and "wore powder, small-clothes, and buckles, and was unostentatious in his manner," tending to keep his hands clasped behind him. Paul had no way of knowing that he would one day serve as Madison's "barber and dressing man" and be the one responsible for his queue and clothes.[3]

As the guests mingled among the three rooms, the servants threaded through them with trays of refreshments. "Wine, punch, coffee, ice-cream, &c., were liberally served," Jennings recalled. Young Jennings may have been among the servers that first night but more likely was a runner, acting on the steward's commands to replenish this from the pantry or tote that up from the cellars. It must have been both a frightening and an exhilarating experience. The carriages, music, mirrors and chandeliers, the sophisticated and political conversation. Paul the observer, Paul the listener, received an eyeful and an earful this evening.

Soon enough, the interesting attendees at Dolley's Drawing Rooms—also known as jams or squeezes—would include statesmen Henry Clay, John Calhoun, and Daniel Webster. Soon enough, too, Paul developed his serving skills. One evening, a young man ill at ease accepted a cup of coffee, but when the First Lady approached him, he was so flustered that he dropped the saucer and unthinkingly shoved the cup into his breeches' pocket. Dolley assured him it was easy to be jostled in the crowd and that a servant would bring a fresh replacement.[4] One imagines Paul, now able to maneuver through the crowd even with a full tray of cups, empathizing with this neophyte's nervousness and tactfully assisting.

JAMES MADISON'S INAUGURATION AS FOURTH PRESIdent of the United States took place on 4 March 1809, nearly three months before Dolley's first Drawing Room. A gun salute sounded to announce the occasion that bright Saturday morning. The President-elect rode to the Capitol for his swearing-in ceremony in a coach led by four fine horses and escorted by two troops of cavalry in full regalia along Washington's wide main artery. Pennsylvania Avenue was "over-spread with persons of every description," noted one citizen, who estimated that she was one of ten thousand people, and added, "Carriages, horse and foot, all were hastening to the Capitol." No preceding event had attracted such multitudes to Washington. At hearing the cavalry bugler's brass notes, pedestrians paused as the official suite passed, but not many noticed the young black footman in place on the back of the carriage. Behind the showy livery, that footman may have been Paul Jennings, ten years old, new to a city that was itself new. In the beginning he found Washington, unformed as it was, "a dreary place," the tentative impression of a boy away from home for the first time. And yet, as his eyes feasted on scenes of presidential splendor that early spring morning, he must have sensed that, homesickness aside, he was at the start of a great adventure. Paul Jennings would come of age in the nation's capital and be an eyewitness to historical events in the process.[5]

Once sworn in, the new President stepped outside the Capitol chamber, reviewed the arrayed military forces, and returned to his home. "After the ceremony was over, I went to pay the visit of custom," wrote future president John Quincy Adams in his diary, explaining, "The company was received at Mr. Madison's house; he not having yet removed to the President's House." Adams would later reside in the same neighborhood where James and Dolley had lived ever since they returned to Washington from their first "autumnal retreat" in 1801. One of the city's longtime residents recalled that while Madison was Secretary of State, "You might have seen him every morning quietly wending his way up to the White House from his residence on F Street." This enclave of town houses of the well connected, located a few blocks to the east of the executive mansion, included William and Anna Thornton's. He designed the Capitol and was superintendent of the patent office; she was a good friend to Dolley and, like John Quincy Adams, a faithful diarist. F Street was blocked with carriages now, the Madisons' reception attracting such crowds that many guests had to wait half an hour to squeeze into the house. Every available space overflowed with well-wishers. The First Couple stood near the drawing room door to receive the company while Paul and the other servers struggled to deliver refreshments to all.[6]

A week later Anna Thornton noted in her diary, "Mr. and Mrs. M. went to the Great House." It was during the Madison administration that the President's house was first referred to as the White House, this designation—one among many—only slowly coming to dominate. Many elements were incomplete when the Madison household moved in. Jennings remembered that the huge east room, where Abigail Adams had hung her laundry nearly a decade earlier, was still unfinished. Dolley and James decided on room functions different from Jefferson's. On the east side of the oval drawing room was the President's sitting room (corresponding to his wife's on the west side), which opened into the cabinet room created via a temporary wall at the south end of the east room, which otherwise ran the length of the house. On the north side of the house was included a room for the President's private secretary, Edward Coles, brother to Jefferson's last secretary and cousin to Dolley.

President Madison left the running of most domestic matters to his wife and instructed Latrobe to work directly with her on the décor, but in at least one domestic matter his preference held sway. That was the placement of the life-size Gilbert Stuart portrait of George Washington, portraying the first President standing at his full six feet three inches. Dolley hung it in the oval drawing room, but her husband thought the state dining room better, and there it went, against the west wall.[7]

The second story was divided into more and smaller rooms than the first floor, mainly bedchambers for the First Family and the many extended kin who lived there from time to time. At the start of the administration, Payne Todd, then seventeen, was attending boarding school in Baltimore. The upstairs family initially included the family of Dolley's sister Anna. Anna had married Congressman Richard Cutts from Maine in 1804. After the birth of three sons, their family had grown to five by the March move-in date. The Cutts family, while a presence at the White House throughout the Madison tenure, moved to their own home nearby on F Street later in 1809. Even married, Anna Payne Cutts remained Dolley's sister-daughter. Dolley's closeness to Anna and to her children grew with the increasing likelihood that she and James would have no offspring themselves. The only known reference to a possible pregnancy is a cryptic passage in a letter written to Thomas Jefferson by Joseph Dougherty, an Irish workman on Jefferson's presidential domestic staff who stayed on for occasional employment under Madison. The letter, dated 15 May 1809, when Dolley was almost forty-one, reads: "Mr. Barry is painting at the President's House but Mrs. Madison cannot abide the smell of the paint: that may be on account of her pregnancy, but I think she will bring forth nothing more than dignity."[8]

Paul, Sukey, and other live-in household members had sleeping quarters on the cellar level (which met the ground on the south side), where rooms opened onto a central corridor that ran the full length of the house. The kitchen, directly under the entrance hall, had great fireplaces at each end, one of which was fitted with the new-fashioned iron range that Jefferson had installed. Opposite the kitchen was the oval room (repeating the shape of the oval salon above it) that functioned as a servants' hall and was equipped with a series of calling bells. During Jefferson's administration, long rows of low, one-story rooms had been added to the east and west sides of the mansion. These provided a meat house; storage for liquors, coal, and wood; and privies. Along the east wing a stable was constructed by the close of Jefferson's administration, and in the first year of Madison's, a carriage house was built near it. "[Mr. Madison] never had less than seven horses in his Washington stables while President," Jennings stated in his reminiscences.[9]

Care of the carriages and horses was the job of coachman Joseph Bolden. In the memoir written by Dolley's niece Mary Cutts (a daughter of Anna and Richard born in 1814), it was noted of Bolden, "with his wages he soon freed himself," indicating that he was enslaved at one time. His wife, Milley, was owned by Francis Scott Key (another of Dolley's cousins), who lived in Georgetown. Key wrote to Dolley in June 1810, "Your Servant Joe has been anxious to purchase the freedom of his wife." Milley joined the presidential household, Key sending Dolley the deed of manumission and she advancing the $200 purchase price for Milley and child, which would be reimbursed by Milley's and her husband's future labor.

Other members of the household staff included John Freeman and his wife, Melinda. Freeman was a slave purchased by Thomas Jefferson in 1804 with the understanding, set by his former master, that he would be freed in 1815. When Jefferson's term ended, Freeman did not want to go to Monticello as his master expected him to. Freeman had married Melinda Colbert (a member of Monticello's Hemings family), who moved to Washington to live with her husband after she was freed in 1808; if she returned to her native state, she would be subject to the Virginia law requiring freed slaves to leave the state within a year of their emancipation. Freeman delicately negotiated with Jefferson, writing him that he would obediently go to Virginia but "I shall be oblige[d] to leave hir and the children." The sympathy ploy worked: Jefferson arranged for his successor Madison to purchase Freeman for $231.81. (Jefferson characteristically did the calculation to the penny based on Freeman's remaining time.) The Freeman family lived in the Madison White House. Melinda Freeman sewed carpets, drapes, and sheets and was paid in cash. She and her husband reported to John Sioussat, the steward.

Jean-Pierre Sioussat was born in Paris, arrived in New York in 1804, and made his way to Washington City, where he first worked in the Merry household while Anthony Merry was English minister. Known as French John, he developed a close relationship with Dolley Madison that lasted until her death. Sioussat arranged for purchase of the pair of giant sculpted eagles that flanked the Pennsylvania Avenue entrance to the presidential mansion. Making household purchases and keeping accounts, along with oversight of the White House daily operations and domestic staff, were among Sioussat's responsibilities.[10]

Dolley's niece described Paul Jennings as "a handsome mulatto boy, and a favorite page of Mrs. Madison's." As footman, his roles included messenger, dining room servant, assistant to the coachman, and other duties as assigned by Sioussat. In his recollections, Jennings identified Freeman as butler and Sioussat as doorkeeper (which Cutts called him as well). Designations aside, there was a clear hierarchy, and Sioussat was at the top. Doorkeeper may not sound as illustrious a title as major domo or maitre d'hotel, but in the White House, then as now, the doorkeeper, who controls access, holds power. It must be Sioussat one White House insider referred to when he described the small room next to the north entrance as being "for the porter, who is always at the door." This is the space reserved for the White House chief usher to this day.[11]

Care and operation of the presidential domicile was a private undertaking at this time, accomplished by about ten persons in Jefferson's household. To round out the number needed to run the Madison White House, there were additional Montpelier slaves in residence along with enslaved and free workers engaged in Washington. It was common for slaves to be hired out by their owners (often themselves residing in the Maryland or Virginia countryside) to city householders. While Secretary of State, Madison signed a five-year contract for the services of one enslaved man, Plato, and hired another, a waiter named George, by the year. The First Lady communicated the terms of a different arrangement in 1804: "Mr. Madison is willing to take David for 400 dollars to be paid at the end of one year from the time of his comeing into service with lawful interest from that date, it being understood that at the expiration of five years he is to become free, & that in the mean time Mr. M. is to be his owner." Dolley and her lady friends borrowed slaves for dinner parties from one another like so many cups of sugar. Also, there are numerous instances of the Madisons employing free persons, white or black, for specific jobs, such as upholstering or gardening.[12]

As for a chef or head cook, no references to this position are known coinciding with the start of the Madison administration other than a casual mention of "the cook" in a September 1809 letter from Latrobe to Dolley. Honoré Julien, Jefferson's French chef, afterward hung out his shingle as a caterer in the city, and the First Lady might have engaged him by the event.

At a White House dinner on 12 November 1812, the guests included author Washington Irving from New York and Mr. and Mrs. William Seaton, he the new coeditor/publisher of the *National Intelligencer* newspaper. First son Payne was home from school and present at the dinner. Paul Jennings was likely present as well, serving, standing, absorbing. Fine French dishes and exquisite wines were offered, the latter a major topic of discussion. Sarah Seaton noted that once the cloth was taken away, "Ice-creams, macaroons, preserves and various cakes are placed on the table, which are removed for almonds, raisins, pecannuts, apples, pears, *etc.* Candles were introduced before the ladies left the table; and the gentlemen continued half an hour longer to drink a social glass."[13]

William C. Preston, yet *another* cousin to Dolley, newly graduated from Washington College in Virginia, was part of the social scene this winter of 1812–13. He was the same age as Payne, and the two young gallants must have enjoyed one another's company. "The season was gay and I very fully participated in it," remembered Preston. Dances, dinners, theater, card games, horse races, picnics—these were some of the ways young elites forestalled ennui.

Directly to the north of the White House was President's Square. It was originally part of the much larger president's private park, most of which was to the south of the mansion, but these seven acres were given back to the city at the recommendation of Thomas Jefferson, who did not want so "ostentatious a 'front yard' for the president of a republic." While the Madison household occupied the White House, it was the only structure facing the square, which itself was a half abandoned apple orchard with a few crooked gravestones poking up in one corner.

During construction of the executive mansion, a score of wooden huts faced the overgrown common, temporary housing for the hired slaves who helped build the edifice in the 1790s.[14]

An observer on the scene in 1809 reported: "The President's house was surrounded by a high rock wall, and there was an iron gate immediately in front of it, and from that gate to the Capitol the street was just as straight as a gun barrel. Nearly all the houses were on that street." Young Paul Jennings ventured through the gate on occasion; on Sundays he was free to explore on his own time. He lamented "that street," Pennsylvania Avenue, not being paved but rather "always in an awful condition from either mud or dust." Another chronicler of the day elaborated:

> Nothing could be more splendid than Washington *on paper,* and nothing more entirely the reverse of splendid than the real city, when, at wide intervals, a few paltry houses were seen to arise amid the surrounding forest. The founders of Washington imagined it would become the seat of a large foreign commerce. This expectation has been disappointed. Washington has no trade of any kind, and there is, at present, no prospect of it ever possessing any. Its only hopes are now founded on its advantages as the seat of government.[15]

A visitor from Massachusetts noted that the "Federal City is called a very dull place, except when Congress is in session. Then, it is dignified, and enlightened by the thundering debates, the splendid equipages of foreign ambassadors, and the smiling beauty of the presidential levees." Washington Irving first arrived in January 1811, in the midst of the overlapping congressional winter session and the social season, and was enthralled by the lifestyle, his mind "continually and delightfully exercised" by the many intelligent people he met. "I may compare a place like this to a huge library," he enthused. But when Congress adjourned he was crestfallen: "You cannot imagine how forlorn this desert city appears to me, now the great tide of casual population has rolled away."

Of course, for tradesmen, shopkeepers, and others not part of the social set, the challenge was to make a year-long living.

Wherever Jennings went, he would see other black people. One visiting Englishman observed, "The waiters in the hotels, the servants in private families, and many of the lower class of artisans, are slaves," while another noticed that blacks were the chief sellers at Washington's three marketplaces. It was a Sunday when the Vice President's son approached the capital for a visit in the summer of 1813, and the road was crowded with slaves returning from town with baskets and tubs. As he noted in his diary, "Their masters permit them on this day alone to make their sales."[16]

In 1810, Washington City itself had a total population of 8,208; about 28 percent were black and, of that subpopulation, two-thirds were slaves. That left 867 free blacks, and Jennings must have met a good number of them, some through John Freeman, who though still a slave himself was scheduled to be freed and had eight years more experience than Jennings as an African American in the capital. Certainly Jennings was exposed to a wider variety of African American modes of life than he had been in Orange County, Virginia.

As everywhere in America, the actions and opportunities afforded African Americans, even if free, were circumscribed by law. There were black codes in the nation's capital as early as 1808, a stinging series of requirements, restrictions, and fines. Persons of color were not allowed in the streets after ten at night, for example, and could assemble—even for a social gathering in a private home—only by permit. Violators who did not meet the fines were subject to imprisonment. However, as historian Constance Green has pointed out, "Provisions of the black code were weapons put to use only when white people became frightened and vindictive."[17]

Two African Americans whose Washington experiences overlapped with those of Jennings and who also left accounts are Michael Shiner and Charles Ball, both born into slavery on Maryland plantations and later leased by their owners to work in the Washington Navy Yard.

The wages of a hired slave belonged to the owner, but arrangements whereby the slave kept a portion of his earnings were common.

Shiner's diary descended in his family for generations and eventually came into the possession of the Library of Congress. Shiner, like John Freeman, was scheduled to be freed when a given term of enslavement ended. His master's will contained this clause: "Having purchased a Negro Man named Michael Shiner for the term of fifteen years only, and having promised to manumit and set him free at the expiration of eight years, if he conducted himself worthy of such a privilege, it is my will and desire and I hereby set free and manumit the said Michael Shiner at the expiration of eight years from the date of said purchase." Some Upper South slave owners at this time recognized that "term slavery," as it has been called, was an efficient form of enslavement. Knowing that freedom lay in his future, a slave was more motivated to cooperate, less likely to run away, while the owner was spared the traditional burden of supporting the slave once his working life was over. When Shiner was freed, he continued to work at the Navy Yard, listed on the employee payroll as receiving 80 percent of the wages of his white counterparts.

The narrative of Charles Ball's life as told to a Philadelphia lawyer was published in 1837. Ball related the story of his first exposure to the new capital:

One Saturday evening, when I came home from the corn-field, my master told me that he had hired me out for a year at the city of Washington, and that I would have to live at the navy-yard. On the new-year's-day following, which happened about two weeks afterwards, my master set forward for Washington, on horseback, and ordered me to accompany him on foot. . . . In the course of a few days the duties of my station became quite familiar to me. . . . I was permitted to spend Sunday afternoon in my own way. I generally went up into the city to see the new and splendid buildings; often walked as far as Georgetown, and made many new acquaintances amongst the slaves, and frequently saw large numbers of people of my colour chained together in long trains, and driven off towards the south.[18]

Acting as soon as the twenty-year ban in the Constitution against such action had expired, the government under the Jefferson administration forbade further international importation of slaves, but the domestic slave trade was robust and went in one direction: south.

Slave pens were located throughout the city, including in the shadow of the White House and Capitol, with auctions of enslaved men, women, and children a regular occurrence. As the plantation economy faltered in Virginia and Maryland while flourishing in Georgia, Louisiana, and Mississippi, the differential in slave prices meant substantial resale profits for traders. The demand for plantation slaves in the Deep South grew so high that blacks, both free and enslaved, risked kidnapping. President Madison's private secretary, Edward Coles, wanted him to do something about "such a revolting sight" on the streets of the American capital as "gangs of Negroes, some in chains, on their way to a southern market." Once, when the President and his secretary together came upon people in irons destined for sale to the South, the younger man recalled that he "jeered" Madison by sarcastically "congratulating him as the Chief of our great Republic" that he was spared the mortification of witnessing such a scene in the company of a foreign minister, a "representative of a nation, less boastful perhaps of its regard for the rights of man, but more observant of them." Coles had grown up in the same Virginia Piedmont as Jefferson and Madison and was a devotee of both statesmen and the natural rights doctrine they espoused. Born in 1786, he was a member of the rising generation that Jefferson predicted would not tolerate slavery, having taken in ideals of liberty with their mother's milk. Sure enough, Coles was convinced that slavery and republicanism were incompatible. Coles claimed he "frequently talked unreservedly about the enslavement of the Negroes" with President Madison, "always expressing freely my opinions." He voiced his "surprise that just men & long sighted politicians should not . . . take the necessary steps to put in train [slavery's] termination."[19]

If young Paul Jennings was present as waiting footman while some of these conversations were transpiring, it would be the start of his own consciousness being raised. Paul, of course, could not freely express his opinions; one imagines these overheard ideas falling like sweet, or bittersweet, tunes onto his ears. A good listener with a good mind, he too could appreciate that all men had natural rights and their enslavement was never justified.

The inconsistency that Edward Coles harped on and Paul Jennings lived with was described most energetically by many a foreign visitor to America's capital. "Washington, the seat of government of a free people, is disgraced by slavery," Englishman Thomas Hamilton expounded. "While the orators in Congress are rounding periods about liberty in one part of the city, proclaiming, *alto voce,* that all men are equal, and that 'resistance to tyrants is obedience to God,' the auctioneer is exposing human flesh to sale in another!" Hamilton related with ironic relish seeing enslaved coachmen of some of the legislators waiting outside the Capitol one rainy day to convey their masters home "when *the rights of man* had been sufficiently disserted on for the day."[20]

◆

PAUL JENNINGS RETURNED TO MONTPELIER with the First Couple for a long stay in late summer and early fall each year of the administration but one (the fateful 1814, when Washington was invaded). By July that first summer he must have sorely missed his mother and other connections in Virginia. Back home the roses and jasmine would be releasing their fragrances into the air and the corn in the field increasing to knee height so rapidly that (some plantation hands swore) you could *hear* it grow. The household had intended to depart for Montpelier earlier, but the President's business held them back until the third week in July. Finally they exited the sweltering city. When the Blue Ridge Mountains came into view on the second day of travel, the party anticipated the prospect of their final destination. "The pretty country begins near Orange Court House, at the place where the land is raised in rounded hillocks and little valleys," penned a visitor who took the same approach to Montpelier during Madison's presidency, and continued: "The layer of earth-mold is thicker there and of better quality. The trees are prettier and better nourished; brooks and springs appear. The atmosphere is purer, the air more healthful."[21] They were home, and planning to settle in for a good two months.

Visitors were part of every stay. Mr. and Mrs. Samuel H. Smith came the first week of August in 1809. Like the Thorntons (who visited Montpelier while Madison was Secretary of State), the Smiths were a prominent couple in Washington and regular guests at the White House. He was founding editor of the *National Intelligencer;* she, Margaret Bayard Smith, an author as well as wife and mother. "Hospitality is the presiding genius of this house," Margaret Smith declared. Indeed. Dolley leisurely welcomed her friend and had a servant bring in punch and pineapples as they chatted in her chamber, even as she claimed, laughing, that there were "three and twenty in the house" at that moment. For the hostess to be able to present a relaxed demeanor to each of twenty-three persons, Paul, Sukey, and the rest of the domestic staff were relentlessly taxed behind the scenes. When it was time to go to bed, one of the housemaids, Nany, led the way upstairs with a candle. Margaret Smith remarked, "You have a good mistress Nany," and Nany allowed that she believed her the best mistress in the world. "The next morning Nany called me to a late breakfast, brought me ice and water . . . and assisted me to dress," Smith recorded in her notebook, impressed with Nany's attentiveness. She was also impressed with the breakfast: "We sat down between 15 and 20 persons to breakfast—tea, coffee, hot wheat bread, light cakes, a pone, or corn loaf—cold ham, nice hashes, chicken, etc."[22]

Margaret Smith's account of her visit did not mention the major construction project at Montpelier just getting under way. Madison decided to have the mansion enlarged and enhanced, including the

addition of flanking brick wings. He also ordered a temple-form sum-
merhouse to be built on one side of the mansion and new houses for
the domestic slaves on the other. By mid-1809 the skilled craftsmen
Jefferson had recruited to the area to remodel Monticello were working at Montpelier, kilning bricks and sawing plank. Madison's ideas for
room use were still in flux when the real construction started late in
1809. As revealed in a letter from his master builder in October of that
year, Madison was envisioning the renovated central space as a dining
room and the large chamber in the north wing addition as a new library, but these spaces instead became a drawing room and master bedchamber, respectively. Benjamin Latrobe, Surveyor of Public Buildings
in Washington, arranged for Madison to buy surplus sheet iron and
glass from the construction of the U.S. Capitol, the sheet iron for the
roofs of the wings and the glass for new windows. The nearly two-year
delay in receiving these goods was symptomatic of the overall building
project, which took over four years to complete.[23]

British minister Francis Jackson was waiting to see the President
when the household arrived back in Washington on 1 October 1809.
After a full morning of meetings, Jackson was grateful that while
he and Madison talked, "a negro servant brought in some glasses of
punch and a seed cake." This was the kind of duty that fell to Paul
Jennings as a White House footman. The diplomat who succeeded
Jackson as British minister was already familiar to Jennings. Augustus
John Foster, who visited Montpelier in 1807 while he was secretary
to the British legation, returned to America in the head diplomatic
position in 1811. Jennings may well have enjoyed his exposure to
newsmakers of the day and come around to agreeing with Minister
Foster, who concluded, "Washington City was, I think, in spite of
its inconveniences and its desolate appearance, the most agreeable
town to reside in for any length of time. . . . There is a great deal of
occupation and of interest connected with public affairs . . . and it is
satisfactory . . . to meet there with so many of the principal people
of the Country."[24]

The yearly visits to Montpelier, while as welcome to Paul and Sukey as they were to James and Dolley—a chance to enjoy the Piedmont climate and reconnect with kin and neighbors—were, of course, working vacations for all. Jennings described in his memoir the interruption of their stay in 1812: "Soon after war was declared, Mr. Madison made his regular summer visit to his farm in Virginia. We had not been there long before an express reached us one evening, informing Mr. M. of General Hull's surrender. He was astounded at the news, and started back to Washington the next morning."[25]

The War of 1812 was the perhaps inevitable culmination of an unsuccessful experiment in commercial coercion going back to Madison's Secretary of State days. Restricting trade had failed to end British impressments of American seaman and other conflicts. After "frequent consultations at the White House as to the expediency of doing it," as Jennings noted in the *Reminiscences,* Congress declared war in June 1812. Augustus John Foster was recalled. Benjamin Latrobe's wife, Mary, remembering the "rational" entertainments the British minister hosted (where new publications and prints were provided for those who did not dance), watched in sadness as his "chariot and four" passed her house in exiting the capital. The stresses of a wartime presidency showed on James Madison at the White House reception that followed his second inauguration on 4 March 1813. Sarah Seaton was in attendance, and observed the chief executive and his guests. "The major part of the respectable citizens offered their congratulations, ate his ice-creams and bonbons, drank his Madeira, made their bows and retired, leaving him fatigued beyond measure with the incessant bending to which his politeness urged him, and in which he never allows himself to be eclipsed, returning bow for bow, even to those *ad infinitum* of [French minister] Serrurier and other foreigners."[26]

Jennings's firsthand accounts on the War of 1812 are those most often quoted by historians since the *Reminiscences* were first published. Jennings detailed many of the machinations of Cabinet and military officers, revealing his political acuity. He chronicled both the political calls and local reactions as the war unfolded: "The people of Washington began to be alarmed for the safety of the city, as the British held Chesapeake Bay with a powerful fleet and army. Everything seemed to be left to General Armstrong, then Secretary of war, who ridiculed the idea that there was any danger."

The result of this leadership gap was a city of residents alternating between we-need-to-do-something anxiety and there-is-no-danger-here placidity. Despite soldiers present in the streets and drilling in front of the White House, the city was mostly business as usual when the Vice President's son, Elbridge Gerry Jr., visited in July 1813. Or, rather, fun as usual, in the case of this twenty-one-year-old. Even when he took his turn among local citizens volunteering to patrol the city at night, he treated the duty as a lark. He would have been a great partner for first son Payne Todd—two bons vivants seeking the high life—but Payne was in Europe at this time. Though his stepfather was disappointed that Payne would not be going to his alma mater at Princeton or to any other college, he handed him an opportunity to accompany the American peace delegation to Europe. Gerry, meanwhile, was soaking in the city's public baths like a Roman epicurean, satisfying a near-constant yen for "*a good high* on some Soda Water," and chasing one pretty girl after another.[27] He was charmed by the First Lady (and it turned out that he was *yet another* one of her cousins), but upon meeting the "most beautiful girl, the handsomest I have seen since I left home," the same day that he "had half promised to take tea with Mrs. Madison," he concluded that tea with the First Lady was "morally impossible under my present situation."

"The President's house is a perfect palace," Gerry declared, and visited several times over the summer. He noted the portrait of General Washington "as large as life" at the head of the dining room and that the east room, or grand council chamber, as he called it, was *still* unfinished. Privileged as the Vice President's son, young Gerry was even "shewn upstairs to [President Madison's] room," perhaps by Paul Jennings. Gerry evidenced scorn for servants in his diary. He missed an invitation and blamed it on "the stupidity of the servants." Another time, after a pleasant evening, Gerry returned to his rented carriage to find the coachman asleep, and he and his companion gave the carriage a violent shake and were "heartily amused" by the coachman's sudden fright. Madison later referred to young Gerry in a letter, aptly enough, as "a dolt."[28]

A year after Gerry's visit, in August 1814, "The enemy had got so near," as Jennings told it, "there could be no doubt of their intentions. Great alarm existed, and some feeble preparations for defense were made." Secretary of War John Armstrong was useless, and the top military commander, General William Winder, was barely more decisive. President Madison himself rode to the front on 24 August, a stifling hot day, and joined the troops at Bladensburg, Maryland. There, less than ten miles from Washington, the Americans came face to face with British regulars; it was their last opportunity to prevent an enemy invasion of the capital. The President countermanded just one of Winder's orders, sending Commodore Joshua Barney's seamen and marines into battle. According to one historian, "That presidential order produced the only redeeming feature of the operations." Jennings related an account of Commodore Barney's force, which included free blacks:

> Com. Barney's flotilla was stripped of men, who were placed in battery, at Bladensburg, where they fought splendidly. A large part of his men were tall strapping negroes, mixed with white sailors and marines. Mr. Madison reviewed them just before the fight, and asked Com. Barney if his "negroes would not run on the approach of the British?" "No sir," said Barney, "they don't know how to run; they will die by their guns first." They fought till a large part of them were killed or wounded; and Barney himself wounded and taken prisoner.

One of Barney's men was Charles Ball, who, after working as a leased slave at the Navy Yard, had been kidnapped and forced to labor in the plantation fields of the Deep South. He eventually escaped and made his way back home. He was posing as a free man "when Commodore Barney came into the Patuxent with his flotilla, [and] I enlisted on board one of his barges, and was employed sometimes in the capacity of seaman, and sometimes as a cook on the barge." Ball manned a cannon at Bladensburg and stood at his gun until the Commodore himself was shot down. The courage Barney's force evinced that day contrasted with the cowardice of the militiamen on the scene, who, as Ball described them, "ran like sheep chased by dogs." (Ball related in his narrative how, sixteen years after the battle, he was kidnapped again and, while on a forced march that would terminate in Georgia, passed the old battleground at Bladensburg and reflected—in irons—on his having "fought in the ranks of the army of the United States in defense of the liberty and independence of that which I then regarded as my country.")[29]

Jennings's identification with and pride in the bravery Barney's men displayed at Bladensburg is obvious. We can guess at his frustrated reaction to some white citizens' state of alarm stemming not just from the encroachment of the British but from fear of the city's black residents. The Madisons' close friend Margaret Bayard Smith called them the "home enemy" and expected trouble from them either by insurrection or by their joining the British. Gerry Jr. had referenced the same worry in his diary the summer before: "Should we be attacked, there will be great danger of the blacks rising, and to prevent this patroles are very necessary to keep them in awe." When such a specter never materialized, Smith was relieved but gained no insight into the true range of attitudes of her African American neighbors.

While the contest at Bladensburg ensued amid the smoke of firearms, the air in Washington was almost as thick with tension and humidity. Jennings went about his usual routine at the President's house, preparing for the three o'clock meal. "I set the table myself, and brought up the ale, cider and wine, and placed them in the cooler." Other households had nervously vacated the city, but the First Lady insisted on setting an example of calm. Sukey was "lolling out of a chamber window" when that illusion was suddenly broken. As Jennings recalled: "James Smith, a free colored man who had accompanied Mr. Madison to Bladensburg, galloped up to the house, waving his hat, and cried out, 'Clear out, clear out! General Armstrong had ordered a retreat!' All then was confusion."

Anna Thornton, a few blocks away on F Street, observed the rider as well: "Saw a man riding as hard as possible toward the President's house—we went up soon after and found that Mrs. Madison was gone."[30] Dolley, before she "caught up what silver she could . . . and jumped into the chariot with her servant girl Sukey," ordered her servants to break the frame and rescue the portrait of George Washington. Jennings held the ladder and, after the enormous portrait, ninety-five inches high, had been freed from its frame, was undoubtedly one of the "two colored boys" who helped a pair of "gentlemen of New York" load the stretched canvas onto the cart they had managed to procure, any wheeled conveyance being now at a premium. The portrait was ferried away to the safety of a barn in rural Maryland. This is the stuff of legend. Because of the impulse of Dolley Madison and the efforts of Jennings and others, Americans today celebrate "the rescue of the portrait of George Washington" instead of ducking the anniversary of "the burning of the White House."[31]

Once the "people running in every direction"—including John Freeman and family rushing off in a coachee with a feather bed lashed to it—eased, the wait for the actual invasion by British troops stretched out. Jennings recalled:

> About sundown I walked over to the Georgetown ferry, and found the President and all hands (the gentlemen . . . who acted as a sort of body-guard for him) waiting for the boat. It soon returned, and we all crossed over, and passed up the road about a mile; they then left us servants to wander about. . . . As we were cutting up some pranks a white wagoner ordered us away, and told his boy Tommy to reach out his gun, and he would shoot us. I told him "he had better have used it at Bladensburg."

This last bit of bravado reveals both Jennings's verve and patriotism.

Soon after Jennings found a place to settle in for the evening, he heard "a tremendous explosion, and, rushing out, saw that the public buildings, navy yard, ropewalks, &c., were on fire."[32] Watching the flames, he perhaps realized that the Madison household would never live in the White House again.

Michael Shiner, who remained in the city throughout the reign of destruction, witnessed the approach of the British troops. The enemy soldiers, having marched from Bladensburg to Washington, came into view as they mounted Capitol Hill: "They looked like flames of fier all red coats and the stoks of ther guns painted with red vermilon and the iron work shind like a spanish dollar." Hearing the tread of army boots was enough for young Shiner, and he started to dart off, but a white woman "caught hold of Me. Wher are you runig to you niger you. What do you recon the Brtish Wants With such a niger as you?" The soldiers plundered and set fire to government buildings through the night, but then a rainstorm, accompanied by terrific thunder, lightning, and hail, came sweeping on and doused the flames. The city still smoldered as the British army left it on Friday, 26 August. Shiner believed their wheels and horses' feet must have been muffled "for they Went a way so easy that you scaresly could hear them."[33]

Before the month ended, the presidential couple, as well as their servants, were reunited at the Cutts town house next to the Thorntons', a few blocks from the White House, now a cracked and blackened shell. City residents feared the British might return. Anna Thornton noted in her diary on 30 August: "We had another quiet night & hope the Enemy will not pay us a second Visit. . . . The President and Lady being next door *we* were guarded at night."

That same day, William Thornton had arranged with John Tayloe for the government's rental of Tayloe's city residence at New York Avenue and 18th Street, called the Octagon, as a temporary President's house. Already in residence when the Madisons arrived in early September was Dolley's parrot, which had been deposited at the Octagon by John Sioussat the evening of the fire. The bird, trained to utter certain phrases in Sioussat's native language, had joined the French minister who was staying at Tayloe's house with his home flag displayed that evening expressly to prevent it from being torched by the British.

It was raining, or at least drizzling, during the first part of September as the Madison household tried to get comfortable in the Octagon. Dolley wrote Mary Latrobe that among the family's personal "valuable stores" that had been lost to the fire were "all my servants' clothes." Up in Baltimore Harbor, meanwhile, British ships were bombarding the American forces at Fort McHenry. The boom of sizzling rockets could be heard in Washington. These were the same whistling rockets whose "red glare" lit up the American flag at the fort and inspired Francis Scott Key (whom Madison had sent to the scene to arrange a prisoner-of-war exchange) to compose the lyrics to the country's future national anthem.[34]

The two sides had basically fought to a standstill. The Madison administration looked to the American and British representatives meeting in Ghent to configure an honorable draw. "We lived [at the Octagon] till the news of peace arrived," Jennings recorded in his reminiscences. All the household members and their guests felt the tension as that wait lengthened into the new year. Harvard professor George Ticknor, a dinner guest in January 1815, described the company sitting in the Octagon drawing room before the meal was served when "a servant came in and whispered to Mr. Madison, who went out, followed by his Secretary." The mail had arrived, and the guests—which included members of Congress and military officers—waited anxiously, but the President returned "with added gravity" and said there was no news. "Silence ensued," reported Ticknor. "No man seemed to know what to say at such a crisis."[35]

Finally, welcome word arrived on 14 February in the hand of a breathless Christopher Hughes, secretary to the American peace delegation in Ghent. The ship that carried Hughes from Europe came to port in Annapolis, and Hughes immediately raced a copy of the treaty the thirty-three miles to Madison in Washington. When the Octagon residents learned that the commissioners had agreed to terms of peace, "We were all crazy with joy," Jennings remembered. The servants' quarters were in the cellar, and Edward Coles's sister, too excited to pull the service bell wire, skipped protocol and hollered the news to the downstairs set: "Miss Sally Coles, a cousin of Mrs. Madison . . . came to the head of the stairs, crying out, 'Peace! peace!' and told John Freeman (the butler) to serve out wine liberally to the servants and others. I played the 'President's March' on the violin, John Suse´ and some others were drunk for two days, and such another joyful time was never seen in Washington."

Madison signed the Treaty of Ghent in the second-floor study of the Octagon. The celebrations were ongoing. "After the news of peace, and of General Jackson's victory at New Orleans, which reached here about the same time, there were great illuminations," remembered Jennings. The victory at New Orleans took place before the combatants knew a treaty had already been agreed to. Never mind; the Americans took nothing but pride in this sound defeat of British ground forces, which made the *status quo ante bellum* terms of the peace treaty much easier to take.

During this time, Dolley Madison was concerned with her husband's fragile health and that of her servants as well. She complained to a friend, "Our servants are constantly sick, owing to the damp cellar to which they are confined." These conditions encouraged relocation of the temporary President's residence to the so-called Seven Buildings. As one traveler explained the local terminology, "Here and there was what is called in the vernacular of the country 'a block of building,' or, in other words, a connected range of shops and dwelling-houses." The Seven Buildings was located on Pennsylvania Avenue about half a dozen blocks to the northwest of the White House. The President's household moved into the corner town house in the spring of 1815. "Whenever soldiers marched by," Jennings recalled that his mistress "always sent out and invited them in to take wine and refreshments, giving them liberally of the best in the house." Special guests included the great hero of the day. "General Jackson came on with his wife, to whom numerous dinner parties and levees were given," Jennings recollected.[36]

By this time, there had been a couple of changes in the domestic staff. John Sioussat left the Madisons' employ after the conflagration of Washington and took a position at the local branch of the Bank of the United States. One of his last services was salvaging some iron kitchen equipment from the rubble at the White House. Meanwhile, a new steward entered the picture. Benjamin Latrobe acted as go-between, recommending a Frenchman named Henry Doyhar to the First Lady and enumerating for Doyhar his future responsibilities and compensation: "Your duty will be to undertake the business of confectionary & cooking with a woman and a young man, pretty good cooks, under you; to market, to set out the table, & superintend the waiting upon the guests, & the arrangement during the dinner in the dining room, to keep correct accounts . . . Your wages are to be thirty dollars a month." Doyhar's tenure was a short one; he complained about the workload and bickered with his fellow domestics. Madison dismissed him after six months.

After July 1815, John Freeman was a free man, working for pay in the President's household and preparing to set up a household of his own. In 1816 he and an associate, John Shorter, purchased a remarkable assortment of goods for $400, including horses and a buffalo cow, a carriage, bed and bedding, furniture, and table wares. (John Shorter had been a stable hand in the Jefferson White House who stayed on for occasional employment under Madison.)[37]

In the summer of 1815, Payne Todd returned from Europe. Though some of his time abroad was put to good use, such as in acquiring artwork for Montpelier, Payne came back hardened in the habits of gaming and drinking that he had indulged in many foreign capitals. Exasperated with his ways, Henry Clay, who had been a member of the overseas peace delegation, asked him point blank, "Will you never gain anything by experience?" Payne's contemporaries, such as William C. Preston and Elbridge Gerry Jr., were also conspicuous consumers and, to use Preston's word, "roisterers," but Preston and Gerry, unlike Payne, eventually pulled away from such behavior and pursued careers. Preston specifically recognized the epicurean lifestyle as a trap that could catch boys of his class in a life of perpetual "riot and dissipation" from which there would be no turning back. Time would prove that for Payne, the answer to Clay's query was sadly No.[38]

Payne Todd had been tested, and failed. The new national capital had been tested, too. There were calls to give up on Washington, given that its public buildings were practically decimated and its coastal location was clearly vulnerable. "Strong efforts were made to remove the seat of government north," Jennings recalled, but in the summer of 1815, "Mr. John Law, a large property-holder about the Capitol, fearing it would not be rebuilt, got up a subscription and built a large brick building . . . and offered it to Congress for their use, till the Capitol could be rebuilt." This "coaxed [the members of Congress] back," concluded Jennings. Even when restoration of the Capitol was well under way, a foreign traveler testified:

> Marks of the late conflagration are still very apparent, while the walls bear evidence of public opinion in relation to the transaction. . . . Some of the pencil drawings exhibit the military commander hanging upon a tree; others represent the President running off without his hat or wig; some, Admiral Cockburn robbing henroosts: to which are added such inscriptions as, "The capital of the Union lost by cowardice;" "Curse cowards;" "A_____ sold the city for 5000 dollars;" "James Madison is a rascal, a coward, and a fool;" "Ask no questions," &c.[39]

Hired slaves provided the labor for the reconstruction of the Capitol, White House, and other public buildings burned by the British. This was evidence enough that though the "Second War for Independence" had been brought to a successful conclusion, America's shameful anomaly remained. One critic taunted, "The man who would study the contradictions of individual and national character, and learn by how wide an interval, profession may be divided from performance, should come to Washington. . . . He will hear the words of freedom, and he will see the practice of slavery." The traffickers in human wares who disgusted Edward Coles during Madison's first term were still on the streets when first-time visitor Jesse Torrey described seeing a slave coffle pass by Capitol Hill on the opening day of Congress in December 1815. Alerted by the chant of a stammering boy . . .

> "There goes the Ge-Ge-orgy men (. . . the general title applied to slave-traders, indiscriminately, is *'Georgia-men'*) with a drove o' niggers chain'd together two and two" . . . I just had a distant *glimpse* of a light covered waggon, followed by a procession of men, women and children, resembling that of a funeral.

Torrey, a Philadelphia physician, rallied to the abolitionist cause. "The tragedy of a company of men, women and children, pinioned and bound together with chains and ropes, without accusation of crime" offended him as a *"native citizen"* who had structured his "life coevally with [the country's] constitutional organization." Moved to investigate, Torrey was shocked to learn "that several hundred people, including not legal slaves only, but many kidnapped freemen and youth bound to service for a term of years and unlawfully sold as slaves for life, are annually collected at Washington (as if it were an emporium for slavery) for transportation to the slave regions." In 1817 Torrey published his evidence and analysis in a book, *A Portraiture of Domestic Slavery in the United States.* Among the individuals he interviewed was a woman named Anna who had shattered her spine when she jumped from a garret over the third floor of a brick tavern on F Street in a desperate attempt to escape from slave traders. Now that she was crippled, the slave traders gave the woman, already involuntarily separated from her husband, to the tavern landlord (as compensation for taking care

of her) but "carried my children off with 'em to Carolina." Not all of
Torrey's arguments focused on heart-wrenching personal testimonies.
He insisted that the act of depriving free blacks of their liberty was "a
violation of the constitution of the United States and an *overt attack*
upon the public liberty" and that even slaves had "moral rights."[40]

The last full year of the Madison administration got under way
with the traditional reception at the President's residence. "On New
Year's day the whole city and most of the members of Congress went to
the President's levee to pay him the felicitations of the season, and gaze
unmeaningly at each other," as one of the members of Congress characterized it. The weather in January of 1816 was severe, and by the end
of the first week there were three or four inches of snow on the ground,
but this did not keep Dolley's Wednesday night Drawing Rooms in the
Seven Buildings town house from flourishing. An attendee at one of
the January assemblages, for which so great a throng turned out that
they were jammed in two large rooms, was impressed that "coffee and
wine and punch were handed about, and whips to the ladies," the latter
presumably a cream drink of the period. One of the most memorable
of all Dolley's Drawing Rooms took place the next month: "The deco-
rations were magnificent, and the building was brilliantly illuminated
from garret to cellar, much of this light being made by pine torches
held by trained slaves." Individuals for such duty could be hired for a
mere 35 cents each for the evening.[41]

The Madisons along with Jennings and the other Montpelier slaves
residing at the city town house took a lengthy hiatus in 1816—they
reached home on the fifth of June and remained a full four months.
This would be the household's last trip to Montpelier before they returned to Virginia for good. One of their visitors over this period was
none other than abolitionist Jesse Torrey. By his own accounting, Torrey's "ardent zeal" for the abolitionist cause was on full display at Montpelier. On reflection, he felt that he had been overly strident in his
appeal and belatedly apologized to the Madisons—Mr. and Mrs.—for
his "crude and incoherent rhapsodies on the subject of African Slavery"

when at Montpelier and in Washington, asking for lenity owing to "the purity of my intentions." (Madison wrote Torrey back and assured him no apology was necessary.)

Back in the city, a new issue had bubbled to the political surface. Massachusetts congressman Elijah Mills announced in a letter to his wife written on Christmas day 1816, "Tomorrow all the gentlemen of our mess have been engaged to dine with the President." (A "mess" was a coterie of like-minded congressmen who took room and board together.) The subject slated to be discussed—presumably while Jennings and his fellow enslaved domestics served a meal in the town house dining room—was "the project lately started for settling, with the free blacks which abound in the South and West, a colony, either on the coast of Africa, or in some remote region of our own country." Mills enclosed an essay for his wife to read that was circulating in Washington on the subject of colonization, which, Mills enthused, "has excited great interest."[42]

With the advent of 1817, the Madison administration was drawing to a close. Congressman Mills attended one of Dolley's last Drawing Rooms on 12 February, a "gay and pleasant evening," though not without sad emotions over the First Lady's imminent retirement. Just that day Mills and his colleagues had "gone through the idle ceremony of counting the presidential votes . . . and proclaiming Mr. Monroe as president-elect." On 4 April, a month after Monroe's inauguration, preparations for the Madison household's departure from Washington were nearly complete, and the now ex-President penned an associate: "The day after tomorrow I shall be on the road to my farm, where I shall be a fixture for the residue of my days." The first leg of the trip was actually accomplished via the new option of steamboat. Come 6 April, the Madison household was moving along the Potomac River by steam power, headed home to spring in Virginia.

There is evidence, however, that Jennings's return to the Virginia plantation was not without contention. Some two months before the April boat trip, Madison had received a letter from his brother William's son, Robert L. Madison, the nephew who had resided at the White House for half a year in 1813. Robert wrote to his uncle on 21 January 1817: "Capt. Eddins thinks that you ought to be apprised that when you were in Orange, your Servants Jim, Abram & Paul observed in the presence of Warrell that they never intended to return to Va: upon being asked what they meant to do, they replyed that their were Captains of Vessels who wanted Cooks & that they would enter into their service." This letter reveals that Jennings and two other Montpelier slaves (who were apparently part of the Madison Washington household, at least at this late date) were hatching a plan to run away. The Captain Eddins referred to was Abraham Eddins, a Montpelier overseer. The identity of "Warrell" is unknown, but most likely he was a local slave in whom Jennings and his cohorts had inadvisably confided.[43]

One imagines Jennings gnawing on the possibility of escape as he walked Washington's city streets over the final six months, his last window of opportunity to act. Jennings's eighteenth birthday was looming. He had come into his manhood in an important place at an important time. He had experienced a wartime adventure and the ever-changing attractions of the theater that was the capital city. Could he go back to the farm for the residue of his days? As the time until the final departure date for Virginia was whittled down from months to weeks, he reflected on all he had learned about himself and about the rights of man. Had Jesse Torrey and his antislavery "rhapsodies" been among the elements influencing him? There were many ways his mind had been exercised and challenged over these eight years. The decision Jennings wrestled with did not center only on personal risk, his willingness to chance being arrested and punished for an illegal run. The ties that bound him to Montpelier were as real as family, as strong as the next man's sense of place. Could he abandon the scene of his boyhood, the home of his mother, never to return?

It is not known if Madison confronted Jennings with the letter from his nephew. Possibly there were negotiations between master and bondman, given that Jennings not only returned to Montpelier but was promoted to a position of greater responsibility. On the steamboat home, James Madison, relieved of his heavy public responsibilities, was described as "like a school boy on a long vacation." As "playful as a child," he "talked and jested with everybody on board."[44] His servant Paul Jennings remained reflective. Whatever he might have told Madison to allay his fears and suspicions was not the whole truth. We can be sure there was a lot on his mind that his master knew nothing about.

CHAPTER THREE

"Enamoured with Freedom"

28 July 1817, the Front Portico at Montpelier

It would have been Paul Jennings who met the special guests and showed them into Madison's study. Later he perhaps slipped back outside to the front portico to see if he could catch a breeze. Throughout this Monday morning, one by one, the gentlemen scheduled for their meeting with the former President had approached the plantation gates. Oncoming visitors were spied by the telescope kept on the portico. Jennings could use a moment to himself now in the breeze, if any was to be had in late July, because he had recently been ill. On Friday, Dr. Charles Taylor, brother to diarist Francis Taylor, had attended him, returning the next day with medicine. Jennings had had yesterday—his one day off of each seven—to rest up and ready himself to assist his master in the care of their guests.

The meeting inside was about the new institution of higher learning—Central College—that Madison was working with Thomas Jefferson on establishing in Virginia, right in Charlottesville, they hoped. The two statesmen, as well as James Monroe, were among the trustees that comprised the college's "board of visitors." John Adams, retired in Massachusetts, took note: "From such a noble Tryumvirate, the World will expect something very *great and very new." As the sitting President busy with other du-ties, Monroe was unable to attend the meeting. Besides Jefferson, two other trustees were present, and Jennings had left the four men discussing potential professors and the plan for the first college building, or "pavilion."*[1]

After eight years in Washington, Jennings was back on the plantation, greeting visitors at the mansion door. The Madisons would receive a multitude of visitors at Montpelier during their retirement despite its rural location. "It is wildly situated—surrounded by forest," recalled one who came ahead anyway. Many guests were invited or at least arrived with letters of intro-duction. Others were ordinary citizens without special connections who came to the door desirous, as one put it, "to take by the hand a man who had occupied so conspicuous stations in our country's history." Among numerous foreign visitors past and to come, the Frenchman, the Baron de Montlezun, had made the trek to see the Sage of Montpelier just the last September. He rhapsodized about the Blue Ridge, like a semicircular amphitheater encasing the view from the portico: "The sight of the mountains refreshes the spirit; they elevate the mind and tend to put the imagination into play." Certainly Jennings was susceptible to such musings as he looked to the horizon. He knew how the appearance of the ridge varied. Some days—especially with the sunset—one could count layer after layer of romantic shades of lavender and blue. Some days the ridge was altogether hidden in haze. But it was always there, twenty-five miles away as the crow flies. Jennings perhaps wondered if he would always be here, a slave on a Vir-ginia plantation. After his experience in the federal city, he—like Madison when he returned from college in Princeton—might well have looked west to the Blue Ridge as representing hope in the future and pondered what would come next for him. Perhaps he overheard enough Enlightenment philosophy to know that it pos-ited a future that was better than the past because application of reason would advance not only science but human harmony as well. He certainly knew of the movement that jelled just the past December into the American Colonization Society; it had been all the talk while Jennings was still in Washington. The West was seen as a panacea to further the goals of this organization—if not actually to relocate free blacks there, then to use the money from sales of western lands to resettle them to Africa's West Coast or the Caribbean. Madison supported this plan as affording "the best hope yet presented of putting an end to the slavery in which not less than 600,000 unhappy negroes are now involved."[2] Jennings had a lot to think about, but, meanwhile, he had gentlemen to attend.

As it turned out, Central College became the University of Virginia by charter of the General Assembly a year and a half after this date. The first board of visitors meeting wherein this conversion was effected was also held at Montpelier, in the snowstorm of late February 1819. As for the immediate future, a week after the July 1817 meeting, Dr. Taylor's next patient at Montpelier proved to be the master himself. The invoice the doctor sent to Madison listed, right after Jennings's treatment, "Augst. 4th A Viset Attendance &c Yr.Self"; the charge was the same at £1.4.0.[3] Was Jennings's illness contagious? Either way, this proximity in the record stands as a metaphor for the close association that Paul Jennings and James Madison would maintain for the next two decades.

PAUL JENNINGS SPENT AS MUCH TIME AS ANYONE on the wide portico supported by classical columns in front of the house; it truly was a major room for the Montpelier residents and their guests. Mary Cutts described the telescope used "to spy the road where carriages and large parties were to be seen almost daily winding their way from afar to this harbor of hospitality" as "part of the portico furniture." The family and their guests gathered on the portico at all times of day and in all kinds of weather. Here, Cutts remembered, "Mr. Madison always exercised in stormy weather, walking his allotted number of miles." Margaret Bayard Smith confirmed this use when she visited the Madisons in retirement with her young daughter: "One time on the portico, [Mrs. Madison] took Anna by the hand, saying, 'come, let us run a race. I do not believe you can out run me. Madison and I often run races here, when the weather does not allow us to walk.'" Smith also described the dinner company relaxing on the portico both before and after the early evening meal was served in the dining room. The view was an irresistible draw: the mountains stretched across the horizon "as far as the eye can reach," fronted by "a broad level field of nearly a mile, bounded by a Forest." Jennings would have seen to the company's refreshment as they chatted, as he undoubtedly did when man of letters James K. Paulding visited for several weeks in the summer of 1818. Paulding recalled: "Our daily routine, with little variation, except Sunday was as follows. After breakfast, between seven & eight, I took my Segar and Seated myself on the western Portico, looking towards the Blue Ridge, while Mr. Madison would commence a conversation, sometimes on Public Affairs . . . sometimes on Literary and Philosophical subjects."[4] We can imagine Jennings, as waiting servant, standing behind the two men and listening in on their conversations.

From such a post, Jennings viewed in the foreground the paling fence running parallel to the house. A perpendicular gravel walk led from its center gate to the steps of the portico. Along that walk was kept a large tin cup, and niece Mary Cutts reported that it "had been there for years; after every rain it was brought to [Mr. Madison] to measure the quantity which had fallen." This was the vessel—overflowing with water each morning when it was checked——that Madison referred to in his letter to Jefferson in connection with the flood of August 1807.

If Jennings scanned to the right, he saw a lawn of green where Moses's blacksmith shop had once been, with the forge observed by Augustus John Foster in 1807. About five years after Foster's visit, Madison had the enslaved hands relocate the blacksmith shop that Moses and his crew had built in this area, restricting the unsightly clutter and its associated noise, smoke, and smells to a farther distance from the mansion. The stretch of land was grassed over, and Madison employed the same skilled joiners from Monticello who had enlarged his house to construct a neoclassical temple—a circle of Tuscan columns—above a twenty-four-foot-deep icehouse. Down a rolling slope from the spot was a pond, probably dammed by slaves for the express purpose of generating ice in winter. The men would cart up great quantities of ice to lower into the cavity, a depth of two stories. An allee of silver pines led from the house to the temple, which, according to Cutts, "was intended, but never used, for [Mr. Madison's] study," perhaps because "it was built over the icehouse which made it very cool."[5] Still, it must have been a pleasure for Madison to admire this symbol of the Roman republic, and Dolley's guests were able to be served iced drinks all through the summer, altogether a satisfying combination of the aesthetic and the functional.

If Jennings looked to the other side, he could not see around the corner to the south yard where his home was, one in a series of outbuildings that included a kitchen, smokehouses, and a stable as well as dwellings for enslaved families. As one visitor described it, surveying the landscape from under the portico, "To the left, peeping through the foliage near the house, you catch a glimpse, at some distance, of the barns and farming arrangements of the estate." Indeed, even visitors approaching the mansion from that direction by the fence-lined road that ran past these outbuildings could barely discern the structures. As Cutts noted, "On the left were clumps of rare trees of which the weeping willow and the silver poplar predominated; these concealed the out buildings so necessary to such an establishment." An antebellum publication on the homes of American states-men delved further into the function of the foliage:

> The [trees] half screen those dependencies of a handsome establishment—
> stables, dairies and the like—which, left openly in sight, look very ill, and
> can be made to look no otherwise, even by the trying to make them look
> genteel: for they are disagreeable objects, that call up (attire them as you will)
> ideas not dainty. As, therefore, the eye should not miss them altogether—for
> their absence would imply great discomfort and inconvenience—the best
> way is to half-veil them, as is done at Montpelier.[6]

The cluster of outbuildings in the south yard may have been screened from visitors upon arrival but was perfectly visible from the mansion's second-floor terrace that overlooked it. This area, with its detached kitchen and two smokehouses, was the service yard for the mansion as well as home to the enslaved domestics. Their daily activities working and living in this yard revolved around washing laundry, preserving meat, and preparing meals for the Madisons and their guests as well as providing for their own households. An 1837 insurance map of the yard coupled with present-day archaeological investigations document the location of three residences, each a duplex for two enslaved families. As one visitor to Montpelier noted of Upper South plantations generally, the "house servants live in detached dwellings sufficiently near to be within call."[7] Jennings, along with others who worked in the mansion or nearby gardens and stables, would have lived in one of the three duplexes that had been constructed during his years in Washington, over the same period that the mansion was enlarged and enhanced.

It is a conspicuous comparison that the spacious mansion was itself a duplex with two generations of Madisons living side by side at the same time that pairs of enslaved families shared duplexes that measured thirty by twenty feet, close to the dimensions of the south terrace, which overlooked them, alone. Each of the three duplexes allowed roughly 460 square feet of living space. The central chimney with back-to-back fireplaces divided the space into two mirror-image rooms, with lofts above; each side was occupied by a household of as many as ten persons. There were no foundations; the cabins were set off the ground on foot-high brick or stone piers. The rooms were drafty and cold in winter, hot and humid in summer. Still, they boasted plank walls (rather than log), glazed windows, wooden floors, and brick chimneys. In the shadow of the big house, the daily lives of house slaves were conducted under the watchful eye of the Madisons and the curious view of their guests. Partly because of this proximity, these houses were better built and equipped than those for slaves sheltered elsewhere on the plantation. Recorded one visitor to Montpelier: "The number of slaves upon the plantation is about 100, 40 or 50 of them only working hands. They are scattered in little settlements over the farm, and reside in distinct families and comfortable dwellings." Cutts described a slave quarter "in 'the Walnut Grove' [which] was a pleasant walk" from the mansion. Housing here included the log cabin of Granny Milly and her daughter and granddaughter. According to Cutts, their dwelling was "an object of interest to Mrs. Madison's [many] relatives, who would save part of their luxurious breakfast, take themselves to those good old people and return with the gift of a potato or fresh egg."[8]

Field hands lived in outlying quarters, near the land they cultivated. Montlezun, visiting in 1816, noted that "[Mr. Madison's slaves] are divided among the numerous farms which constitute his holdings," and added, "Some of these farmhouses are very pretty, built of wood, clean and comfortable." If Montlezun was not referring to the south yard duplexes, then likely he meant the overseers' houses at the outlying farms, which presented a striking contrast to the field slave cabins. Typical dwellings for these enslaved families were described by one visitor to Montpelier who observed such housing as he traveled through Virginia and Maryland: "The negro huts are built of logs, and the interstices stopped with mud, of which material also the floor is composed. At one end is an enormous large chimney made of logs, which are of a large size at the bottom, and gradually smaller towards the top. The lower part of the chimney, in the interior, is covered with earth or mud, to prevent its catching fire."[9]

Archaeologists at Montpelier have excavated a wide variety of ceramics, table glass, furniture tacks, and clothing notions at the south yard site; in comparison, material remains uncovered at the former quarters of field slaves were meager. Their crude cabins would have been sparsely furnished with straw mattresses on the earthen floor, a couple of blankets and items of clothing, and a cooking pot with a few assorted bowls and utensils. In his "Instructions for the Montpelier Overseer and Laborers," Madison directed that the men constructing stables "season the timber . . . by putting it in the lofts of the Negro Cabbins."[10] This shows that the slave had no privacy that the master must, in the end, respect.

After his retirement, "[Mr. Madison] amused himself chiefly on his farm," Jennings recalled in his reminiscences. A fortnight before the July 1817 meeting of the college trustees, Madison had written to his brother-in-law Richard Cutts, "I am just closing my wheat harvest." A visitor who arrived one May recalled that the center road to the mansion "was an almost imperceptible rise through a fine waving and rippling field of grain," while another who approached by this same route in the month of August passed "through a very large field, lying in fallow at this time, and shewing here and there, huge splotches of the dark red soil, common to this whole region." For the first decade or so of his retirement, while he was still "hale and vigorous," Madison would call for his horse Liberty, "riding out generally twice a day," according to a visitor present in August 1820, "to observe the progress of his rural domain." Paulding, on the scene two summers before, noted that Madison "never encumbered himself with a servant on these occasions," though he accompanied his host on these rounds during his stay. "By and bye," following their morning talk on the portico, as

Paulding reconstructed it, "The Horses were brought, and we set out on a tour to visit the different parts of the Estate where farming operations were going on." They encountered innumerable gates, and Paulding was impressed with Madison's ability "to open the Gates, which he did with a crooked stick, without dismounting, a feat which required no little skill." One day, Paulding remembered:

> We rode to a distant part of the Estate bordering on the Rapidan River—I think it is called—a ferocious stream, and subject to occasional inundations. There had been a heavy shower the day before; the river had overflowed its banks, and covered two or three acres of fine meadow with gravel some inches deep, so that it was completely spoiled. "Why this is a bad business Tony," said Mr. Madison. "Yes, masser ver bad—ver bad indeed"—answered Tony—then scratching his grey head, he added with perfect simplicity, "I tell you what Masser—I tink the Lor amighty, by and large, he do most as much harm as good."[11]

The elderly Tony might have been William Gardner's father, whom Madison had referred to as "old Anthony" two decades earlier.

When Montlezun visited two years before Paulding, the Frenchman observed, "The products of this region are: wheat, tobacco, wool, cattle and hay." He noted that "The President's estate contains five thousand acres. . . . Right now, the grazing lands around the house are of small extent, but they are going to be considerably enlarged." A later visitor enumerated:

> [The plantation's] crops have often amounted to 24 hogsheads of tobacco worth $200 per hogshead; 4000 bushels wheat; 6000 bushels corn, besides flax, hemp, all kinds of vegetables, and a large quantity of the choicest fruits. There are about 100 head of cattle, mostly of the North Devonshire breed, and a few of the Durham. The former are thought to produce the most superior working oxen, the latter the best cows. There are perhaps two dozen horses, 50 hogs, 100 sheep, and quantities of poultry.[12]

Cutts recalled that "the pet Durhams were allowed to come near the house," and she and Jennings both described Madison's partiality for horses in their memoirs. "He was very fond of horses, and an excellent judge of them, and no jockey ever cheated him," Jennings stated, and Cutts wrote of Madison's chosen mount:

> His favorite horse "Liberty" which had grown old in his service, was petted, fed and stalled alone; he well deserved his name; not a gate which he could not open—nor, any outrage which cattle could commit was not, by the negroes, ascribed to "Liberty." Mr. Madison, in his humorous way, often repeated these amusing and generally false tales of his disused horse, but never curtailed his freedom.

After his daily ride around the plantation, Madison was welcomed back to the front porch by his wife. Though it may have been Dolley who would "meet him at the portico door with refreshment in her own hands," Jennings would not be far behind and probably was the one who had prepared the cool drink and handed it to his mistress.[13]

"A handsome mulatto boy, and a favorite page of Mrs. Madison's" was the way Mary Cutts described the young Paul Jennings. "This boy when he became a man," she continued, "was a very efficient one." In 1820, Jennings was rewarded for his performance to date by being promoted to the position of James Madison's valet or personal man-servant. "I was always with Mr. Madison till he died, and shaved him every other day for sixteen years," Jennings stated in the *Reminiscences*. A dozen years after Madison's death, when Jennings was a free man and his story appeared in an abolitionist newspaper, his years of service as Madison's personal attendant were given as twenty-five. A subsequent issue amended this number to sixteen. It must have been Jennings himself who corrected the Washington correspondent, not only confirming the figure in the *Reminiscences* but showing that Jennings counted precision among his virtues.[14]

As personal manservant, Jennings was responsible for Madison's toilette and wardrobe. He appeared in Madison's room early each morning, on alternate days ready with a mug of hot water for the shave. When it came to the barbering, it seems that he shared the task with Dolley; he did the shaving and she the hairdressing. According to niece Mary Cutts, Madison trusted only his wife to powder his hair, which was pulled back into a small queue and tied with a black ribbon. Cutts also noted that "[Mr. Madison] was long sighted in one eye, and short with the other, in consequence; he never shaved with a glass." He must have been relieved to rely on Jennings's steady hand here.[15]

After leaving Washington, Madison never altered his style of dress, which thus became increasingly old-fashioned. "He was very neat, but never extravagant, in his clothes," recalled Jennings. "He always dressed wholly in black—coat, breeches, and silk stockings, with buckles in his shoes and breeches. He never had but one suit at a time. He had some poor relatives that he had to help, and wished to set an example of economy in the matter of dress." Madison's having only one suit would mean constant upkeep by Jennings, who would brush Madison's suit, shoes, and boots daily. He probably did this at the end of his long workday. Madison typically retired about ten o'clock, then read in bed, sleeping only four or five hours a night; as it was, then, Jennings's duties began before the sun came up each morning. An African American butler who authored a butler's handbook in 1827 boasted that he knew "his" pantry so well he could put his hands on whatever was wanted in the dark.[16] Perhaps Jennings mastered this trick, too. The pantry at Montpelier, next to the stairs that descended to the cellar kitchen, opened to the passage that led from the dining room to the Madisons' bed chamber.

James Madison was characterized by Benjamin Ogle Tayloe (son of the owner of the Octagon) as "a well-bred, Virginia gentleman, very hospitable and liberal in his entertainments, with great powers of conversation, replete with anecdotes and well constituted to shine in society."

This last phrase was apparent only to those close to Madison; it came through not in large receptions but rather in smaller settings like dinner parties. Margaret Bayard Smith was one such intimate. Madison was solemn in public life, but she described how around the dining room table at Montpelier the company "often laughed very heartily" at his amusing stories. The dining room directly adjoined Madison's study where Jennings spent so much time in his master's company. One wonders if they passed long periods in silence when alone or if they tended to chat and gossip. Did Madison try out his characteristic ribald jokes and anecdotes on his attendant? Certainly Jennings would have heard them over and over serving and standing in the dining room. Cutts revealed that among the many anecdotes that enlivened Madison's conversation were any number of "repetitions," which his guests nevertheless enjoyed, though more in watching "the play of his countenance" than in hearing the story again.[17]

Was there serious conversation between Jennings and Madison about the world or each other, either in the study or when the two men traveled together? A cousin of Madison's, Sarah Conway, remembered visits to Montpelier as a young girl and is the source for the following summary of Jennings's valet duties as given in Gaillard Hunt's 1902 biography of Madison: "[Madison] was always neat in his dress and was assisted in his toilet by Paul (Jennings), his body-servant, and Paul always accompanied him when he travelled." Thomas Jefferson had summarized the requirements of a trained manservant in an advertisement he placed in a Philadelphia newspaper: "Wanted, A Genteel Servant, who can shave and dress well, attend a gentleman on horseback, wait at table, and be well recommended."[18]

Jennings served as travel companion to Madison on his sojourns to the University of Virginia and nearby Monticello and, on the only lengthy trip he made during his retirement, to Richmond in 1829. Madison's responsibilities at the new university, first as board member and then as Jefferson's successor as rector, entailed regular trips to Charlottesville. There in 1826 in the midst of an early winter snow, it was Jennings whom Madison referred to in the "we" of the letter he penned Dolley the night of December 4: "Here we are snug in a warm room consoling ourselves on our escape from the Storm." Jennings's name comes up in other letters between Madison in Charlottesville and Dolley at Montpelier— casual references to his running an errand ("Send Paul for my books lent to [Jefferson granddaughters] Mary and Ellen") or passing on a message from a third party ("Paul tells me he saw John Carter from whom he learned . . .").[19]

Jennings recalled in his memoir, "After Mr. Madison retired from the presidency, in 1817, he invariably made a visit twice a year to Mr. Jefferson—sometimes stopping two or three weeks—till Mr. Jefferson's death, in 1826." Dolley often accompanied her husband on these visits, and even after Jefferson's passing, they usually lodged at Monticello during trips to Charlottesville because they were close to his daughter Martha and her large family. Jennings had friends at Monticello, too. His counterpart there as butler and Jefferson's personal manservant was Burwell Colbert, brother of Melinda Colbert Freeman, with whom Jennings had worked at the White House. The siblings were grand-children of Elizabeth Hemings, children of her daughter Betty Brown (niece and nephew to Sally Hemings). Jennings got to know Melinda's brother not only from the many times that he accompanied the Madisons to Monticello but from the occasions when Colbert accompanied Jefferson to Montpelier.

There were other opportunities for Montpelier and Monticello slaves to interact. In 1820, for example, Jefferson invited Madison to send one of his slaves to Monticello to learn the art of making good ale, claiming "Our malter and brewer is uncommonly intelligent and capable of giving instruction if your pupil is as ready at comprehend-ing it." The man with the malting and brewing expertise was Elizabeth Hemings's son Peter Hemings.[20]

Reminiscences related by Peter Fossett, yet another member of Monticello's Hemings family, provide a lens into Madison's visits

and his interactions with Jefferson's enslaved domestics. Remembered
Fossett:

> Mr. Madison used to come and stay for days with Mr. Jefferson. He was
> a very learned man . . . a kindly looking old gentleman, and his coming
> looked for with pleasure by the older servants for he never left without leav-
> ing each of them a substantial reminder of his visit. . . . [Mr. Monroe's and
> Mr. Jefferson's] companionship was not as close as that existing between Mr.
> Jefferson and Madison. [Monroe] was more of a statesman than a scientist,
> while Madison and Jefferson were both. On the north terrace of Monticello
> was the telescope, and it was here that Madison and Jefferson spent a great
> deal of their time.[21]

Fossett's accurate assessment of the relationships among the three Presidents is evidence that slaves were often more astute in their insights
than they tended to be credited with.

According to Jefferson's overseer Edmund Bacon, a slave whom the
former President had given to his grandson escaped from Monticello
in a Montpelier cart with the assistance of Madison's servant. Jefferson
wrote to an associate in Washington of Thruston Hern's disappearance
in June 1817: "A young negro man, named Thruston, brother to Edy,
who while I was in Washington was in the kitchen under the instruction of Mr. Julien, has escaped. . . . He is supposed to have gone to
Washington and to be lurking under the connivance of some of his
sister's old friends." Bacon reported that the runaway "went off with
Mr. Madison's servant" and made his way to Washington by passing
himself off as one of Madison's slaves.[22]

There is a distinct possibility that Paul Jennings was the Madison
servant who assisted Hern in his escape. According to Jennings family tradition, their ancestor used his literary skills to forge passes and
free papers for slaves. It would seem, especially given the alert from
his nephew Robert, that Madison was less than "prudent" in allowing
Jennings to return to his enslaved friends in Virginia, for he, like Wil-

liam Gardner before him, had become "tainted" with ideas of liberty. Jennings "sighed for freedom . . . [was] enamoured with freedom," wrote Mary Cutts. If the Jennings family tradition is true, there is no indication that Madison was aware of such actions; had he been, it is not the least bit likely that he would have tolerated them. On the other hand, though Cutts imparted a patronizing air in her description of Jennings sighing for freedom, Madison would have recognized— theoretically—the legitimacy of his manservant's longing for his natural birthright. After all, Jennings was exposed to the theoretical underpinnings to support his innate yearning for freedom directly from the master, the country's premier political philosopher. It was not all anecdote-telling that transpired in Madison's study. Jennings would have been privy to countless discussions on literary, historical, and political subjects. As Thomas Jefferson's granddaughter Ellen Randolph wrote of the level of discourse at Monticello, "The conversation that I hear is completely the feast of reason."[23] Though hardly an invited guest, Jennings was present at the feast and an intelligent individual motivated to take advantage of his position. And while learning is gratifying in its own right, Jennings could understand as well as Madison the profound connection between it and liberty.

Madison's major endeavor during his retirement years was to review and organize the papers of his life's work promoting individual rights and self-government, in particular his notes from the Constitutional Convention. Benjamin Latrobe's son John visited with Madison in his study during this period and remembered that "The story of the Constitution of the US was amply discussed." Young lawyer Henry Gilpin, who stayed overnight in 1827, concurred, calling it Madison's "favourite topic"; he listened late into the evening, enthralled as the sage expounded on the document's finer points. Margaret Bayard Smith experienced lengthy conversations at Montpelier's dining room table as "living History," her host elaborating on "the formation and adoption of the Constitution, the Convention and first congress, the characters of their members and the secret debates."[24]

Another frequent topic of discussion was the colonization of freed blacks to Africa's West Coast. Madison joined the American Colonization Society around 1819 and displayed a certificate testifying to his membership on the dining room wall. It hung next to an engraved copy of "Memorial and Remonstrance," his thesis on religious liberty. Among the many other prints displayed in this room—where Jennings spent so much time waiting on diners and just waiting—was one of an "African king." There were books and prints throughout the house. Some of the maps and pictures were from Madison Sr.'s time. Recognizing their educational value, he specified in his will that they should "belong to my mansion house, so that those who have not been advanced in my lifetime, shall have an equal share with those who have." His son added to the cultural display, and Margaret Smith, for one, responded, declaring that the many portraits and paintings in the drawing room "gave activity to the mind, by the historic and classic ideas that [they] awakened." She claimed she went to bed at Montpelier with her mind overflowing with ideas.[25]

As for Jennings, his exposure to the visual and auditory "feast" at Montpelier was a daily education. The light, the knowledge was shared with him, even if inadvertently. Thus enlightened and informed, he pondered on ways to secure his birthright, the gift Nature had bestowed. Yes, he sighed for freedom, but he did not choose life as a fugitive, as Thruston Hern did. Instead, for the time being, Jennings fashioned a life of meaning while still enslaved. He learned to balance his divided loyalties carefully. He knew how to succeed within the system in which he was trapped. He was good at what he did, always the unobtrusive figure in the background, there to attend to his master's needs, to anticipate his needs. Madison saw Jennings as trustworthy and capable, and he, in turn, had reason to take pride in his skills and usefulness. But Jennings was also good at gaming the system, judging when to stretch or risk his "place," and not lacking for courage to follow through.

Like Burwell Colbert at Monticello, Jennings, besides serving as the master's valet, was the butler or houseman and held the responsibility of head servant. Jennings was the "courteous, well-bred and well dressed" servant who answered the rap at the door of one caller and came out to greet another even as he ascended the portico steps. One of a pair of visitors ushered into the drawing room noted, "*En atten-dant* let us look around it." As butler Jennings would wear a suit (with trousers, not outdated knee breeches with hose like Madison). He may have started his day in other garb, or at least covered his suit with a baize apron, given that, as houseman, chamois in hand, he oversaw certain cleaning chores. Once fires were built up as necessary and the morning cleaning of lamps and goods from plate to glass to mahogany was under way, Jennings consulted with the cook in the cellar kitchen, then laid the breakfast table.[26]

The professional know-how that Jennings mastered included set-ting a proper table and sideboard. One Montpelier visitor recalled that at another Virginia planter's mansion, it was not the mistress but the family servant who superintended the setting of the table. It may have been the same in the Madison dining room, where the table was "set with a liberal display of silver and fine china," though Jennings would be careful to privilege Dolley with as much sway as she cared to hold. He was, indeed, as courteous and well bred as he was well dressed. Some of that training came from his own mother, some from Sious-sat and Freeman at the White House, and some from Mistress Dolley. Mary Cutts wrote that "never to contradict . . . was one of the earli-est lessons [Mrs. Madison] inculcated in the young people by whom she was always surrounded." Experienced housemen like Jennings and Colbert—who began their apprenticeship as young boys in the big house—were expert at this. The skill set they developed focused as much on manner as methods. Jennings related the following anecdote in his reminiscences:

[Mr. Madison] often told the story, that one day riding home from court with old Tom Barbour (father of Governor Barbour), they met a colored man, who took off his hat. Mr. M. raised his, to the surprise of old Tom;

to whom Mr. M. replied, "I never allow a negro to excel me in politeness."
Though a similar story is told of General Washington, I have often heard
this, as above, from Mr. Madison's own lips.

For the record, Jefferson's eldest grandson, Thomas Jefferson Randolph, told the same story, except in his version he is riding along
with his grandfather who admonishes him when he neglects to return
a black man's greeting, alarmed his grandson would "permit a negro
to be more of a gentleman" than he was.[27] One imagines Jennings and
Colbert, for whom being exceedingly polite, agreeable, *and tactful* was
second nature, given their occupation, inwardly cringing each time
they overheard this oft-repeated "lesson."

A document in the William Cabell Rives Papers at the Library of
Congress reveals that during the period of Madison's retirement, the
number and age distribution of slaves at Castle Hill, the Rives plantation located about midway between Montpelier and Monticello, and
the fraction of individuals fit for field labor were strikingly similar to
the numbers at Montpelier. The Castle Hill data for the total enslaved
population of one hundred people breaks down in this way:

46 laborers (18 men, 16 women, 12 children)
8 "employed in the duties of the household"
8 "entirely useless"
38 children not employed

Given the match in data for the two plantations, the further break-
down of those "employed in the duties of the household" at Castle
Hill ought to apply closely at Montpelier as well. Under "necessary
to carry on the work of the household," the document lists "a cook,
a coachman, a gardener, a washerwoman, a house man with a boy to
assist him, two or three housemaids and a servant of all work, wood
cutting etc."[28]

Sukey, Dolley's lady's maid, was one of the house servants at Montpelier, and Nany, whom Margaret Bayard Smith interacted with during her 1809 visit, was another. With Jennings filling the houseman position (and sharing the coachman role as well), the "boy to assist him," once he reached six or so, was Sukey's son, Benjamin Stewart. Among others, like Ben, receiving early training in the mansion were Ralph Taylor and his future wife, Catharine. Eventually—in the widow Madison's house in Washington—this couple would succeed Paul and Sukey in their roles. As for cooks, the name of one, Ailsey Payne, is known from an interview she gave a newspaperman when an old woman. Ailsey Payne described herself as a "house gal" at Montpelier and a cook there for thirty years.[29]

Jennings, in the leadership role as principal servant, set the standards for management of the household, and it was his responsibility to ensure that its enslaved members were fit for skilled service. Presumably, he was respected and admired by the household staff. He could read and write and used his literacy—according to oral tradition—to forge passes and free papers. He had the ear of the master and the confidence of the mistress. Only Dolley's control of the household keys exceeded Jennings's.

Madison's mother had her own enslaved domestics to wait on her in her suite of rooms. When Mary Cutts wrote about Mother Madison's "use of the servants who had grown old in her service" (the last phrase the same one she used to characterize Madison's pet horse Liberty), she specified Sawney. Calling him "Old Sawney," she described him as "the very picture of Time with his scythe."

"We continue well," Madison began one of only three extant letters to his mother, "I pray that you may also enjoy the same blessing." Jennings later used this same expression in a letter to Sukey: "I am well and I hope thes fiew lines may finde you injoin the same blessing." (Poor spelling notwithstanding, Jennings writing "injoin" for "enjoying" hints at his Southern accent. His great-granddaughter, well spoken in every way, pronounced her surname as "Jennens" in 2008, which must be the pronunciation that came down to her from her father and grandfather, the latter Paul's son Franklin.)[30]

When callers came for Mother Madison, Jennings would show them through the entrance foyer's arched opening that led to the south side of the house. But as Cutts recalled, James and Dolley's visitors also appreciated an opportunity to pay their respects to the old woman:

> Mrs. Madison Senior, or "the old lady" as she was usually called, kept up the primitive hours for meals to which she had been accustomed, and her time for receiving visits from the guests of her son was after her dinner and before his. . . . They esteemed it a privilege to be taken at two o'clock, her audience hour, from the pictured hall and mirrored walls, to the old time wainscoted and closseted rooms of this most excellent woman! . . . The "old lady" had her separate garden and gardener, and allowed no innovation on the primitive style.[31]

Mother Madison's and her son's households each had a separate cellar kitchen as well as a detached kitchen in the yards that flanked the mansion. James Paulding confirmed that at "upwards of ninety years of age, the old Lady seldom joined the family circle but took her meals by herself, and was visited every day by Mr. & Mrs. Madison." Judith Rives, mistress of Castle Hill, visited Mother Madison in the late 1820s and was amazed at her constitution, reporting that she had her windows open on a sharply cold winter day and declared, "It would be impossible for me to live without air." But by the time Ben Stewart came along, Mother Madison was bedridden in her chamber: "I only remember that she kept candy for the servants, and we used to go there to get it."[32]

Meanwhile, the nuclear family on the other side of the house sometimes included Payne Todd and sometimes not. He had impressed Montlezun in 1816, the only one in the Madison family with whom the Baron could converse in French. Certain other visitors referred to him positively as well, some of them aware that it was he who had, as Cutts put it, "With a refined taste, purchased many gems of art and paintings which . . . adorned Montpelier." But it was all surface charm, and even that faded as Payne's addiction to alcohol deepened. As Cutts admitted, he "lost the power of applying himself to any pursuit" and increasingly as time went by was "a drawback to [his mother's] happiness." One of Dolley's friends compared Montpelier to the Garden of Eden, and James and Dolley to Adam and Eve, but Payne, according to his cousin Edward Coles, was the snake in the grass.[33]

Montpelier residents during Madison's retirement often included extended kin of both James and Dolley. Dolley missed living with her younger sister, and that made Anna Cutts's many long-term visits to Montpelier with her children all the more precious. Mary, who later chronicled domestic life at Montpelier, and her sister Dolley and her brothers Thomas, Madison, and Richard were in residence nearly every summer. From childhood the Cutts siblings looked on the Virginia estate as a second home and took pride in their familiarity with it. During his retirement, Madison had a sister and brother and numerous nephews and nieces living in Orange, and they were regular guests at Montpelier. One of the nieces, Nelly Willis, daughter of his deceased brother Ambrose, became Madison's ward. Another niece was his brother William's daughter, Rebecca Madison Chapman. One of Rebecca's sons, Alfred, would play a small but significant part in Paul Jennings's life in freedom in Washington, facilitating his initial employment in the Department of the Interior when Chapman was a clerk there in the early 1850s. For it was not only observing and listening that Jennings took advantage of, but "meeting"—that is, making contacts. Chapman was just one in a long line of contacts—individuals with power and influence—on whom Jennings could call for patronage of one kind or another. He had absorbed the lesson spelled out in the 1827 butler's guide: "You should likewise be civil and polite to all visitants who come to the house . . . for it is a great advantage to a servant, to have the good wishes of those ladies and gentlemen that visit . . . because you may perhaps one day or other, have access to their good word, &c."[34]

The advantages that Jennings had working in the mansion and shadowing Madison meant encountering not only the master's peers but his own besides. When Jennings accompanied the Madisons, he met his counterparts at the various plantations they visited. Since these same manservants and lady's maids traveled with their masters and mistresses, when company came calling at Montpelier, it included both the gentry and their enslaved attendants. Dolley loved to entertain. The backyard at Montpelier was the scene of many a fete. The First Lady seemed breathless but not weary when she wrote her sister Anna the day after a Fourth of July bash in 1816:

> Yesterday we had ninety persons to dine with us at one table, put up on the lawn, under a thick arbor. The dinner was profuse and good . . . the day was cool and pleasant; half a dozen only stayed all night with us, and they are now about to depart. Colonel Monroe's letter this morning announces the advent of the French Minister, and we shall expect him this evening, or perhaps sooner. I am less worried here with an hundred visitors than with twenty-five in Washington.

The Montpelier house servants could not have shared Dolley's outlook in making light of providing meals and accommodations for so many guests, much less to the legendary standards of the *mistress's* hospitality. A family relation remembered that on one occasion during the former President's retirement, the Madisons "invited every family in Orange County to an entertainment, and the grounds were covered with tables to accommodate the people, the more distinguished guests and elderly people being entertained in the house." And it was not just the enslaved domestics who labored to provide an experience that one guest characterized as "a bit of faery in the prosaic world." Slaves, not fairies, had literally moved the earth to create the beautiful back lawn where the couple hosted so many gatherings, manually removing soil from hillocks and filling in depressions. One visitor marveled at the effect: "The lawn is beautifully even and level and is of great extent." Back in 1807, Augustus John Foster had observed that while Madison fancied a naturalistic "English Park" for Montpelier, such landscaping would be very expensive, and the enslaved hands were fully occupied already. But Madison had put those laborers to work creating pleasure grounds, and by 1816 the Baron de Montlezun appreciated the way that to both west and east, the house's "contours are softened by pleasant lawns bordering on woods laid out in park-like vistas at unequal distances."[35]

The spacious drawing room that opened from the front portico extended to the back porch on the opposite side. A guest described the drawing room's "three windows to the east, reaching down to the floor & opening upon a piazza & so upon the lawn." An elderly woman who visited as a young girl called up an olfactory memory: "Into [this room] came the sweet odors of the Jessamine and roses, which twined around the pillars of the rear porch." The guests stepped from this porch onto a broad lawn edged with shade trees and flowering shrubs. At the lawn's border was a formal terraced garden, four acres enclosed by a wooden fence where fruits and vegetables as well as ornamentals were nursed. This terraced landscape was laid out by Charles Bizet, the French gardener recommended to Madison by James Monroe. Bizet trained certain "black aids" in the fine art of gardening once they had completed the "prosaic" work of forming the steep terraces. Mary Cutts claimed that Bizet and his wife "were great favorites with the negroes, some of whom they taught to speak French."

Cutts included in her memoir a vivid pen portrait of the prevailing class levels socializing in a kind of parallel—or, perhaps more accurately, sequential—fashion at festive barbecues on the Montpelier back lawn. As she explained:

> Barbecues were then at their height of popularity. To see the sumptuous board spread under the forest oaks, the growth of centuries, animals roasted whole, everything that a luxurious country could produce, wines, and the

well filled punch bowl, to say nothing of the invigorating mountain air, was
enough to fill the heart with joy! . . . At these feasts the woods were alive
with the guests' carriages, horses, servants, and children—for all went—
often more than a hundred guests. . . . After the crops, "farmer's topics," and
politics had been discussed . . . if not too late, these meetings were termi-
nated by a dance, as there were generally some violins taken by their merry
owners, and good musicians were these "Uncle Tom's" and "Uncle Sam's."
The Negroes, like the birds of the woods, have their sweet wild notes, filled
with melody—but their songs and dances need no encomium![36]

To serve all these guests, the cooks could keep going up to four kitchens—the detached kitchens that flanked the mansion, as well as the
two cellar kitchens—at all hours. One of the Montpelier guests remembered that to ensure "the liberality of entertainment provided"
at her own nearby plantation, "lambs and poultry of every description were freely sacrificed on the altar of hospitality." As busy as the
household staff was, one of Jennings's responsibilities was to model a
calm, efficient manner; it would not do for guests to be put off by surly
waiters. Eventually, as Mary Cutts recalled, it was the slaves' turn to
let loose and make merry among themselves and their visiting peers:
"The slaves animated by the sight of the enjoyment of their masters
and mistresses, of whose feast they have partaken, when their duties
are over, assemble in the largest cabin, call in house servants and field
hands, tune up the violin and make the plantation resound until morning with their gaiety and mirth." One of the fiddlers was Paul Jennings,
who had acquired his musical proficiency in his early years. John Finch,
an Englishman who visited Montpelier in 1824, recorded his impressions of black Virginians' fondness for music-making:

Every negro is a musician from his birth. A black boy will make an excellent
fiddle out of a gourd and some strings. . . . The banjo is another instrument
they are fond of, but the supreme ambition of every negro is to procure a real
violin. By saving the few pence which are given them, selling chickens, and

robbing a little, if necessary, they generally contrive to make up the sum. An instrument of music seems necessary to their existence.[37]

Making friends outside his home plantation, like Burwell Colbert at Monticello, for example, expanded Jennings's circle. Developing a love interest among the young women he encountered warmed his heart. Fanny Gordon was lady's maid to the Madisons' near neighbor, Jane Taylor Howard. She and her husband, Charles P. Howard, whose farm bordered Montpelier's eastern edge, were regular guests of the Madisons. Paul Jennings and Fanny Gordon, operating in the same social circuit, as it were, must have interacted fairly frequently. At some point an attraction sparked between them, and friendship advanced to courtship.

FANNY GORDON WAS BORN INTO SLAVERY at Greenfield, the plantation of Erasmus Taylor, youngest brother of James Madison's grandmother Frances. Greenfield, a few miles to the north of Orange Court House, was one of the four tracts awarded to James Taylor's sons when he subdivided his enormous acreage. Erasmus and his wife, Jane Moore Taylor, had seven children, the youngest a daughter named for her mother. Young Jane married Charles P. Howard in 1793. Her bridegroom was from Philadelphia; his father had acquired interests in Orange, and Charles moved to the area about 1790. He was a merchant who made regular trips back to Philadelphia, where the Howards were a well-established family with Quaker connections. Charles himself had been received into the Philadelphia Friends Meeting when he was sixteen.[38]

Fanny was born at Greenfield three decades after Jane. Jane's father, Erasmus, died in 1794, a year after she married. In the 1795 inventory of slaves prepared following Erasmus's death, there is no mention of a Fanny. However, in the document establishing the "final distribution" of slaves in 1800, the name Fanny appears along with a few other new names, those of children born in the five-year interim. Judging by her value at £18, Fanny was born about 1798. The "final distribution" lists which slaves will go to the sons and sons-in-law of Erasmus Taylor, meticulously calculated so that the worth of the persons distributed allows for equity among the recipients.[39]

There are nine names listed in a group of slaves bequeathed to Charles Howard, but the document makes it clear that his "lott" totaled ten people. The tenth was a woman named Kate. Either Kate or one of the other two women willed to Howard had to be little Fanny's mother. Erasmus Taylor's will specified that Kate would be retained by his wife while she lived, presumably because Kate was her personal maid. (Her significantly higher value among the enslaved women supports this.) Since Fanny became lady's maid to daughter Jane and, as has been discussed, such skilled positions tended to be passed down, Kate is the most likely candidate for Fanny's mother. Dolley Madison referred to the familial component associated with personal servants when she advised her sister Anna, who had just acquired a new maid, to try to attach the woman—"now that she is your own"—to herself and her children.

Charles Howard, despite his Quaker background, found himself not only living in the South and husband to a Virginian but the owner of ten slaves. As the years went by, that number grew by natural increase, and the Howards and their enslaved families settled on an 890-acre estate known as Howard Place, which was contiguous with Montpelier land. Mary Cutts noted in her memoir that Jane Taylor Howard was cousin to James Madison and that she and her husband were "near and highly respected" neighbors of James and Dolley and frequently at Montpelier.[40]

In a note to Madison from his neighbor Charles Howard dated 8 March 1818, the writer jotted, "I send by Paul" a file of newspapers that the former President had inquired about. The note and newspapers were hand-delivered, the courier perhaps only too happy to perform errands that took him to Howard Place. If not by this date, then soon enough, Paul Jennings was keeping company with a woman there. Fanny Gordon had (at least) one child by a previous marriage, a daughter, Elizabeth. Given that Kate was Fanny's mother, three generations in the female lineage made Howard Place home. Jane Howard's mother had waived her life interest in Kate in 1800. She became "Old Kate" eventually, listed on a Howard Place inventory in 1856 with a negative value or "charge" of $300. But she certainly was of value when training her daughter in the refined skills of a lady's maid such as hairdressing, fancy needlework, and laundering of fine fabrics. Dolley Madison noted in 1818 that "good [lady's maids] are rare & as high as 8 & 900$." As Jane Taylor Howard's personal maid, Fanny's responsibilities were care of the mistress, her chamber, and her prized things. An 1825 book, *The Duties of a Lady's Maid with Directions for Conduct, and Numerous Receipts for the Toilette,* reveals that, as with butlers of the period, as much emphasis was placed on "duties of behavior" as on "duties of knowledge and art."[41]

PAUL JENNINGS AND FANNY GORDON MARRIED in 1822. Slave marriages were not recognized by law. As the bride's brother Edmund Spotsey later explained, "They were married according to the manner of slave law in Virginia. Each master gave consent. Paul Jennings and Fannie Jennings were given a marriage supper at her master's home." Thus was the bond between man and wife solemnized. The couple did not live together. Jennings at Montpelier was a good two hours' walk from his wife at Howard Place. A skilled horseman, he reduced his travel time considerably when he was allowed to take a mount to the Howards' farm. With his attendance on Madison so constant, it is likely that he commuted to see Fanny only weekly, on Saturday evening, to spend all of Sunday together, the one day slaves traditionally had off.

Paul and Fanny had what was known as an abroad marriage. Owners of large slave populations generally preferred that their slaves chose spouses on their own plantation. Some, like Thomas Jefferson, even offered incentives for those who took a mate "at home"—a pot, sifter, or mattress cover. But new love is priceless, or at least worth more than a household accoutrement to most individuals lucky enough to find it. So abroad marriages for Virginia slaves in this period were common, and masters for the most part accepted them, though at least one in Orange County, namely diarist Francis Taylor, did not quite get it. When his manservant Frank came to him for permission to marry a woman enslaved on a nearby plantation, bachelor Taylor was taken aback, surprised that his constant companionship was not enough for Frank's emotional well-being.[42]

Abroad marriages were more complicated. If the owners of the husband and wife lived close enough for the couple to get together at least a couple times a month, then the status quo usually held, as with Paul and Fanny or Frank and his wife. However, if the distance was great enough, or if an owner later moved away from the area, then one master customarily bought one of the spouses rather than see the couple separated. Exceptions, however, were far from uncommon. Such accommodation was strictly the call of the two owners, who needed to agree on a deal. For example, Madison received a letter in 1824 from neighbor John Henshaw who was planning to relocate to Missouri. He offered Madison $300 for his enslaved man Jesse, who wished to be purchased in order to go with his wife pending Madison's approval. Jesse applied his suit "very pressingly," and Madison presumably acquiesced as Jesse's name drops from the known records.[43]

Children belonged to the master who owned the wife. If it was the wife who was to acquire a new master, she was commonly purchased with her young children, though children over twelve were not included in that category. Again, to whatever degree the decisions were, or seemed, arbitrary, they were the owners' prerogative. The historical literature is full of examples of masters' and mistresses' self-serving justifications of decisions that went against the pleas of their human property. These were the occasions when a slave's wiles went point for point, action for action, against the master's authority, but, given the master's upper hand and the slave's extremely limited range of acceptable language and behavior, when the slave "won," it was a well-earned victory indeed. It is telling how whites routinely described slaves as ignorant and thoughtless until one escaped or otherwise outwitted an owner; then the characterizations suddenly shift to intelligent and conniving. Of course, the victories to be silently savored were those where the master never realized he had been bested.

A year after his manservant took a wife, Madison commented on slave marriages and abroad marriages specifically. The vehicle was a series of responses, dated 28 March 1823, to a questionnaire sent him by Jedidiah Morse, a minister from Connecticut, regarding slavery. Madison agreed to provide answers applicable to Virginia. One question was *Is it common for slaves to be regularly married?* "Not common; but the instances are increasing," Madison replied. The next question was *If a man forms an attachment to a woman on a different or distant plantation, is it the general practice for some accommodation to take place between the owners of the man and the woman, so that they may live together?* Madison's answer: "The accommodation not infrequent where the plantations are very distant. The slaves prefer wives on a different plantation; as affording occasions & pretexts for going abroad, and exempting them on holidays from a share of the little calls to which those at home are liable." Did Madison think this of Jennings, who would, after all, be his most immediate example? If Jennings ever figured that there were any advantages to having a wife abroad, with his children as they came along owned by a different master than he was, he would have sadly recalculated when he was living in Washington with the widow Madison while his family remained in Virginia. But surely Jennings would have preferred all along a domestic arrangement like Ralph and Caty Taylor's—husband, wife, and children sharing the same dwelling where they gathered each evening for a family meal. As it was, Jennings did not spend even enough time with his young children to teach them to read and write. Madison's responses to Morse on slave marriages are perplexing, even the first one. What can he mean by replying that it was not common for slaves to be regularly married? In a letter four years earlier, he himself had referred to slaves "connected as they generally are by tender ties with others under other Masters." All in society understood that these ties were accepted as marriages and the partners referred to as husband and wife, just as all understood that the bonds held no legal standing.

Madison's cavalier response to Morse on abroad slave marriages, to which his factotum would have taken considerable umbrage, is symptomatic of the reality that however close Madison and Jennings became, they never closed the deep divide between master and bondman, white elite and black servant. Their limits to understanding or appreciating the other's perspective were underscored by some of Madison's other responses to Morse's questions to which Jennings would have taken exception. "The remarkable increase of slaves . . . results from the comparative defect of moral and prudential restraint on the Sexual connexion," he declared. And when asked about free blacks, it was one thing to characterize them as a destabilizing element because they would side with their enslaved brethren in a case of slave insurrection, but Madison denigrated all people of color by describing free blacks as "generally idle and depraved, appearing to retain the bad qualities of the slaves with whom they continue to associate, without acquiring any of the good ones of the whites."[44]

◆

EDWARD COLES RESIGNED HIS POSITION as Madison's private secretary in 1815, but his relationship with the Madisons continued. He was Dolley's cousin, after all, thus part of the family's social network. Moreover, he would remain an outspoken antislavery activist "leaning into" his former mentor and a rising agent in the development of Paul Jennings's thinking. Coles would come to Montpelier and, as conscience articulated, speak aloud daring ideas that Jennings could only dream of saying. How he must have savored hearing them communicated directly to his master. Coles had a radical idea when he visited in the spring of 1819: he was going to free his slaves. The impulse itself was far from new. Coles had been incubating the idea even before he inherited twelve slaves from his father in 1808. As his kinswoman Mary Cutts put it, "Early in life he was imbued with the belief that the possession of slave property was essentially wrong—from that moment all the energies of his enthusiastic nature were bent on the manumission of his own." Others would theorize; he would act and his deed would, he hoped, make a statement resounding enough to inspire others to action.

Coles hoped for verbal public support—at least—from the two prestigious retired Presidents who had inspired him, but neither Jefferson nor Madison came through for him. To Coles, slavery was not an issue to be dealt with when the time was ripe or the endless complexities were ironed out just so by legislative bodies. It was an emergency-level moral imperative. With an abundance of personal courage, Coles proceeded to act on his convictions. He had unknotted a series of difficulties and tied up the last details. Now it was April 1819, and he was set. Coles had already sent his slaves ahead to Pennsylvania. They would not know until he joined them there that they were to be freed on the spot and welcomed to join their former master in relocating to Illinois, where they would have land and employment and thus the opportunity to "add to their self-esteem and their standing in the estimation of others." Coles stopped at Montpelier literally en route to consummating his vision, to live the moment that had been twelve years in the making. When the weather turned miserable, he was prevailed upon to stay for two days, longer than he had intended.[45] He must have been excited but apprehensive, and likely poured out his hopes, even as the spring rains came down, at the dining room table and in Madison's study for the household inmates, white and black, to appreciate. When Coles finally rode away with the picture in his mind of what he was about to do, the members of the household who saw him off returned to their immediate business with the same picture, dissolving in seconds for some but embedded in the imagination of others.

With the memory of Coles's April visit only two months past, Madison sat down and penned a letter to Philadelphian Robert J. Evans (which was published in the *Daily National Intelligencer*) replete with his ideas on emancipation and colonization. Though Madison was still pondering Coles's words and actions, full of can-do spirit as they were, his own extended remarks and proscriptions tended to a conclusion that slavery was impossible to eradicate. One of the conditions for emancipation that he listed was consent of the slave, who would need to agree "that his condition in a state of freedom be preferable in his own estimation to his actual one in a state of bondage." This was easy to meet; its inclusion in a series of formidable challenges is evidence that paternalistic slaveholders pretended that their slaves were not chafing under a lack of liberty. Another condition for emancipation was "permanent removal" of freed blacks "beyond the region occupied or allotted to a White population." Madison went on to present his scheme for the colonization to Africa not just of blacks already free but of all people of color, for he saw in colonization the green light to proceed with full, if gradual, emancipation. He later referred to colonization as "relief from the greatest of our calamities." Participation would be voluntary, and Madison admitted that securing willingness among both masters and slaves would be a "hindrance." The owner would be compensated by the government for his human property. What was the slave's motivation to abandon his homeland? For this Madison had only to offer the black man's cognizance that he would be a second-class citizen in American society or, in a word, unwanted.[46]

In Madison's mind, emancipation and colonization had to be coupled. For most whites, "objections to a thorough incorporation of the two people are . . . insuperable," Madison wrote, and they included the "lasting peculiarities" of blacks and a fear of their "vindictive recollections or the predatory propensities which their State of Society might foster." Madison's ultimate message was that *until* the second step, colonization, was ready to be implemented, the first step, emancipation, should *not* be attempted. He advocated the "double operation" or none at all.

Drew McCoy, a leading historian of Madison and slavery, has documented Madison's increasing desperation over the issue of slavery in his thoughtful work, *Last of the Fathers.* Madison allowed that he had been in even greater despair before he latched onto the concept of colonization. But that was like holding on to air in the cup of one's hand. Desperation led to delusion. Madison was deluding himself as to the workability of his emancipation/colonization scheme. The numbers involved, both dollars and population (Madison's estimations were based on 1.5 million slaves), were overwhelming, and so were the details, such as obtaining individual consents from slaves and their owners in order to add to the "list of emigrants" to Africa. Over the ensuing months Madison corresponded with Robert Walsh Jr. on the Missouri Compromise and the extension of slavery into new states. On that issue Madison, like Jefferson, averred that dispersal of slaves over a greater territory was the best option, as if the slave population was a constant—also delusional.[47]

Like most members of white society, Madison compartmentalized the "issue of slavery" from the base injustice being perpetrated on real people in real time. His support of emancipation seemed to have more to do with achieving a "slave-free" future for the country whose reputation as a republic of liberty was being undermined and even mocked than with freeing fellow countrymen from bondage. The inability of Madison and others to treat the emancipation of human beings as an imperative so urgent that further debate was unthinkable was centered not on slavery but on race. Slavery had to go: Madison recognized it as the same "moral, political, and economical" evil that Coles did. The young activist was chomping at the bit to do something about it. The sage held back, chewing over the issue in the faint hope of arriving at a full solution. The sticking point was the freed blacks: What do "we" do with "them"? We certainly cannot share "our" country with them. One would be hard pressed to find more than a handful of white men and women in America then who did not concur.

The penultimate question on Jedidiah Morse's 1823 questionnaire was *Is there any general plan of emancipation in progress, and what?* Madison gave a one-word answer: "None."[48]

♦

THE ENERGIES AND THOUGHTS OF MOST enslaved people were focused on day-to-day living—work, fellowship, meals, and interactions with owners and overseers. Former North Carolina slave Thomas Lewis commented with pith on the last-named item: "There is no such thing as being good to slaves. Many white people were better than others, but a slave belonged to his master and there was no way to get out of that." As Frederick Douglass put it, "The feeding and clothing me well, could not atone for taking my liberty from me."[49]

Just as slaves had their individual ways of coping with the social order of slavery, so too did their owners. James and Dolley displayed contrasting styles. He was the more temperate, known for his "equanimity of disposition" in all matters. This served him well in dealing with the pressures of the presidency and the vicissitudes of farming, such as the periodic floods to which he reacted with such dispassion. This personality trait also translated to his being held in good stead by his enslaved men and women. Jennings stated, "I never saw [Mr. Madison] in a passion, and never knew him to strike a slave, although he had over one hundred; neither would he allow an overseer to do it. Whenever any slaves were reported to him as stealing or 'cutting up' badly, he would send for them and admonish them privately, and never mortify them by doing it before others." An elderly slave whom one Montpelier visitor came upon while negotiating the interminable gates that led to the mansion was quoted as saying: "Mr. Madison was a good master" who "would not let his overseer make fight with the men."

Madison had an easier-going relationship with enslaved individuals than Dolley, who was more highly strung. Gaillard Hunt obtained first-person testimony for his 1902 biography from Nancy Barbour, an ex-Montpelier slave "still living at a great age in the village of Orange." She declared, wrote Hunt, that Madison "never got angry with any of them, and they preferred going to him with requests to going to his wife. She recalls one instance of his personal castigation of a slave, when Reuben, a worthless scamp, returned from some unlawful errand with a palpably false excuse and was punished by three light taps on the shoulder from his master's walking stick." But true corporal punishment was occasionally the order of the day, as revealed by Payne Todd, who told a visitor in 1836 that no Montpelier slave "had been flogged for several years." Payne admitted in his journal to whipping a slave himself during an earlier episode, on reflection acknowledging that he was "in bad temper" while his victim "perhaps was not in fault on the occasion and wept very bitterly."[50]

Dolley was more demanding, less forgiving than her husband. She had an increasingly volatile relationship with Paul's close friend Sukey, who was trained as Dolley's maid at a young age. Sukey was skillful and efficient enough that Dolley did not want to replace her even though she was intermittently frustrated with her. In 1818, as she informed her sister, Dolley temporarily banished Sukey to one of the plantation's outlying farms, complaining "Sucky has made so many depridations on every thing, in every part of the house that I sent her to Black Meadow last week but find it terribly inconvenient to do without her, & suppose I shall take her again, as I feel too old to bring up another— so I must let her steal from me, to keep from labour myself." Sukey and her mistress continued to have their ups and downs. In 1833 Dolley was panicked when she reported (again using a variant spelling for her maid's name) that "my most efficient House servant Sucky lies very ill with bilious fever." But two years later it sounds as if Dolley subjected Sukey to a thorough shaking-down when she wrote to a niece about missing bushels of chestnuts, noting pointedly, "Sucky had nothing to do with any of them I assure you."[51] The relationship between the two women continued down a path to disintegration (as we shall see), culminating, in what can be likened to a horror-filled divorce wherein only one party had legal recourse, with Sukey losing everything.

◆

BY 1824, THE RURAL ROUTINES SET during the first part of Madison's retirement were in place and so was Jennings's own domestic mode of living, balancing his job at Montpelier and his family at Howard Place within the slavery system. In the spring of that year, Englishman John Finch visited; his account illustrates how the days flowed by at this time.

When Finch arrived on a Saturday with letters of introduction, Jennings was the valet at the door who informed him that Mr. Madison was out riding about the plantation, even as he ushered their guest into the drawing room. If the two men conversed while waiting for Madison's return, Finch might have mentioned—given the many presidential portraits painted by Gilbert Stuart in the room—his recent visit to the Monroe White House, where he took particular notice of George Washington's life-size likeness in the oval salon. If he did, Jennings would have had quite a tale to share concerning the general's picture himself. When Henry Gilpin arrived three years after Finch, the Madisons were likewise out, but he was escorted inside and amused himself looking at artwork until Dolley appeared in straw bonnet and shawl and her husband in "breeches & old fashioned top boots." In welcoming visitors in his master's absence, Jennings was following expected protocol. One first-time traveler to the South who stopped at a plantation mansion hoping to take a respite was astounded when the enslaved butler, whose master was out of town altogether, took the initiative to invite him, a gentleman unknown to the family, to stay overnight.[52] Of the many myths connected with the American South of this period, the extremely liberal dispensation of hospitality, even as authorized by an enslaved member of the household, is not one of them.

The second day of John Finch's visit was a Sunday, and it rained without letup. No matter the weather, Sunday meant church for most of Montpelier's enslaved residents; they had umbrellas for shelter from the rain. Finch commented that some slaves in the region used proceeds from sales of chickens or other goods to "purchase a little better clothes for Sundays." Madison described for Finch's countrywoman Harriet Martineau, who visited some years later, how seeing some of "his negroes go to church one Sunday . . . gayly dressed, the women in bright-coloured calicos" had astonished "some strangers who had an idea that slaves were always whipped all day long." In a response to a query about slaves' religion or religious instruction from Jedidiah Morse's questionnaire, Madison explained, "There is no general system of religious instruction. There are few spots where religious worship is not within reach, and to which they do not resort. Many are regular members of Congregations chiefly Baptist; and some Preachers also, tho' rarely able to read." It is not known what Jennings's religious persuasion was at this time, though he was probably not a "freethinker" of the type Augustus John Foster noted was so prevalent in the home state of Madison and Jefferson.[53] Jennings may have appreciated the civic religion of republicanism, but true faith in old-time religion was too welcome a comfort not to be embraced by most enslaved Virginians.

After a splendid meal, Finch remembered, the servants withdrew and "The Ex-President said very calmly, that in an afternoon, it was Sunday, he could not have the servants to wait on him, as they made it a holiday." The host and his visitor threw wood on the fire themselves as they conversed. The retreating servants had left a stack nearby, perhaps chopped by the master himself. Jennings stated in the *Reminiscences* that Madison cut his own firewood for exercise. Jennings would have spent this rainy Sunday at Howard Place with Fanny, the two of them feeding the fire in her cabin against the spring dampness. Fanny was already mother to Elizabeth when she married Paul, and they probably had their own baby to coo over by now.

By Monday the spring rain was just a memory. Under a fair sky, Madison and his guest rode all over the plantation and woods. They drew up where some "negroes were employed in clearing new ground for a crop of tobacco, cutting down the trees, and making a rail fence," and Fitch witnessed an example of Madison's easy accessibility to his laborers. "There was more independence of manner about the negroes, when conversing with their master, than I expected," he recollected. "One of them was unwell, and he made known his complaints to Massa with great confidence of having a favorable hearing. The Ex-President sent him to the house to get some medicine."[54]

As 1824 proceeded, visitors formed an all-but-continuous queue to Montpelier's front door. But no company in 1824, or any other year, compared to the pomp and circumstance that attended the November visit of the Marquis de Lafayette. He had been invited by President Monroe to travel across the Atlantic for a triumphal return tour of America as the Nation's Guest. General Lafayette received the belated gratitude of citizens in every one of the twenty-four states for his role in winning the War of Independence. He slept in many more places than George Washington in his travels did. Every town wanted him for a dinner or ball or, if that was not possible, then at least for a procession down their main road or an ale in their local tavern. Even given the nonstop celebrations, the general's reunions with Jefferson at Monticello and Madison at Montpelier, with a trip to the new University of Virginia in between, were highlights of the tour.

Madison did not wait for Lafayette to come to Montpelier for his first sight of the old hero; he and Jennings traveled to Monticello the day of his welcome, 4 November. They arrived at dusk, just in time for Madison to join the select guests at Jefferson's dining room table for dessert. If, as waiting servant, Jennings was not privy to this first conversation, he certainly was to some that followed during Lafayette's sojourns at Monticello and then Montpelier, a total of two weeks. One of the topics the general repeatedly brought up was slavery. Lafayette reasoned that he was being endlessly feted across America for one reason, his love of liberty. Though Madison pronounced Lafayette "as American as any Frenchman can be," in fact he had come to a foreign country's aid in 1776 only because he could not resist a fight for human freedom. But now, near half a century later, even sons of liberty like Jefferson and Madison were still slaveholders! Lafayette minced no words in letting these prestigious retired statesmen know of his disapproval. They let him shake his finger at them but had little to say in their defense, having come to the point where, as historian Joseph Ellis put it, they seemed to regard "silence as the highest form of leadership" on the issue of slavery. Indeed, Madison assured the general that just to allude to the subject in any legislative body would be like adding a spark to a mass of gunpowder.[55]

Once the dinner honoring Lafayette in the rotunda of the university had taken place, Madison and Jennings returned home to prepare for the general's visit. These were "stirrin' times at Montpelier," recalled former cook Ailsey Payne, who could not read or write but related her memories to a newspaperman. The whole house was "gone over to make it look as fine as possible." The silver was shined, and it and the china and glassware were displayed just so on the dining room sideboard, showing that "degree of taste and neatness" that, the butler's handbook promised, "will strike the eye of every person who enters the room, with a pleasing sensation of elegance." The sideboard groaned with three generations of silver, remembered Mary Cutts, while another relation recalled, "The table appointments were massive." Houseman Jennings monitored all this while Cook saw to the food. "In the ice house," she recounted, "we had mutton, beef, chickens, turkeys, ducks, shoats." The Madisons had ridden out to meet the general's carriage, and when finally the entourage approached, the servants peeking through the windows were ready in their Sunday best. Dolley had seen to that since she "didn't want no slouchy lookin' gals inside Montpelier." Or men either: local merchant records show that

Jennings, along with Madison and Payne Todd, acquired new clothes this fall. Ailsey Payne reported that she never saw so many carriages lined up or so much handshaking going on as when "General Fay-ette" came.[56] We can visualize Jennings opening both halves of the French doors and welcoming the guests flowing in as he accepted hats and dispensed guidance. It would take all the efficiency he was noted for to attend to the company even before the first course was served or glass of champagne poured.

Lafayette probably stayed in the same second-floor guest chamber that the Baron de Montlezun recalled occupying eight years earlier. A spacious room with a classically ornamented fireplace mantel, it not only looked out to the Blue Ridge Mountains from two large side-by-side windows but allowed private access to the adjoining north terrace as well.

In the passage outside this guest room was a walled-off space within which was a ladder that led to the attic, and it was on that level, under the enormous center pediment, where Madison kept his favorite fortified fruit of the vine. Madeira is the only wine whose flavor and aroma improve with heat. It was Jennings's job to climb to the "Madeira closet" and decant several bottles' worth at a time from the barrels there. He would also descend to the wine cellar and do the same for the light varietals that were stored at the cooler subterranean temperature. According to Jennings, Madison himself imbibed temperately, but he sometimes entertained hard drinkers who pushed the decanters about the table and "put away his choice Madeira pretty freely."[57]

Lafayette's private secretary, Auguste Levasseur, kept a diary of the historic trip. He wrote that during their four days at Montpelier, the company assembled there "was almost entirely composed of the neighbouring planters" and that "Lafayette, who though perfectly understanding the disagreeable situation of American slaveholders, and respecting generally the motives which prevent them from more rapidly advancing in the definitive emancipation of the blacks, never missed an opportunity to defend the right which all men without exception have to liberty."

Levasseur had a special curiosity about the slaves. At Monticello, he had sought out the genuine article and asked them directly if they were happy. They assured him that they were perfectly happy. Englishman John Finch, too, observed slaves closely during his travels; he first stated that "the muscular strength of the blacks is not so great as that of the whites," but then wondered if perhaps the difference was actually the level of exertion that enslaved and free laborers put into the task. Levasseur thought he had the inside line on slave labor:

> [It] is easily understood [that] the free worker, paid by the day knows that, if he does not bring all his strength and all his intelligence to his work, the one who pays him will stop employing him. . . . The Slave worker, to the contrary, knows that, whether his work is poor or valuable, his lot will always be the same. . . . Without worries as without hopes for the future, the Slave worker can have, ought to have, but one desire, namely that of rest.

For all Levasseur's reflections on American slaves, his insights are lacking. On attitudes toward work, he neglects to consider slaves' individuality. Some surely found gratification in doing as little as possible. Some, like Jennings or Monticello's expert cabinetmaker John Hemings, sought satisfaction in acquiring skills and taking pride in work well done. As for Levasseur's conclusion—"What does it matter to him, indeed, that the prosperity of his master grows or diminishes! Aren't the results always the same for him?"—the short answer is no, the status quo was not guaranteed.[58] Levasseur was missing levels of complexity that slaves understood all too well. Their future well-being was tied in with the master's. If he was failing, they could be forced to work more; if he failed, they could be turned into ready cash.

Lafayette, like his secretary, was curious to interact directly with some of the enslaved residents, so he walked over to Montpelier's Walnut Grove slave quarters. As Cutts has it, Lafayette said, "one of the most interesting sights he had witnessed in America was when he visited the log cabin of Granny Milly, 104 years of age, whose daughter and grand daughter, the youngest nearly 70, were retired from their labors." Granny Milly rummaged in an old chest to show off her "only treasure . . . an old worn copy of Telemachus, which had been given to her as a keepsake by the wife of the gardener." An earlier visitor from France, the Baron de Montlezun, had been equally astounded at the "numerous cases of longevity" among the area's inhabitants and noted in his journal, "These last few days I saw a Negro ninety-five years old engaged in splitting wood; he belongs to President Madison."[59]

One member of Lafayette's entourage who would have been of particular interest to Jennings and vice versa was Lafayette's manservant, known in most accounts only as Bastien, but who, like Jennings and all the Montpelier workers, had a full name. Sebastien Wagner, in his late thirties at this time, was characterized as "quiet, sober, honest and sensible." He and Jennings were counterparts—valets serving famous personages—even if one was an American black slave and one a white employee of German origin working for a Frenchman. Perhaps Jennings had learned some French colloquialisms from gardener Bizet to insert here and there into their broken communication. Bastien Wagner and Lafayette shared a bond like Jennings and Madison's. Lafayette's valet de chambre became "indispensable for his comfort." Back in France, Wagner would remain at Lafayette's side until the general passed away a decade later, then would carry the old soldier's sword on a black pillow in his funeral procession.[60]

One pair from Lafayette's entourage not present at Montpelier in November 1824 was antislavery activist Frances Wright and her sister and traveling companion, Camilla. They intended to come along with the general from Monticello, but Camilla took sick. Instead, the two made the trek to Montpelier from Washington the first week of March in the next year. The outspoken Fanny Wright undoubtedly gave Madison as much of an earful on slavery's shame as her mentor Lafayette had some three months earlier. Of course Madison readily agreed that slavery was an evil of great magnitude, as he later wrote Wright after she forwarded a printed copy of her plan for the gradual abolition of slavery. Their point of departure was that Wright, like Edward Coles, had determined to do something about the evil *immediately.* As with Coles, this translated not only to taking action on slave emancipation but, just as important, to affording blacks a fair chance to exercise their qualities and abilities.[61]

Is it any wonder that Jennings, exposed to such perspectives, personally acquainted with activists like Jesse Torrey, Edward Coles, and Fanny Wright, was enamored with freedom or might aspire to one day take his own stand as an abolitionist? Madison's study was a crucible of ideas, not all of which were Madison's or even acceptable to him. Jennings and other waiting servants were like part of the wallpaper. Rarely were they sent out of a room where white people were talking because a sensitive political topic was about to be explored; certainly it was no matter if the conversation included items that belittled blacks. It was all part and parcel of the pretense that slaves were either like children and not tuned in or not understanding what was being said, or did not mind being made fun of and could just put up with being insulted, or should not have been listening in the first place. The slaves knew the game and played their practiced part. Naturally they were interested in what the "higher-ups" might reveal of concern to them, but they were trained to maintain poker faces. No matter what they overheard, they did not react visibly, much less speak up. If their opinion should be *asked for,* they knew better than to respond with anything that was the least controversial. When the English writer and antislavery promoter Harriet Martineau visited in 1835, Madison expounded hour after hour on all aspects of slavery and colonization. Martineau claimed, "During all our conversations, one or another slave was perpetually coming to Mrs. Madison for the great bunch of keys; two or three more lounged about in the room, leaning against the doorposts or the corner of the sofa."[62] That household servants were present is not a surprise. That they remained while hot-button topics were being analyzed is not a surprise. What is a surprise is Martineau's description of their disposition: slaves did not generally lounge and lean in a room with the master and mistress and their special guest (Jennings would have elbowed them right up if they tried). Most students of plantation life would suspect that Martineau chose her words imprecisely here. Lounging and leaning? Unlikely. On hand and listening? Absolutely.

Edward Coles was at Montpelier on many occasions over many years. Jennings had the opportunity to get to know him, and Coles had his own reasons to be interested in the thoughts of an intelligent and experienced enslaved man like Jennings. It is possible they had private conversations wherein Jennings expressed himself honestly and at length; that is to say, conversations during which he dropped the demeanor and dissembling just detailed and communicated unguardedly with Coles. If so, each would have learned a great deal from the other. To the established power structure, Edward Coles, Fanny Wright, and Jesse Torrey were extremists, tolerated only because they were rare types predicted to be ineffectual; to a reed-slender liberal element in society, they were cutting-edge political activists; to Paul Jennings, they were pure inspiration.

The last visitor of note in 1824 was Daniel Webster, who was destined one day to help Jennings travel the road to freedom by arranging for his final toll. For now, the renowned statesman and orator was one more important guest to whom Jennings attended. Webster arrived on Saturday, 11 December, in the company of fellow New Englanders George and Anna Ticknor, he the Harvard professor who had dined with the Madisons in Washington in 1815. The trio had traveled from Washington to Fredericksburg by steamboat on the ninth. The next day they made it by carriage to an inn just five miles from Orange, but the shadows were too long and the road too rough to go on. The innkeeper where they dined, Ticknor recalled, "dropped his knife and fork with astonishment, as he was carving a very nice turkey, when he understood that he was talking with Mr. Webster of Massachusetts; but he was nothing daunted, and they had a great argument upon the question of internal improvements, the Virginian confessing that if the power were not in the Constitution, he wished it was."[63]

The next morning Madison sent his coachman to meet the party when they reached Orange Court House. In all likelihood this was Jennings, given that he acted as coachman in addition to his other duties, and that it was James and Dolley who received their special guests directly when the carriage drew up to Montpelier's portico. Jennings would have remembered Webster from Washington although Webster probably did not remember him, a liveried lad serving refreshments at Dolley's Drawing Rooms. Webster was now a congressman from Massachusetts, active in that body again after a six-year absence. Just the autumn before the Montpelier trip, Webster made his first visit to Marshfield, a Massachusetts farm in full view of the sea that he would eventually purchase and that Jennings would travel to in the future as a Webster household employee.

The company was treated with "much hospitality," recalled Webster, and Ticknor elaborated on the regular pattern of Montpelier domestic life:

> We breakfasted at nine, dined about four, drank tea at seven, and went to
> bed at ten; that is, we went to our rooms, where we were furnished with
> everything we wanted, and where Mrs. Madison sent us a nice supper every
> night and a nice luncheon every forenoon. From ten o'clock in the morning
> till three we rode, walked, or remained in our rooms, Mr. and Mrs. Madison
> then being occupied. The table is very ample and elegant, and somewhat
> luxurious; it is evidently a serious item in the account of Mr. M.'s happiness,
> and it seems to be his habit to pass about an hour, after the cloth is removed,
> with a variety of wines of no mean quality.

The intellectual repartee made the visit just as agreeable. The threesome would go on to Monticello to visit Jefferson; they had not planned to make this first stop as long as they did, but conversation with the Sage of Montpelier was just too stimulating to rush off. Ticknor reported that after a long and pleasant dinner the first evening, as the company headed back to the drawing room, "Mr. Webster said to me, in an undertone, *'Stare hic;'* for he was afraid I might say something of going away the next day; but I had no such intention." The party finally reached Monticello on Tuesday morning. After returning to the capital, Webster allowed, according to Ticknor, "that he had been very much impressed by Mr. Madison's conversation, and that it had fully confirmed him in an opinion he had for some time entertained that Mr. Madison was 'the wisest of our Presidents, except Washington.'"

There was a sad element to Webster's Virginia trip. At Monticello, he received word that his two-year-old son, Charles, was seriously ill. The boy died while Webster was still with Jefferson, but he did not get this saddest news until he was back in Washington.[64] "Little Charley" was the second child Webster buried; he would not be the last.

Jennings would not meet Webster again for more than a dozen years, but when he did, he would be reminded that it helps to have acquaintances in high places. Occasionally such positions were reversed, and it was Jennings who served as contact of interest. When, some years after Webster's visit, Christopher Hughes, who had been secretary to the peace commissioners in Ghent in 1814 and knew Jennings from Washington, arrived at Montpelier unexpectedly, he was thrilled to discover that access to the sage was facilitated via a familiar face. In a letter he wrote from Montpelier three days into his visit, Hughes took the time to describe how this initial reception set the tone for what would be the most "interesting and instructive and delightful days" he ever passed:

> I arrived at Mr. Madison's on Friday, at Midday; the Carriage was ready to take the President his daily drive; as I stepped from a rusty Orange Court House Gig, some 30 yards from the door, the Coachman exclaimed, "Is that Mr. Hughes?" So thought I, I am not forgotten by the *helps.* "How do you do Paul?" "Lord, Sir," said he—"I knew you directly: Master & Mistress will be delighted to see you! They often speak of you."
>
> In I walked![65]

CHAPTER FOUR

"Not Even Paul"

Wednesday, 11 November 1829, home of Andrew and Sally Coles Stevenson, Richmond, Virginia

Paul Jennings stood in the front doorway of the Stevenson town house holding James Madison's olive-colored overcoat. It was the coldest morning yet. Madison was gathering up his papers for the day's legislative session. Since it was not due to start until eleven o'clock, Jennings would let his master decide if the air was still chilly enough for the overcoat. Madison walked from the home of his host to the delegates' chamber in the neoclassical state house each morning but Sunday. He was seventy-eight years old but, as one colleague observed, "walks without a staff." His manservant was there to accompany him and offer his arm as needed.[1]

The Madison household had been in Richmond for over a month now. Jennings informed James Monroe of the arrival of his master and mistress on 3 October, two days before the Virginia convention commenced. Madison and Monroe participated as elected delegates to the convention, which had been called to reform the commonwealth's constitution. Some combination of duty and honor, and perhaps missing some of the rough-and-tumble of political life as well, brought the two former Presidents out of rural retirement.

The other delegates were suitably impressed, as was the whole town. On the last day of October, the former Presidents had attended a performance at the Richmond Theater together. "On the entrance of these patriarchs, the audience, with one accord, rose and greeted them with cheers, and the house rung, for a few minutes, with the most deafening applause," the newspaper reported.

Jennings could not help but take some residual pride in the honor virtutis premium *(as the newspaper put it) shown his master. When Jennings escorted Madison to the state house and left him at the chamber door, he could watch the old statesman, in breeches and powdered hair, work his way slowly but deliberately to the very front and take a chair at the extreme right.*[2] *Just as at the national Constitutional Convention forty-two years earlier, Madison was intent on processing every word and gesture. Jennings might have been pleased on occasion by his association with Madison, yet he had reason to be somewhat embarrassed by his appearance. As valet, it was his job to see that his gentleman was attired in the latest fashion. Noticing that almost all the other delegates wore trousers, he would be forced to acknowledge his failure in this regard.*

We can be sure Jennings gave that little thought on Sundays, his one day to take in Richmond on his own time. This was his first return to a real city in a dozen years. He had known Edward Coles's sister Sally, now Mrs. Andrew Stevenson, since his days in the White House. He never forgot how she called down the cellar stairs to him and the other servants at the Octagon when news of peace reached Washington, setting off rounds of celebration for the household. It was exciting to be in the commonwealth's capital now. There was a lot more to look at in each block between the Stevensons' and the state house than in the whole five miles between Montpelier and Orange Court House. Richmond was a town of sixteen thousand. The proportion of free people among the black population was very much higher than in Orange.

If Jennings missed city life, it was not with the same poignancy and intensity that he came to miss his own family, especially when Sunday circled around, the day he normally spent in their company back home. He had a son and daughter now. Felix was his boy, and the baby was named Frances, after her mother. It had been a month and counting since he had seen them, and he had no idea how much longer the Madison household would remain in Richmond; neither did he have any say in the matter.

PAUL JENNINGS'S FAMILY GREW AS HE AND FANNY had children. His struggles to be an involved parent were hindered by living on a different farm from his family and by his master's increasing dependency on him. An eyewitness on the scene in 1824 described Madison as "quite the Farmer, enthusiastically fond of all its employments, and wearing pantaloons Patched at the knees." But by the end of the decade, that image was fading, to be inescapably replaced by one of a housebound old gent in a dressing gown relying on his personal attendant to ease his increasingly thin frame and stiff joints onto a couch. One traveler closed his account of being in the sage's presence in 1824 by writing, then underlining, "His mind is his all." Fittingly enough, as Jennings characterized it and as visitor after visitor during Madison's last years ratified, "his mind was bright" through to the very end; apparently it was built for endurance as well as brilliance.[3]

The year 1829 was one of transition. It signaled the start of Madison's final decline as his health problems mounted. Ironically, the year also included the first and last time in his nineteen-year retirement that Madison acted on a public stage outside of the Piedmont or traveled so far, going the eighty miles to Richmond as a legislator at the state constitutional convention. It was also in 1829 that Madison faced the extreme embarrassment of having to bail his stepson out of debtor's prison. The year began in sadness for the household when Mother Madison died in February.

Twenty-eight Februarys had passed since her husband died, and she was three years shy of one hundred. By July, the inventory of Nelly Conway Madison's estate was completed. Nineteen slaves (eleven men, five women, and three children) were listed with her other property. The most valuable individual was Edmund, worth $380. One man, Peter, was worth "nothing." Three people were worth less than nothing; they were a drag on the estate, equating to negative sums that needed to be subtracted from the final balance sheet. One of these "old negroes" was Sawney, and this document reveals that, at seventy-eight, he was the same age as James Madison. For Sawney and the two other "old negroes," Violet and Lucy, it was estimated that "the value of [their] support (including necessary clothing) for the remainder of their lives" was $60 each. The ages of Violet and Lucy were not given, but one of them may be the servant referred to by a visitor present in 1826, impressed that Mother Madison and "her waiting woman" had both reached the advanced age of ninety-four.[4]

One of the two appraisers for Nelly Madison's estate was none other than Charles Howard, who was active in these kinds of services in the community. He officially witnessed the calling together of Mother Madison's enslaved people on 15 August 1829. Once gathered, they were informed that "by the will of their mistress they were allowed to choose for their masters or mistresses" among the heirs. Only the three oldest—Sawney, Violet, and Lucy—opted for James Madison. Apparently the others did not think it a good bet to throw in their future prospects with Madison's. In the end, to keep the accounting among heirs equitable, six or eight of Nelly Madison's slaves were offered up to the highest bidder in front of the local hotel in Orange. The rest of her property, the household goods, was sold, too, and among the buyers was one slave, Sawney. He spent 12½ cents to purchase a coffeepot, seven bottles, and a tureen top.[5]

How much longer Sawney lived to use these items is not known. His name never comes up again in the historical record. A Montpelier slave from cradle to grave, surname unknown, Sawney presumably was buried in the slave cemetery, a fieldstone marking his life. What lessons did Paul Jennings draw from observing and interacting with Sawney, whom he knew from his earliest memories? We can imagine him at Sawney's burial, thinking back on conversations they had about their travels with James Madison and what adjustments they made upon returning to the farm.

◆

PAYNE TODD, MEANWHILE, WAS WANDERING among the cities of the Eastern Seaboard, drinking and gambling and leaving a trail of debts in his wake. Unable to maintain a lead on his creditors, he landed in debtor's jail in June 1829. His mother and stepfather, after so long enduring "his strange absence and mysterious silence," were now forced to absorb the unwelcome news: Payne was "boarding within prison bounds!" Bailed out by Madison, the same scenario replayed the next year. Payne, even as he approached forty, was still unable to learn from experience, and with drink his master, his best days, such as they were, were behind him.

Payne's behavior made Dolley "wretched," her husband reported, and for familial warmth from the younger generation, she turned to her nieces and nephews. Among this set, Annie Payne, daughter of her brother John, developed a close relationship with Aunt Dolley at this time and would serve as live-in companion in her widowhood. John Payne had moved to the Montpelier neighborhood earlier in the 1820s and was one of several "secretaries" who assisted in the care and copying of Madison's papers.[6]

In May 1829 Madison contracted influenza, and could not shake off the illness all summer. This was compounded by a bout with the intermittent "bilious attacks" that he had been subject to since he was young. A third malady, and the one that would plague the rest of his retirement years with misery, was diffusive rheumatism. And yet this was the moment that Madison's political career came full circle. He would close it as he began it, fifty-three years apart, as a delegate from Orange to the state constitutional convention. In 1776, the capital was Williamsburg, but since 1780, it was Richmond. "Mrs. Madison accompanied him and enjoyed the hospitalities of that city," recorded Mary Cutts. Jennings and at least three of his enslaved coworkers completed the entourage.[7]

Despite his lingering illness, Madison was determined to participate in the convention, and the activity actually improved his health. The two major issues were suffrage and representation. The reformers from the western districts wanted an end to suffrage being limited to landholders and opposed slave population being factored into representation apportionment in the legislature. Needless to add, there were many more large land- and slaveholders in the eastern districts. The intent of counting slaves was to put more political power in the hands of the masters, hardly to allow the slaves the kind of true representation that the colonists had demanded from England, the mother country they rebelled against when such representation was not granted. The hypocrisy behind counting slaves is transparent: slaves were property unless it helped their owners gain legislative influence by pretending that slaves were people whose voices were taken into account in the legislative agenda.

Though initially he seemed to side with the reformers, as the convention dragged on, Madison came to see how entrenched the eastern slave owners were in their position. When Madison rose to speak on Wednesday, 2 December, he advocated compromise, suggesting adoption of the three-fifths "federal number" (the fraction applied to enumerating slaves in the U.S. Constitution for apportionment of representatives). In his attempt to justify counting slaves (even if at a three-fifths rate), Madison issued statements of lofty sentiment, to wit: "It is due to justice . . . to our character as a people, both abroad and at home, that [slaves] should be considered, as much as possible, in the light of human beings, and not as mere property . . . the mere circumstance of complexion cannot deprive them of the character of men." But, in fact, these sentiments—so affecting when quoted out of context—were made in service to a shell game. Even granting Madison's sincerity in the sentiments themselves, as historian Drew McCoy does, expressing them in support of a power grab for slave owners was pure manipulation, yet one more form of exploitation of enslaved African Americans. Madison was truer to his own convictions when he reread the speech in later life and added a corrective note: "Men cannot be justly bound by laws in the making of which they have no part."[8]

When Madison finished speaking, "The members rushed from their seats and crowded about him," but it seemed as if he and they knew that their homage was for the sum of his toils in the field of statecraft rather than for the remarks just delivered. This was to be Madison's only major speech during the three-month convention. One delegate noticed that the former President occasionally would put his hand to his powdered head, but rarely did he raise it to indicate that he wished to hold forth. He had narrowed his objective down to prevention of outright "abortion" of the proceedings. In the end, reforms were few; the eastern slave owners held on to an excess of power. Once again, unity—union—took precedence over other considerations, no matter how high the principle or deep the distress.[9]

On 4 December, when Dolley put pen to paper in reply to her brother's letter from Orange, she mentioned her husband's speech two days earlier, but her focus was on domestic matters. Full of household news and gossip, she began by passing on the message that "Paul is much oblig[ed] by news from his wife & children—& when opportunity offer[s to] send he woud to write him." Before Dolley shifted to white society gossip ("now for ourselves . . ."), she completed the requests from members of her enslaved staff: regale Sam's wife by the news that he is well and sober, tell Ralph his mother sends her love for now and to expect a gift when she gets home, and let Sarah's husband know she wants to hear from him. Paul's wife and Sarah's husband were likely illiterate, but their spouses hoped they might enlist someone with writing skills to act as amanuensis as they dictated. That particular letters are from illiterate individuals is not always apparent unless a line such as one in an 1837 letter from an enslaved Virginian to her daughter gives it away: "You must not expect [me] to write to you Often as it is some trouble to get a person to write for Me." That Jennings's letters to his family in Orange were written in his own hand must have made them all the more treasured. We can imagine Fanny listening as one of the Howards, perhaps, read his letter aloud to her, and she then retrieving the paper, folding it carefully, and placing it in her skirt pocket.

That Felix was the firstborn among Paul and Fanny's five children can be surmised by circumstantial evidence. Dolley's 4 December 1829 letter referred to "children," so there must have been more than one child by this date. At least approximate birth dates are known for four of the children, with only Frances born before the letter's date. No birth date is known for Felix. Since Paul and Fanny married in 1822, and Frances was not born until about 1827, it is likely that Felix was born during the first five years of the marriage. We can picture Felix in his mother's cabin at Howard Place, playing with his older half sister, Elizabeth, while their mother cares for toddler Frances and, if it is a Sunday, missing his father's presence.[10]

A buzz developed in Richmond's African American community in December that Jennings, with his aptitude for networking, surely heard about. Two months earlier, David Walker, a free black originally from the South, had published a pamphlet in Boston titled *Appeal to the Coloured Citizens of the World*. It advocated common cause among slaves and free blacks, and that cause was nothing short of revolution against the oppressor. Walker opposed colonization, declaring that America belonged to all who helped build it; indeed, averred Walker, "America is more our country than it is the whites—we have enriched it with our *blood and tears*." Within weeks the *Appeal* was circulated among people of color as far south as Georgia. Walker himself sent thirty printed copies to a Richmond contact, accompanied by the only

extant letter in his hand, dated 8 December 1829. In it Walker instructed the booklets to be sold at twelve cents each or given away if
the would-be recipient had no money. It is likely that Jennings either
read Walker's *Appeal* or was apprised of its content and that its rhetoric
added to his politicization. One of Walker's goals was to instill pride in
African Americans and a belief that they could be their own agents in
effecting change. The white powers-that-be were horrified when they
discovered that Walker's "incendiary" pamphlet was being circulated
among Richmond's African Americans that winter. Copies were confiscated, and Walker's letter ended up in the governor's hands.[11]

Jennings would have particularly pined for his family over Christmas, so he must have been gratified when he learned that the household would spend the holiday at home. One ex-Virginia slave, thinking
back, swore that slaves lived just for Christmas to come around. It was
the only time the whole year that they were, by tradition, granted several consecutive days off. The period when Paul was in Richmond was
by far the longest separation he and Fanny had known, but some slaves
were able to reunite with their spouses only during the annual holiday
break. Christmas was on a Friday, so most likely Paul enjoyed at least
a three-day weekend catching up with Fanny and the children. The
household was back in Richmond before the year was out, then finally
returned to Montpelier for good in mid-January. "We reached home
the fifth day after leaving Richmond," Madison remembered, "much
fatigued, and with the horses almost broken down by the almost im-
passable state of the roads." All were glad to be back. Even Dolley had
tired of socializing.[12]

◆

THE RELATIONSHIP BETWEEN MASTER AND MANSERVANT
became more intimate as Madison's neediness increased. "The last few
years of his life," wrote Mary Cutts, "his fingers were so affected by
rheumatism that he dined at his small table, in his room (having his
dinner cut for him) placed sufficiently near the door of the dining

room for him to converse with the guests." One such guest noted, "A diffusive rheumatism has confined him mostly to his room and bed. But his sickness has found all that alleviation which judicious thought-fulness could minister." Madison's constant caregivers were two: his wife and his personal attendant. Dolley wrote to a niece that "His hands and fingers are still so swelled and sore as to be nearly useless, but I lend him mine." But it was more likely Jennings's hands that cut Madison's food and Jennings who provided the bodily ministrations designed to relieve the old man's pain, including lifting him into tepid salt-water baths and wrapping oiled silk bandages on his legs. Jennings would be careful to minimize the indignity of these, mostly ineffectual, treatments to which the former President submitted. Madison wrote of his obstinate disease, "It disables my pen, & my hand from holding a Book or handling my papers."[13] Dolley and other relatives assisted Madison in this regard, but his manservant, literate and available, may have stepped in to help as well.

A "martyr to rheumatism," as Cutts called Madison, it got so he could not walk from one room to another without leaning on his at-tendant's arm. These two men moving as a unit became a common sight for Montpelier's residents. Jennings, while strong, was not much taller than his master had been in his prime, though the elderly states-man became smaller with the passing years of poor health. His foot-steps got smaller, too, so Jennings patiently maintained their slow pace as a couple.

The Madisons' nephew James Madison Cutts married in late De-cember 1833, and the wedding journey included a stop at Montpelier. Dolley Madison's biographer Maud Goodwin apparently learned the family story of that visit from Adele Cutts, daughter of the union be-ing celebrated. "As the coach drew up before the door, Mr. Madison came out, leaning on the arm of Paul Jennings, to greet the guests, and though too feeble to join the family at dinner, he stood at the door which opened between the general dining-room and his own, and rais-ing his glass, drank to the health of the bride."[14]

Jennings is certainly the servant who impressed University of Virginia professor George Tucker: "[I have] sometimes been struck with the conferences between [Mr. Madison] and some trusty servant in his sick chamber, the black seeming to identify himself with his master as to plans of management, and giving his opinions freely, though not offensively, as if conversing with a brother." The fact that Jennings's familiar manner came across as inoffensive to Madison's peer reflects on Jennings's finesse and highly honed skills as personal attendant and the resultant trust and ease he built up in his relationship with Madison.[15]

Over the last few years of Madison's life, his study or sitting room doubled as his "sick chamber." Here he was served many of his meals, here he kept both a couch and bed, and here he met with his numerous visitors. He deteriorated from a vigorous and ambulatory retired President to an increasingly feeble and hurting old man restricted to two rooms, his study and the private bedchamber that he and his wife shared. Eventually Dolley described her husband as "my patient" and claimed that he walked only from the bed in the one room to that in the other. These two rooms were separated by a large "closet." The study had two doors; the other opened directly onto the dining room. These three rooms then—dining room, bedchamber, and study (plus closet and pantry)—made up the north side of the main story.[16]

When he first planned the north addition in 1809, Madison and his builder discussed the wing room being used for a new library, but instead it became the master bedchamber and the library remained upstairs. We can imagine Dolley coaxing her husband into agreement that this large, light-filled room would make a splendid private chamber for them. Dolley had a bad knee and "disliked the fatigue of a staircase." Thus she was, as Mary Cutts noted, "accustomed to have her private apartments on the ground floor at Montpelier."[17]

Cutts described how one mounted the south staircase and "enter[ed] the library," where Madison's collection of about four thousand books and pamphlets was kept. Ben Stewart, Sukey's son, recalled that three rooms comprised the library. This description matched the upstairs suite: the space one stepped onto from the top of the stairs was actually a spacious landing that could easily accommodate bookcases, and directly adjoining the landing were the main library room with corner fireplace, and a walk-in "closet" with built-in shelves that was lit by a large window. The latter room was reminiscent of Abigail Adams's prized "reading closet"; it was a place where Madison could "indulge his relish for the intellectual pleasures of the closet." When Madison could no longer negotiate the stairs, young Ben (who was about ten when his master died) transported his books and papers back and forth for him. "He kept his papers filed in pigeon holes," remembered Stewart, "I had to put them away for him many times."[18]

Dolley referred to her husband's study or sitting room as "the small chamber," distinct from the commodious master chamber. It was relatively small but crowded with furniture: French bed (with canopy of crimson damask), couch, desk, small dining table, easy chair, rocking chair, and so many books that one of Jefferson's grand-daughters visiting with her mother called the room "Mr. Madison's library." Ben Stewart was familiar with the easy chair. He described it as a "great English arm chair" and recalled how Madison liked to sit in the garden in the shades of early evening and he would carry the chair out for him. We can visualize Stewart placing the armchair under a bower of fruit trees, the old man following slowly behind on the arm of Paul Jennings.[19]

The rocking chair was a gift from Christopher Hughes, the dip-lomat who came unexpectedly in 1833 and, delighted to have been recognized, conversed with Jennings on the portico. Though Hughes "found Mr. Madison on his legs" when he entered the mansion, and the next day Jennings drove the two men along the plantation roads in the carriage, Hughes also reported that "Mr. Madison is very thin, & suffers from Rheumatism . . . & lolls, or reclines, occasionally, on the bed." It occurred to Hughes that a rocking chair might be just the thing for easing the old statesman's joint pain, and after his visit he had one sent to Montpelier. Later visitors mentioned the new piece of furniture, one of them noting that Madison "scarcely ever goes out of his room but takes exercise in a rocking chair," and another recalling, "He reclined upon his sofa all the time we were with him, excepting that occasionally he would change his position by sitting a short time in a large armed rocking chair, observing, as he would seat himself, that he 'found some relief in that machine.'"[20]

When Hughes encountered Madison "on his legs," he was enjoying one of his periodic rallies. During another rally in the early 1830s—a time when the old man was feeling particularly chipper—the family was visited by the young daughter of an old friend of Dolley's. Madison's antics on this occasion perfectly illustrate what Margaret Bayard Smith called just a few years earlier "the sportiveness of his character," elaborating, "Mrs. M. says he is as fond of a frolic and of romping with the girls as ever. His little blue eyes sparkled like stars from under his bushy grey eye-brows. . . . Nor have they lost their look of mischief that used to lurk in their corners." The young visitor, who signed her recollections "M. T." and who can be identified (from hints in her narrative) as a niece of Sarah Pendleton Dandridge, described Madison as "much emaciated." Though "he lay most of the time on a couch in the middle of the room adjoining the dining-room, wrapped in a black silk dressing gown elaborately quilted, and did not look larger than a boy of thirteen," he was not too ill for a little fun . . .

At dinner the first day I was attacked by ague, and Mrs. Madison, leading me into the next room, placed me on his couch. I awoke an hour or two after in a high fever, and the look on his face which has outlived all others in my recollection is that of amusement which lighted the wan features on beholding the expression of bewilderment and confusion which overspread mine as I opened my eyes, half delirious, and found him lying beside me.

Dolley had a lighter side, too. As M. T. tells it, she had an antidote for her husband's flirtatiousness:

Mr. and Mrs. Madison would in private sometimes romp and tease each other like two children, and engage in antics that would astonish the muse of history. Mrs. Madison was stronger as well as larger than he. She could—and did—seize his hands, draw him upon her back and go round the room with him whenever she particularly wished to impress him with a due sense of man's inferiority.[21]

These are the kind of behind-the-scenes behaviors that Paul Jennings was very familiar with. He knew all sides of his master and mistress. Jennings was almost as at home at Howard Place as at Montpelier. The 1830 federal census reveals that Charles P. Howard headed a household of thirty-seven people, two free—himself and his wife—and thirty-five enslaved (a natural increase from the ten people bequeathed him in 1800). Among the bondpeople were Paul's wife, Fanny Gordon Jennings, his son and daughter (Felix and Frances) and their half sister Elizabeth, plus these children's maternal grandmother, Kate, and uncle Edmund Spotsey. So at least six, and probably more, of the people of color at Howard Place were Jennings's kin connections. Paul and Fanny had two more children by the year Madison died. John (also known as Jack, and with the middle name Willis) was born about 1834 and Franklin in 1836.[22]

James Madison's physical slide was accompanied by other kinds of decline at Montpelier. A visitor in the 1820s claimed that the drawing room furniture "had the appearance of Presidential splendor," while Margaret Bayard Smith drew a comparison between Mother Madison's rooms and those of the younger Madisons, noting: "By only opening a door the observer passed from the elegancies, refinements, and gayeties of modern life, into all that was venerable, respectable, and dignified in gone-by days." But by the next decade, visitors' descriptions made it sound like what Smith took for "modern" was now judged as "rather of ancient date." According to a caller present in May 1833, the drawing room furniture seemed "of that rich old cast, which . . . carries us back to other days, and reminds us that we are in the houses of our ancestors." When Madison's former colleague Charles Jared Ingersoll visited three Mays later, he reported that the Montpelier mansion was "decayed and in need of considerable repairs."[23]

Montpelier's deterioration was echoed by that of Virginia generally, documented in Susan Dunn's work, *Dominion of Memories: Jefferson, Madison & the Decline of Virginia*. Ingersoll's phrase could just as well be applied to the infrastructure of the entire state. There was not a traveler to Montpelier who did not complain about the road conditions. One aptly commented, "Here it is 'unconstitutional' to have good roads." Madison told one guest, "A neighbor of mine describes our roads thus, 'You may mire a horse in them in the winter; & straighten a nail on them in the summer.'"[24]

But this was as nothing compared to the wear of the soil itself. Back in 1802, Madison exclaimed, "I am a farmer, and am willing to flatter myself that my farm will be better for my presence." Madison was president of the five-county Agricultural Society of Albemarle and a leading expositor of the most advanced approaches to soil management. Be that as it may, and even as Jefferson (in his hyperbolic fashion) was referring to Madison as "the best farmer in the world," the most productive days of the Montpelier plantation were over. Virginia's plantation economy was failing everywhere. There were three kinds of related causes: the traditional, the cumulative, and the contemporary. The traditional causes were, of course, the pest and weather problems farmers always have had to contend with. One submission of evidence, excerpted from Madison's letter to his nephew and fellow farmer James Madison Hite suffices: "The appearance of the fly in the Wheat, and the damage to the corn, are complained of here as with you. The Tobacco Crop is also understood to have generally suffered much in both quality & quantity, by the wetness of the season, & by the frost; or by culling it, prematurely from a fear of it." It is when a run of bad years ensues that the farmer's challenge becomes the family's disaster. The cumulative problem was, as Ingersoll put it in the account of his Montpelier visit, that tobacco was "injurious to the ground" by exhausting its nutrients and had led to the increasingly "worn soils of Virginia." The contemporary cause was the financial Panic of 1819, which sent crop prices (when one could bring in a crop) and land values (for depleted soils that were poor producers) plummeting.[25]

All of this was aggravated by labor issues. "Farming and slavery are incompatible with one another," a fellow Virginia planter lamented to Madison; and all the "scientific farming" in the world could not keep Thomas Jefferson from concluding, "I am not fit to be a farmer with the kind of labor that we have." The master of the Montpelier plantation concurred. Ingersoll recalled that Madison "spoke often and anxiously of slave property as the worst possible for profit," adding, "He is now in debt." Ingersoll also reported that, while Madison owned one hundred people, "Nearly two-thirds of his slaves are too young or too old to work much, while the support of so many is very expensive. It takes nearly all he makes to feed, clothe, and preserve them."[26]

To conserve financial resources, Madison let his gardener go. "We dismissed our gardener . . . and called in three black men, who understood the business—and we hope to have from them as many good things as usual," Dolley wrote niece Mary Cutts. Next, Madison sold Montpelier acreage, devalued as it was, and moved the families living on—and off—that land to the remaining farms. This meant that the ratio of people to acres increased even as the soil productivity decreased. Ironically, since Madison had so few working hands among his "too many" slaves, he had to hire prime enslaved laborers.[27]

Amid all these factors tending to economic disaster, there was one surplus Virginia commodity in high demand, and that was the slaves themselves if sold to the Deep South, where the cotton business and the people business to power it were booming. When Madison spoke of slave property as "the worst possible for profit," he meant if slaves remained on their Upper South farms. He understood that the value of his slaves was greatest as articles of traffic to the Deep South. He stopped short of sale to commercial traders, but he did resort to sale. In the early fall of 1834, Madison sold sixteen people to his relative William Taylor, who owned a Louisiana plantation. Madison attempted to explain himself in a letter to Edward Coles dated 3 October 1834: "Finding that I have in order to avoid the sale of Negroes sold land till the residue will not support them, concentered and increasing as they are, I have yielded to the necessity of parting with some of them to a friend and Kinsman who I am persuaded will do better by them than I can, and to whom they gladly consent to be transferred."

The sale enabled Madison to pay off $6,000 to creditors (though this was not the whole of his indebtedness). Of the sixteen people who relocated to Louisiana, the name of only one, Betty, is known, and then only because she became the object of contention between Madison and Taylor. Taylor claimed in December that the condition of "the girl Betty" was poor enough that he considered that it canceled the balance ($800) he still owed Madison. This complication after the sale "gave him much trouble," Madison's great-nephew and neighbor John Willis recalled many years later, and was especially aggravating as the transaction had "caused him to break in on fixed principles" to begin with, referring to Madison's resolution not to traffic in people.[28]

◆

BY THE TIME THE CALENDARS READ 1835, there were no more rallies left in the man now referred to as "old master" by his slaves. Madison's wife and manservant spent most of their time in the first-floor rooms of the home's north side and felt the strain that round-the-clock caregivers are subject to. For Madison, enduring a self-described "constitution crippled by disease," two spaces—bedchamber and study—became his whole world. His day started with Sukey delivering his breakfast, often directly to his bed in the master chamber or, if he had already moved to "the room he occupies during the day," to the little table there. One overnight guest recalled that upon rising at seven in the morning, Mr. Madison had already had breakfast when he and his hostess were served a meal of "fine coffee, cold boiled ham, herring, warm and cold bread, and tea." Jennings had stored away the master's suit; the clothes he now helped Madison's aching limbs into were soft pantaloons and long dressing robes. Jennings still shaved Madison every other day, but what hair remained on his head was covered by a nightcap or kerchief. These varied in color while the tufts of hair that stuck out were white. Family members recalled that Madison liked to be read to; perhaps Jennings took his turn at this. In the end, Madison did not walk from bedchamber to study, even with his valet's support, but rather was transported on a contrivance. This is revealed in a letter from Dolley's brother John Payne to one of their nephews, dated 20 June 1836: "A simple contrivance, carrying [Mr. Madison] on a couch from his bed to his sitting room, and back in the same manner, relieves him from the fatigue of walking."[29]

The world continued to come to him. One tourist "resolved to stop, and to visit almost the last of the Romans"; another spoke of "treading on sacred ground" at the "abode of the sage." Madison's voice and mind stayed strong. As Jennings testified, though he "was unable to walk and spent most of his time reclined on a couch . . . with his numerous visitors he talked with as much animation and strength of voice as I ever heard him in his best days." When Benjamin Latrobe's son John called, Madison told him that "his lungs were the strongest part of him that was left." As for his mind, brother-in-law John Payne, even as he enumerated the debilities attendant on what turned out to be the aged philosopher's last month, concluded, "In no respect is a difference of aspect presented by his mind."[30]

One of the last in the long line of visitors over James Madison's nineteen-year retirement, Harriet Martineau, confirmed that Madison's voice was clear and strong and "his relish for conversation could never be keener." The English writer and social theorist arrived as the February snows of 1835 were melting. She found Madison wrapped in a gown with "a warm gray and white cap upon his head, which his lady took care should always sit becomingly." Day after day, Madison and Martineau conversed while the house servants listened in between chores. Martineau, an outspoken supporter of abolition, reported that her host "talked more on the subject of slavery than on any other, acknowledging, without limitations or hesitation, all the evils with which it has ever been charged." Nearly deaf, she employed an ear trumpet, with its curved stem over a foot long terminating in a large bell. She sat at the arm of the sage's easy chair and aimed the bell so it would catch and amplify his remarks. Out they flowed:

> He told me that the black population in Virginia increases far faster than the white; and that the licentiousness only stops short of the destruction of the race; every slave girl being expected to be a mother by the time she is fifteen. He assumed from this, I could not make out why, that the negroes must go somewhere, and pointed out how the free states discourage the settlement of blacks. . . . Africa is their only refuge. He did not assign any reason why they should not remain where they are when freed. . . . One third of his own slaves were under five years of age. He had parted with some of his best land to feed the increasing numbers, and had yet been obliged to sell a dozen slaves the preceding week. . . . He accounted for selling his slaves by mentioning their horror of going to Liberia, a horror which he admitted to be prevalent among the blacks.[31]

Indeed, in 1833, the same year that Madison became president of the American Colonization Society, a committee of Orange's prominent citizens had been appointed by the court to canvass the area's free people of color and determine what number of them would avail themselves of a recent Act of Assembly providing for their transportation to Liberia. No enthusiasm was ascertained. Referring back to her discussion with Madison years later, Martineau clarified that he, given "the unwillingness of the negroes to go [to Liberia], . . . had just sold some of his slaves, instead of compelling them to emigrate." Madison's sale of sixteen slaves in early fall 1834 and twelve more in February 1835—"break[ing] in on fixed principles" again—equaled twenty-eight people who were apparently given the false choice of consenting to be sold or going to Liberia (false, because certainly Madison would not have followed through on forced removal from the country).

Warming to his subject, Madison shared with Martineau the sufferings of slave mistresses, "declaring that he pitied them even more than their negroes, and that the saddest slavery of all was that of the conscientious Southern women. They cannot trust their slaves in the smallest particulars, and have to superintend the execution of all their own orders; and they know their estates are surrounded by vicious free blacks, who induce thievery among the negroes, and keep the minds of the owners in a state of perpetual suspicion, fear, and anger." Martineau's host spoke these words, she remembered, "with deep feelings." One wonders what feelings the slaves present, most likely including Paul and Sukey, listened with, especially when Madison informed his guest "of the degradation of [slaves'] minds, of their carelessness of each other in their nearest relations, and their cruelty to brutes."[32]

◆

ABOUT THREE YEARS BEFORE MARTINEAU'S STAY at Montpelier, during the Christmas holiday of 1831, Edward Coles had paid Madison a visit. According to Coles, the two had a long talk that culminated in Madison agreeing to free his slaves in his will. Coles followed up their conversation with a letter dated 8 January 1832 wherein he reviewed some of the ethical, financial, and operational issues they covered. "You seemed to think," Coles wrote, "there would be much difficulty in their emancipation, subsequent support, and transportation out of the Country in consequence of the advanced age and helpless situation of many of your slaves, and their matrimonial connextion with the slaves of your neighbors." Coles felt he had a solution that would address these concerns and those that Madison had of course expressed for his widow's safety and comfort:

> My plan would be to provide that at the expiration of a specified number of
> years after your death all persons under a specified age should be free, and all
> above that age should continue as slaves, and be bequeathed to your heirs,
> who should be bound to support them. In fixing upon the time at which

they were to be emancipated I should be governed by the circumstances of the estate—the amount of debts—the means left for the support of Mrs. Madison—and also the necessity of retaining the slaves in service until they should have acquired by their labour the means of transporting themselves to Africa.

For parties like Jennings with abroad spouses, Coles suggested that perhaps "exchanges" could be made among the neighboring owners, but where this could not be worked out, Coles bluntly concluded that spouses "would have to choose between their natural love of liberty and the endearing ties of family."[33]

Coles voiced his personal support for colonization and belief that it was "impossible for the races ever to live harmoniously together" in this letter, and in one to Thomas Jefferson's grandson not ten days earlier he revealed a disdain for African Americans, referring to them as an "ignorant, immoral & degraded race." A significant motivation for Coles in urging Madison to free his slaves in his will, one he returned to again and again in his January 1832 letter, was the sage's legacy. "To restore to your slaves that liberty and those rights which you have been through life so zealous & able a champion," Coles prodded, " . . . is absolutely necessary to put a proper finish to your life and character."

Two months after Harriet Martineau's visit, in April 1835, James Madison prepared his last will and testament. He had made his final decision on what the disposition of the slaves residing at Montpelier at the time of his death would be.[34]

◆

"HAVING OUTLIVED SO MANY OF MY CONTEMPORARIES . . . I may be thought to have outlived myself." Still flashing a sense of humor, Madison would in fact outlive every signer of either the Declaration of Independence or the Constitution. Thomas Jefferson and John Adams had both died on the Fourth of July 1826, the fiftieth anniversary of the Declaration, and James Monroe died exactly five years later,

Independence Day 1831. Five years after that, the last week in June 1836, the fourth President lay near death in Orange, Virginia. Mary Cutts picks up the tale from there: "He lingered several days and the physicians would have prolonged his life until the 4th of July—but he would not be unnecessarily stimulated and died in the full possession of all his noble faculties." James Madison missed the Fourth of July death date shared by three of the first five Presidents by six days (and thus sidelined what truly might have been a revival of civic religion in America).[35]

"Here is a great and shining light, which by its brightness had illuminated the world for half a century," wrote one of his last visitors, "But we perceive that the flame begins to fade and flicker in the socket, and that soon it will be seen no more." Madison himself had likened his father's death thirty-five years earlier to a flame gently going out. On his own last day—28 June 1836, a Tuesday—Madison was transported from bedchamber to study and served his morning meal. The clock read approximately half past six. Paul Jennings, who had lived more constantly and more intimately with the great man than anyone save his mother and his wife, left the only eyewitness account of the historic scene and employed the same candle imagery:

> I was present when he died. That morning Sukey brought him his breakfast, as usual. He could not swallow. His niece, Mrs. Willis, said, "What is the matter, Uncle Jeames?" "Nothing more than a change of *mind,* my dear." His head instantly dropped, and he ceased breathing as quietly as the snuff of a candle goes out.

Jennings's description of Madison's death can be compared with that in Gaillard Hunt's 1902 biography:

> On the morning of June 28th he was moved from his bed to his chair as usual, and his niece brought him his breakfast and left it with him, urging him to eat. When she returned to the room a few minutes later he was dead.

No one was with him at the time; he made no parting speeches and took no
sorrowful farewells.

Madison asserted in 1829 that slaves "may be considered as making a
part, though a degraded part, of the families to which they belong."
But in the family version of the sage's last moments—apparently con-
veyed to Hunt by Madison cousin Sarah Conway—Paul and Sukey
have disappeared. The two household stalwarts remain as they began:
always present and yet invisible.[36]

James Madison was carried to the family graveyard two days later,
followed "by an immense procession of white and colored people," as
Jennings well remembered. But it was a simple burial; the memorials
with their long and laboriously crafted eulogies would come later. Governor James Barbour, one of the pallbearers, standing next to Jennings,
heard his sobs and sighs. It was not only the former President's body
servant who wept, he testified, but all the hundred slaves who turned
out for the momentous occasion in their best clothes. Their lamenta-
tions were not only for Madison but also were an expression of anxiety over the inevitable changes his death would mean for them. They
may have known then and there, perhaps not by announcement but
through the grapevine, that by the terms of Madison's will they were
bequeathed to the mistress. What had happened to Edward Coles's all-
out campaign to convince Madison to free his slaves in his will? If Jennings expected this to happen, he must have already turned over in his
mind ways to move on to the next step and secure the freedom of his
wife and children. Charles Howard's presence that day among the pall-
bearers reminded Jennings that this man owned *his* family. Jennings
had to be at least as disappointed as Coles, who agonized to his sister,
"Mr. Madison's course has been most unfortunate for his memory, &
for the peace & happiness of his Widow . . . he has now died without
having freed one [slave]—no not even Paul."[37]

The grief-stricken widow did not attend the burial. Instead, as it
was revealed many years later, she was in her chamber with Madison

niece Nelly Willis. There, Willis claimed, Dolley "took from the drawer two sealed papers, the one endorsed 'My will, opened and resealed by myself' the other endorsed 'To be opened only by my wife should she be living at the time of my death.' The last paper of which nothing more was ever heard was thought to have contained written directions on the subject of the slaves." All these details were contained in a letter to Edward Coles written for the now-arthritic Nelly Willis by her son John. Earlier Coles had been told by one of the Taylor clan that his cousin Robert Taylor had drawn up Madison's will and that Madison said at the time that he wanted to free his slaves but the difficulties could not be overcome while his wife was alive, but that she knew his wishes "and would carry them into effect at her death." Paul Jennings provided corroboration for the notion that Madison had extracted a promise from his wife to free their slaves. Jennings shared his background with a newspaper correspondent in 1848, and the resultant article claimed that "Immediately after the death of her husband, Mrs. Madison promised to set the man free, as she knew was the wish and expectation of Mr. Madison."[38]

Coles took some satisfaction in believing that his mentor, whose reputation remained of great moment to him, had made provision to free his slaves, after all, via an understanding with his widow. Small comfort, this, to the Montpelier slaves themselves, for their mistress was not even abiding by the sale terms set by her husband's will. The relevant passage, which the slaves knew in detail, read: "I give and bequeath my ownership in the Negroes and people of colour held by me to my dear wife, but it is my desire that none of them should be sold without his or her consent, or in the case of their misbehaviour; except that infant children may be sold with their parent who consents for them to be sold with him or her, and who consents to be sold." Two months after her husband died, Dolley was selling slaves, with or without such consent. Coles was an eyewitness, writing in horror to his sister Sally:

Reports has gotten abroad that she (Mrs. Madison) wished to sell many of them (her slaves) & every day or two (while I was at her house in Aug:) a Negro trader would make his appearance, & was permitted to examine the Negroes. It was like a hawk among the pigeons. The poor creatures wd run to the house and protest agt being sold, & say their old master had said in his Will that they were not to be sold but with their consent. She sold while I was with her a woman & 2 children to her Nephew Ambrose Madison who lives near her. The woman protested agt being sold & the more so as her Husband was not sold with her.[39]

Paul Jennings, husband and father, must have witnessed the wrenching scene as well. His master's last utterance had included the order of the day: *change*. He braced himself for more of it.

◆

JAMES MADISON WENT TO HIS GRAVE with the same attitude that he expressed in 1788: "Great as the evil [of slavery] is, a dismemberment of the union would be worse." Edward Coles and Fanny Wright, for all their radicalism, did not go the distance. When Henry Gilpin traveled into the Piedmont counties, he talked of finding himself "among a race of gentlemen of old families, large fortunes & aristocratic habits." These were Coles's people, and, in the end, he reverted to type. He could not visualize a pluralistic America with free blacks being integrated into white society. Fanny Wright, too, became convinced that a fully mixed society would never work.[40] They differed from Madison in feeling that some action, some start was better than none to eradicate the shame of slavery. Madison admired the attachment to human freedom evinced by Coles and Wright, but he disagreed with their means; he thought their plans were destined to fail and were reckless besides. But all shared the same ultimate goals: effect a slave-free America, *and* keep black and white, equally free, geographically separate.

If not, the thinking went, due to deep-seated prejudices and the blacks' predicted proclivity toward vengeance, the inevitable will happen: race war with one or the other race being exterminated. White activists sincerely cared about the people (as opposed to "the cause") whose fates they were debating to different degrees, but few truly put them front and center. Madison can be credited with sticking to his scruples in maintaining that blacks needed to assent to emigration as a prerequisite for colonization. He had to know that insisting on individual consent was a deal breaker, but he never dropped it as a precondition.

Consider: a people forced across the ocean as articles of traffic, treated like livestock for generations even as they labored for the American dreams of others; if and when freed, restricted by law and custom, and then blamed when lack of opportunity led to idleness; and finally told that the oppressor now wants to remove them, transport them to Africa. But the "them" were a new people: they were African Americans with roots in this land that were many generations deep.

The vision for the future that Madison and, representatives of the next generation, Coles and Wright, favored—not just a slave-free America but a white America—was not to be. It was too late to undo the sins of the past, at least by any of the emancipation/colonization schemes being proffered. The two races would not go to war, but the slave-owning and slave-free sections of white society would. They fought a vicious contest that nearly resulted in one section being wiped out and did result in hundreds of thousands of America's young sons being slaughtered. Madison's union survived the civil strife—battered and bloodied, but still a union. And still debating "the Negro problem." Frederick Douglass later articulated what Paul Jennings's point of view might have been in response to the endless temporizing: "There is no Negro problem. The problem is whether or not the American people have loyalty enough, honor enough, patriotism enough, to live up to their own constitution."[41]

Paul Jennings's daguerreotype superimposed on his 23 April 1844 letter to Dolley Madison. Jennings, newly arrived at Montpelier, wrote to his mistress back in Washington: "I write you a fiew line to let you know that I arrive safe home with the horses an wagon . . ." (Paul Jennings's likeness courtesy of the family of Sylvia Jennings Alexander; letter courtesy of the Dolley Madison Papers, Manuscript Division, Library of Congress, Washington DC)

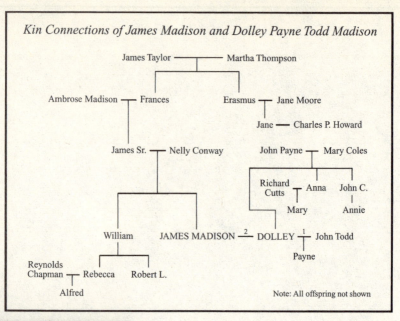

Kin Connections of James Madison and Dolley Payne Todd Madison

James Taylor ——— Martha Thompson

Ambrose Madison — Frances   Erasmus — Jane Moore

Jane — Charles P. Howard

James Sr. — Nelly Conway   John Payne — Mary Coles

Richard Cutts — Anna   John C.

Mary   Annie

William   JAMES MADISON —² DOLLEY ¹— John Todd

Payne

Reynolds Chapman — Rebecca   Robert L.

Alfred

Note: All offspring not shown

James Madison during retirement. This likeness was engraved after a drawing by James Longacre, taken from life at Montpelier in 1833.

Daguerreotype of Dolley Madison and her niece Annie Payne taken by Mathew Brady in Washington in 1848. (Courtesy of the Greensboro Historical Museum)

Paul Jennings's home was in the south yard at Montpelier. The Madison mansion's terrace overlooked this yard with its three duplexes for six enslaved households, detached kitchen, and two smokehouses. (Render by Chad Keller, Institute for Advanced Technologies in the Humanities, University of Virginia)

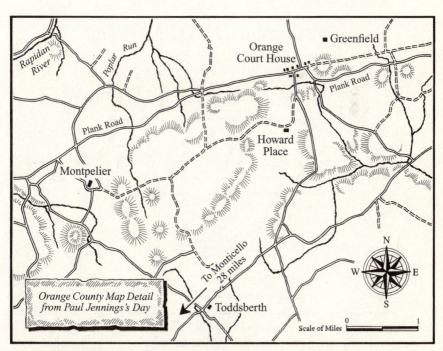

Paul Jennings lived at Montpelier while his wife and children, owned by a different master, lived at Howard Place. The family regularly gathered only on Sundays.

The front elevation of Montpelier painted in 1818 by Baroness Hyde de Neuville. The artist and her husband, French Minister from 1816 to 1821, were among the many notable individuals whom Jennings knew from both Washington and Montpelier. Notice the enslaved woman and child walking toward the temple in the watercolor. (Réunion des Musées Nationaux/Art Resource, NY)

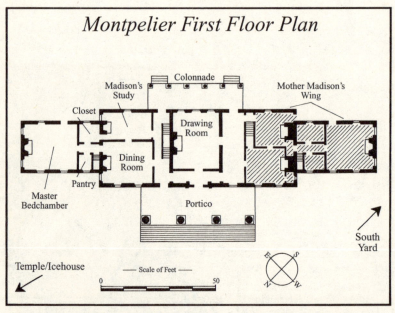

The floor plan identifies the study where Madison and his manservant spent so much time. Jennings was the "trusty servant in [Madison's] chamber," who seemed, as one visitor noted, "to identify himself with his master as to plans of management, and [give] his opinions freely, though not offensively, as if conversing with a brother."

This watercolor of the northeast corner of President's Square (later known as Lafayette Square) was painted by Baroness Hyde de Neuville in 1822. It features St. John's Episcopal Church and the house built for the Cutts family that the widowed Dolley Madison and household would later occupy. The White House sits at the square's south edge, a block away. (Collection of the New-York Historical Society)

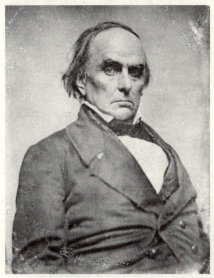

Daniel Webster. Jennings knew him not only as the fiery orator but as farmer and fisherman as well. (Library of Congress Prints and Photographs Division)

John Brooks Russell. The "JBR" of the preface to A Colored Man's Reminiscences of James Madison, Russell worked with Jennings in the pension office in the Department of the Interior. (Courtesy of the Massachusetts Horticultural Society)

(above left) *Franklin Jennings in about 1895 with two of his grandchildren, Frances and Henry Early. (Courtesy of the family of Sylvia Jennings Alexander)*

(above right) *Franklin Jennings stands at the gate of the K Street House that he and his wife Mary Logan Jennings acquired through her family. It is in the same Northwest Washington DC neighborhood where Paul Jennings and other ex-slaves of Presidents lived in the nineteenth century. (Courtesy of the family of Sylvia Jennings Alexander)*

Franklin Jennings was proud of his service in the Civil War and is shown here attending a reunion of veterans. The identity of the flanking figures is unknown; the three men in the middle, right to left, are Franklin, his son William, and his friend John S. Brent (son of Paul Jennings's close friend John Brent), who also served in the 5th Massachusetts Colored Cavalry. (Courtesy of the family of Sylvia Jennings Alexander)

Two grandchildren of Paul Jennings at an extended family gathering. Hugh Jennings (center) was the son of Franklin Jennings, and his first cousin Pauline (in hat and gloves) was the daughter of John W. Jennings. The occasion is the sixty-second wedding anniversary of Hugh and Alice Butler Jennings (right) in 1958. (Courtesy of the family of Sylvia Jennings Alexander)

(left) Sylvia Jennings with her husband John C. Alexander. Sylvia Jennings was the last-born grandchild of Paul's son Franklin. She became the keeper of the Jennings family oral history. (Courtesy of the family of Sylvia Jennings Alexander)

(right) Sylvia Jennings Alexander and her daughter Mary Alexander at their home in Virginia on the day the author first met them in June 2008. Notice the daguerreotype of their ancestor Paul Jennings on the wall behind them. (Collection of the author)

(above left) Pauline Jennings Marshall, Paul Jennings's granddaughter, at her home in Georgetown. Pauline and her husband, Dr. Charles Marshall, were both children of former slaves. (Courtesy of Kay W. Springwater)

(above right) Four generations later, Raleigh Marshall, a graduate of James Madison University, lives in the same house as his great-grandparents. (Courtesy of the Montpelier Foundation)

The Paul Jennings descendants pose under the George Washington portrait in the East Room of the White House on 24 August 2009, the anniversary of the day their ancestor helped Dolley Madison rescue this national icon. Back row, left to right, Barbara Allen behind Mildred Allen, Ron Springwater, Jennifer and Hugh Allen, Samson Marshall, Raleigh Marshall, Raphael Jenifer, Hugh Alexander, Fawn Jordan; Center row, left to right, Jazmine Allen, John Sales, Kay Springwater, Nikki Marshall, Margaret Jordan, Angela Hayes and Daryl Toliver, Seated, left to right, Lisa Collins, Elsie Harrison, Cindy Jenifer with Jonah and Khadijah, Yvonne Alexander. (Courtesy of the Montpelier Foundation)

CHAPTER FIVE

"Change of Mind"

February 1837, Paul Jennings prepares the Washington City house for use by the widow Dolley Madison and household

In the third week of February, Judith Rives, the Madisons' Albemarle County neighbor, in Washington because of her husband's Senate career, wrote a letter to Dolley Madison at Montpelier:

> I took the liberty of going to your house a few weeks ago, and walking all about it. . . . On asking the little girl who came to the door if there was any one there, she said, "there was a gentleman." I was about to retreat, supposing it was Mr. Todd, when she told me it was only a colored gentleman—good Uncle Paul then stepped forth, and quite justified her appellation by inviting me in, and escorting me about in the most gentleman-like manner.[1]

Paul Jennings, nearly thirty-eight, had returned to President's Square for the first time in twenty years. The previous summer, James Madison had died, and change had been the watchword ever since. Mistress Dolley decided she would make use of her city house on President's Square and sent him ahead to ready the dwelling. It was only February, but already the town noise was *gathering, as was that of spring's first frogs, in anticipation of the new Martin van Buren administration. The atmosphere must have reminded Jennings of James Madison's inauguration twenty-eight years earlier.*

As President Andrew Jackson prepared to close shop at the White House up the street, Jennings took stock of a President's Square much altered, starting with the name. The Marquis de Lafayette's return to America as the "nation's guest" in 1824 had occasioned the name shift in his honor, though the Lafayette Square designation took only slowly. Dolley, for example, continued to use "President's Square" on her letters. The common itself was no longer an abandoned apple orchard but had been landscaped in advance of Lafayette's visit. The restored White House now sported porticoes at both the north and south fronts: a bold rectangular porte-cochère covered the north entrance, and a semicircular portico graced the south. Half the building's charred and weakened exterior walls had been rebuilt, in the course of which the workmen dug out, in partial preservation, the dinner display that Jennings had prepared the day the British torched the mansion in August 1814. The George Washington portrait had long ago been retrieved from the Maryland farmhouse where it had rested in safety for several weeks after the fire and returned to Dolley Madison, who had made sure that it was hung in the Monroe White House.[2]

Not until the last years of the Madison administration had the square begun to buzz with construction. Even as the White House was being repaired, the cornerstone was laid for St. John's Church on the opposite edge of the common, and the first Episcopal service was celebrated there six months before the Madison household retired to Virginia. On Jennings's return to Washington, he counted about half a dozen homes facing the square. The one to which he attended was a colonial-style dwelling, two-stories-plus-attic high with cellar below, where his quarters were fixed. Sitting on the square's northeast angle, cater-corner to the church, the house was originally built for Richard Cutts and family in 1820. Cutts's commercial concerns lost money due to the War of 1812, and additional financial problems later culminated in insolvency; he was even briefly jailed. The Madisons stepped in and bought the house from him, and the Cutts family continued to occupy it. Dolley never had the opportunity to visit over the twenty years she was back in Virginia, as much as she would have liked to, musing, "How happy I should be if [Montpelier] joined Washington." Now she would alternate her living arrangements by season, winters in the city house and summers at Montpelier.[3]

Former White House steward John Sioussat renewed his services upon the former First Lady's return to the capital. He did this strictly in a neighborly way that included his arranging for a glazier or other workmen as necessary and looking out for the sometimes-wandering cow Dolley kept in her backyard even while the household was at Montpelier.

As for Jennings himself—his young manhood was behind him, and he was still a slave. Nevertheless, he had applied his intelligence, experience, and motivation over the intervening years, taking advantage of opportunities to pursue that most American of promises: the right to rise. The contrast with Dolley's son is striking. Payne Todd, now forty-five and with neither occupation nor spouse, seemed to lack purpose altogether. The winter before— hopelessly alcoholic, bloated from overindulgence—he spent several weeks under the weather in his room at Montpelier, where his friends entertained him all day. Finally he emerged from his chamber, as his mother wrote a friend, "with the loss of only a little plumptitude"[4] Of course one could say that Payne took advantage of his situation, too. He certainly had taken advantage of his mother and stepfather time and again, slowly draining their finances and goodwill.

*The little girl in Judith Rives's letter had identified Jennings
as "only" a colored gentleman. Jennings's rise would always re-
quire unremitting resistance against legal, social, and psychological impediments.*

JAMES MADISON'S DEATH, IF NOT UNEXPECTED, WAS
nevertheless devastating for Dolley. "Rebellion was useless so she bore
it, as she had borne every change in life, for good or evil," her niece
philosophized. While Jennings was sent ahead to Washington, Dolley
nursed her inflamed eyes behind closed bed curtains at Montpelier.
She never made it to Washington the first winter after her husband's
death, but after several restorative weeks in the summer of 1837 at
medicinal springs in the Blue Ridge Mountains, she determined not
to spend another lonely winter season shut up by snows in the countryside. Her sister Anna had died in 1832, but Dolley looked forward
to living near her nieces and nephews (Richard Cutts and his children
had good-naturedly vacated the Lafayette Square house and moved to
nearby 14th Street) and her many old friends in the capital. Moreover,
as Mary Cutts explained in her memoir, the "massacre of the whites"
in Southampton County, Virginia, only a few years previously "had
struck terror to the heart of every slave owner. For the first time in her
life she was desolate, and feared to remain" on the plantation.

Some of this trepidation preceded Nat Turner's murderous ram-
page of 1831. John Finch, the Englishman who visited Montpelier
in 1824, reported that insurrections were not frequent in the Upper
South but did occur, including murder of overseers or owners. Just
as significantly, while they might pay lip service to the sentiment that
their slaves were devoted to them and did not want to leave, masters
feared such insurrections. Wrote Finch, "During the holidays, when

the slaves resort to the large towns, there is some apprehension of their rising and the militia are assembled." He also noted, "None of the slaves are allowed to sleep in the planter's house."[5]

Dolley reacted to Turner's rebellion in a letter to a niece dated 16 September 1831: "I hope the bustle and alarm of insurrections are over . . . I cannot help myself if I am in danger. I believe there is none at present." But just a week later, there was angry excitement in the Madisons' home county when the Orange postmaster confiscated a copy of the abolitionist newspaper the *Liberator* from the incoming mail before it reached the local free black to whom it was addressed. After the newspaper was circulated among Orange's white citizens, the postmaster forwarded it to the governor along with a missive denouncing abolitionists' motives as wickedness and avarice and declaring that, notwithstanding respect for freedom of the press, "in times like these" such seditious incentives to insurrection ought to be prohibited. Five years later, the *Liberator's* founder, William Lloyd Garrison, pulled no punches in his comments on James Madison, even as the sage was being eulogized by President John Quincy Adams following a procession in his memory in the nation's capital. Garrison applied the derisive term he popularized, "man-stealer," to the fourth President, and lamented, "Alas, for the memory of Madison, that he left more than one hundred slaves in bondage, not having principle or generosity enough to emancipate one at his death!"[6]

Now, without her husband's protection, Dolley would limit residential oversight of the plantation to just part of the year and, to make ends meet, rent her Washington house while in Virginia. Annie Payne, daughter of Dolley's brother John, was her faithful companion. The two women slept behind a locked door at the city house and presumably at Montpelier, too.[7]

When Dolley was in residence on Lafayette Square, Jennings assumed the household roles of butler and coachman. Sukey, too, was usually at the city house in season with one or more of her children, though the young ones seemed to get on Dolley's nerves. Preparing for one winter in the city, Dolley hesitated to have Sukey attend her, complaining to her niece that "Little Ben is too bad and George is worse—I have sent him to Coventry—so I dont know how I am to be waited upon in the Capital." George (presumably, like Ben, Sukey's son), must have been banished to a distant quarter of the Montpelier plantation, as Sukey herself had been in 1818 when Dolley was peeved with her.[8]

By 1838, Dolley referred approvingly to "our amiable neighbors of the whole square" in a letter to Margaret Bayard Smith, who kept house one street over. The home next to Dolley's along the square's east edge belonged to Benjamin Ogle Tayloe, son of the owner of the Octagon. His wife Julia came to appreciate Jennings's proficiency and occasionally forwarded notes next door asking if Dolley might "loan Paul" to wait at her dinner parties.

Directly opposite Dolley's house, on the southwest corner of the square, was the handsome redbrick house built in 1818 for Stephen Decatur, hero of the Tripoli wars. Just two years after its construction, Decatur died an inglorious death there following a duel. His widow rented the house to a series of notables including the French minister and his wife, the Hyde de Neuvilles, Henry Clay, and Martin Van Buren, all of whom had visited the Madisons in retirement in Virginia. Jennings might have recalled seeing Clay and Andrew Jackson at Montpelier in 1832 when, as opposing presidential candidates, they had to maneuver at the last minute to avoid running into one another during their homages to former President Madison.[9]

The year before Jennings returned to Washington, Susan Decatur sold the house to John Gadsby, proprietor of the popular National Hotel on Pennsylvania Avenue. One foreign dignitary, after attending a lavish party at Gadsby's residence, wrote of his host, "He is an old wretch who has made a fortune in the slave trade, which does not prevent Washington society from rushing to his house." Gadsby attached a slave quarters to the dwelling in the form of a long ell with iron-barred windows. Here, claimed longtime neighbor Sarah Vedder, Gadsby kept "negroes until they were sold to Georgia," adding that "sometimes at night you could hear their howls and cries." Nearby ran a long hedge of crabapple and hawthorn, which Vedder remembered perfumed the neighborhood for weeks in spring. Such sights, sounds, and scents were part of Jennings's environment in Washington. He undoubtedly formed acquaintances among the enslaved African Americans on the Gadsby family's domestic staff (as distinguished from those individuals held temporarily for transport to the South). These included a woman just Jennings's age who also had a connection to a Virginia president and his plantation: Nancy Syphax, born the year George Washington died, was the daughter of a Mount Vernon slave named Eloisa.[10]

Hired slaves and free blacks filled the service positions at the city's hotels. An Englishman staying at the Indian Queen, a first-class hotel like Gadsby's, claimed he "saw only decent-looking waiters and house-maids, observant of all external proprieties of demeanor, discharging their several duties with exactitude, and distinguishable from European servants by nothing but colour." Jennings's former White House co-worker John Freeman was employed as a waiter at Gadsby's inn in the late 1820s. He, wife Melinda, and their children were settled in their own home in northwest Washington. Freeman was an activist when it came to race issues and may have introduced Jennings to like-minded associates.

It was from Gadsby's hotel in April 1841 that Solomon Nor-thup—whose narrative, *Twelve Years a Slave,* would later be widely circulated—was kidnapped. Northup arrived there in the company of two white men who had lured him to Washington on the pretense of employment but who in fact plotted all along to sell him to slavers. The inn, as one patron described it, was "like a little town, with more wooden galleries, flights of steps, passages, door-ways, exits, and en-trances, than any building I ever saw." This is the maze that Northup tried to find his way out of after being drugged by his companions. He lost consciousness; when he regained it, he was fettered in irons, des-tined to endure a dozen years illegally enslaved on a Louisiana cotton plantation.[11]

If blacks had reasons to be wary of whites, many whites felt the reverse was true. Sarah Vedder, Dolley's neighbor, told the story that one night "there was a fearful noise in the streets. At that time there was much talk of an insurrection of the negroes; we all thought they were at their dreadful work of destroying the whites, but in the morning we heard that all the confusion, whooping, blowing horns and ringing bells was the burying of the 'sub-treasury bill.'" This was in 1841, a full decade after Nat Turner's rebellion. It was six years after the incident most resembling a race riot that the city of Washington had known, and the mob violence in that case was perpetrated by indignant whites reacting to rumors of misdeeds by individuals. The so-called Snow Riot can be traced to an incident involving Dolley's good friend Anna Thornton, now widowed as well. Thornton's slave Arthur Bowen entered her house in an inebriated state one hot summer night holding an ax. He fled without raising the ax, and later Thornton tried to underplay the incident as a drunken misunderstanding, though too late to stop a mob from the white underclass from unleashing pent-up racial tension by descending on black-run businesses, destroying property and wreaking havoc. A special target was the Pennsylvania Avenue restaurant of Beverly Snow. The black restaurant owner, it was rumored, had spoken disrespectfully of wives of white mechanics at the Navy Yard. "The mob raged with great vigor," recorded African-American diarist Michael Shiner, still a Navy Yard employee. The Snow Riot took place two years before Jennings returned to Washington, but its repercussions were felt long afterward. Restrictions on free blacks were tightened, and certain African-American leaders abandoned the city in fear for months or years.[12]

The composition of the city's white, free black, and enslaved populations had shifted from Jennings's first period in Washington. In 1840, compared with 1810, the total Washington City population had grown by nearly 200 percent, to 23,364. The growth was due totally to sharp increases in numbers of whites and free blacks; the slave population was dropping. The proportion of free blacks to slaves had reversed.

In 1810, the ratio of slave to free black approached two to one. Now, thirty years later, the free black to slave ratio was nearly three to one. The overall white to black ratio stayed exactly the same at 2.6 to 1. Still enslaved, Jennings was part of a true minority.

As for the city itself, the Capitol structure had risen in renewed splendor, its two wings flanking a dome-topped center. Author Charles Dickens, visiting Washington in 1842, described "three handsome buildings in stone and marble" in addition—the Treasury, Post Office, and Patent Office Building. Pennsylvania Avenue was finally paved, or "macadamized," and some initial efforts at improved drainage had been undertaken. But overall, visitors in the 1830s and 1840s voiced comments not so different from their counterparts twenty years earlier. Actress Fanny Kemble, in town to perform at the Washington Theater, found the national capital "a rambling, red-brick image of futurity, where nothing *is,* but all things *are to be.*" Her countryman Dickens picked up on the same theme:

> It is sometimes called the City of Magnificent Distances, but it might with greater propriety be termed the City of Magnificent Intentions; for it is only by taking a bird's-eye view of it from the top of the Capitol, that one can at all comprehend the vast design. . . . Spacious avenues, that begin in nothing, and lead nowhere; streets, mile-long, that only want houses, roads and inhabitants; public buildings that need but a public to be complete; and ornaments of great thoroughfares, which only lack great thoroughfares to ornament—are its leading features.

And yet, Dickens conceded, Washington was "a pleasant field for the imagination to rove in."[13]

Dolley Madison was like a queen dowager. Over the twelve years that she lived a block away, five Presidents transitioned into the White House, from Martin van Buren to her husband's cousin, Zachary Taylor. Every New Year's and Fourth of July holiday, hundreds of citizens followed up a reception at the White House with a call to pay their respects at the widow Madison's residence, which one late-nineteenth-century commentator referred to as "the only secondary, or ex–Presidential Court, ever held in Washington." Dolley had not been forgotten over her years in Virginia. An 1833 newspaper article lamented the current White House assemblages and retraced the former First Lady's heyday: "The grace, beauty and elegance of her drawing rooms are talked of with enthusiasm by all the old *belles* and battered *beaux* in these regions. Mrs. Madison was made for society; she knew its minutest stop, and touched each with the finger of power." Now her home was again a rallying point for the most influential people in the capital's social and political circles.

Daniel Webster was a frequent guest at Dolley's house. As President John Tyler's Secretary of State, Webster bought a three-and-one-half-story Federal-style dwelling along the same north edge of Lafayette Square as St. John's Church in 1841, the first time he had his own home in the capital. Before the year was over, Caroline LeRoy Webster was back in the city after a long absence and presided with her husband over lavish gatherings at their newly repainted and richly furnished residence. City chronicler Samuel Busey claimed that the soirée the Websters threw on 26 January 1842, was "the crowning entertainment of the season, which surpassed in brilliancy any social assemblage which had occurred in the city for a decade or more." Dolley Madison "was often to be seen at the Websters' evening receptions" reported another regular guest, "wearing her old-time turban and kerchief."[14]

One of the great draws at Webster's home was the culinary fare prepared by his African-American cook, Monica McCarty. More than a decade earlier, Russian minister Baron de Tuyll, renting Susan Decatur's house, had exclaimed, "Washington with its venison, wild turkeys, canvas-backs, oysters, terrapins, &c. furnishes better viands than Paris, and only wants cooks." No such lament could have been issued had the baron been on the scene for McCarty's repasts. Liking company at dinner and proud of his cook's expertise, Webster would dash off a note to a friend, "Come and dine with me tomorrow" or "I found a famous possum in market this morning, sir, and left orders with Monica, my cook, to have it baked in the real old Virginia style."

In April 1842 English diplomat Lord Ashburton (Alexander Baring, 1st Baron Ashburton) arrived in Washington and rented a house on the opposite side of St. John's Church from Webster's residence so that he and the Secretary of State might more easily negotiate a treaty between their two countries. Statecraft aside, the presidency of John Tyler ushered in a pronounced renewal of high-society revelry in the nation's capital. Literary lights Charles Dickens and Washington Irving were in town, helping to make this the most stimulating of times. Once Lord Ashburton joined the Lafayette Square social scene, Samuel Busey extended his earlier claim, declaring:

> Washington society enjoyed a season of gayety unequalled in the history of the half-century. Balls, evening parties, and receptions and dinners succeeded in such impetuous haste that it seemed like a continuous stream of fashionable display and brilliant entertainment in which the two distinguished diplomats engaged in the negotiation of the treaty to adjust the differences between England and this country vied with each other in rivalry for the social honors.[15]

Webster and Ashburton famously negotiated a treaty settling the Canadian border and other issues, resulting in a major enhancement of U.S.–British relations. Getting there—even as Busey indicated—had been a pleasure since Webster and Ashburton, who had brought along not only a diplomatic staff but a butler and cook, competed in their hosting of elaborate dinners. Webster served American delicacies prepared by Monica McCarty in authentic American style, and Ashburton admitted in the end that they surpassed his European fare, fine as it was. With Webster and Dolley two blocks apart and regularly exchanging social invitations, certainly Jennings got to know Monica McCarty, who, like Nancy Syphax at Gadsby's house, was his contemporary.

Eventually, the costs of living well caught up with Webster, especially after he felt compelled to relinquish his position as Secretary of State in May 1843, he and President Tyler falling out over the issue of Texas annexation. Webster was a horrendous financial manager and never could hold on to his money. By the following spring, he was renting out his house on the square. Though he would remain a presence in Washington, practicing law, Webster would not hold public office again until 1845.[16]

Dolley Madison's second tenure on Lafayette Square would be as long remembered as her first. In her 1874 book, *Ten Years in Washington,* newspaperwoman Mary Clemmer Ames wrote of Dolley's signature accouterments, "Mrs. Madison's turbans are as famous in Washington to-day as her snuff box." Dolley was addicted to tobacco, the labor-intensive, soil-depleting crop grown by slaves throughout the Upper South. Neighbor Sarah Vedder recollected seeing Dolley in her white crepe turban dozens of times, sitting on the front stoop of her home, "surrounded by young girls, laughing and talking, for she was fond of young company."

Like Daniel Webster, Dolley Madison was living above her means. Paul Jennings later recalled the high style of the mistress's receptions at the Lafayette Square house, as did Ben Stewart, who claimed, "She served wine and cake to each caller, and spent a fortune in entertaining." All the great men of the day came to the house, Stewart continued, and he remembered as a teenager being charged with walking President van Buren back to the White House: "Van Buren . . . often ran in after dinner and spent the evening, and I remember they used to send me along with him to see that he got home to the White House all right. I don't know whether he was afraid or not but I always went along." Jennings and Stewart both remarked on Dolley's dresses and turbans. Though she continued to be well dressed, Stewart admitted that in her later years her turbans were fashioned at home by her maids. In high social demand, invitations to the former First Lady abounded, so she was just as often at the receiving end of dinners and entertainments.[17]

Dolley may have been content living in Washington, but Paul Jennings had a conflict. His wife and children were back in Orange County, Virginia. His fifth (and final) child, William, was born about 1842. Seeing his family only once a week had been bad enough, but now he was away from home for months at a time.

As for the Montpelier enslaved community at large, Dolley faced the reality that her plantation had more slaves than the land could support. As Edward Coles had explained to his sister Sally in November 1836: "Mr. Madison . . . has left so many more [slaves] than can be judiciously employed on his estate that his poor Widow is compelled, it is said, to sell many of them. Thus he has imposed on his widow a most painful task, one which he ought to have performed himself." Acting in concert with her son, Dolley continued selling slaves. In an 1844 letter Payne boasted, "As to the negroes, I take some credit on this score on none having been disposed of but agreeably." Mother and son felt justified and self-satisfied so long as the sales were to neighbors or to Madison kin. When George Waggaman, senator from Louisiana, wrote to Dolley that he had been informed by her son (never one to be inflexible over scruples) that she "would be willing to dispose of the negroes on your estate" and that he was "wishing to increase my stock of negroes in Louisiana," Dolley politely turned him down, extending her "regret that I cannot at this time transfer my colored people to a gentleman for whom I have so great a respect. I had not at any period intended to part with more than half about fifty, owing to their reluctance to leave this place or its neighborhood." The mistress of Montpelier also turned away prospective overseers with violent tendencies, declaring, "No whipper of Negroes shd ever have our people . . . to tirenize over."[18]

It may be that even as deeds of sale were being written, Paul Jennings was secretly forging free papers for slaves. As previously noted, that is the oral history handed down to Jennings's great-granddaughter. There are half a dozen Jennings letters known, five to Dolley and one to Sukey. Examining the extant letters written in his own hand, one would assess his excellent handwriting as an asset for a would-be forger, and his syntax perhaps acceptable; his spelling left much to be desired, but then most letter writers were poor spellers in the 1840s, the decade in which all the letters were written.

As to his own freedom, Jennings's hopes rose again with the February 1841 will of Dolley Madison. It contained the term "I give to my mulatto man Paul his freedom," the only slave so treated. Sukey was not so lucky. She and her sons and daughters were willed to niece Annie Payne. The fateful phrase, not even set off by a proper comma, was inserted among a list of bequests to Annie, namely "three thousand dollars, with my negro Woman and her children one third of my wearing apparel, my forte piano and the furniture of my chamber, with my private papers to *burn*."[19]

Newspaper accounts in 1848 described Sukey as the mother of five children, the youngest, Ellen Stewart, born about 1833. Reconstructing an accounting of Sukey's children requires a careful melding of sources including Montpelier records, contemporary letters, 1848 abolitionist newspaper accounts that relate the stories of Paul and Sukey (without using their names), and 1880s newspaper articles written about and by Ben Stewart. The most direct evidence that Ben Stewart is Sukey's son is his own statement identifying his mother as the maid of Dolley Madison who was with her when she escaped the White House on the approach of the British in 1814. From Jennings's memoir, we know that was Sukey. Ben, by his own account, was sold by Dolley in 1843, not with his consent and not to Madison kin or neighbors but to "Georgians." He was about eighteen at the time. "During the days of her poverty she sold off her servants one by one, and I remember I was bought by a Georgia man and taken to that state," recalled Stewart. "I suppose she got about $500 for me, and if she did I was very cheap at that." The Dolley Madison letter quoted previously where George is mentioned in a context suggesting he might be brother to Ben is the only inkling of a possible fraternal connection. The name "George," at any rate, drops from the Madison records after 1843; that may be because George was sold around the same time as Ben. Ben Stewart reported that his mother, grandfather, and great-grandfather were Montpelier slaves but did not include his father, indicating—and this would be consistent with other evidence—that Sukey found her mate "abroad." Stewart, the only surname on record for any of her children, is probably Sukey's name as well, and—noting that it is the most prevalent surname known among Montpelier slaves—was perhaps the name of her father (rather than of a husband).[20]

Sarah Stewart (precise relationship unknown) wrote three extant letters from Orange to Dolley at the Washington house; the first was dated 19 December 1843 and included the line "tell Suckeys family is Well and Pauls family is Well also." What was left of Sukey's family did not remain well for long. A month later Payne wrote his mother of Sukey's older daughter: "Becca I did not tell you I sold to Mr. John Chapman for 600 and odd dollars." This sale was apparently not final, as in November of that year, Payne posed this curious request of his mother: "Pray try and get out of Sukey who was the father secretly of Becca for it may be of advantage in the Sale—As to Paul—he is out of the question from Colour." It would seem that Dolley did not know who the father of Sukey's daughter was, and Payne briefly considered—and just as quickly rejected—the possibility that he might be Jennings. Meanwhile, in the summer of 1844, Sukey's son William was about to be sold to John Chapman's brother Alfred. (The Chapmans were a local Orange family, and, as has already been mentioned, Alfred Chapman, while working as a clerk in the Department of the Interior, later helped Jennings secure a government job.) William's sale was not finalized either, in this case because the fifteen-year-old's illness and death intervened. Identifying Rebecca/Becca and William as children of Sukey rests on Sukey's full name being Susan, since in both cases the messages in letters sent from Orange to Dolley at the city house that make the mother-and-child connection are directed to "Susan." One message reads, "Tell Susan that Rebecca has a fine daughter named Susan Ellen after her Mother"; the other, "William is lying at the point of deth we expect him to die before many day . . . I wish you to let Susan know about her son." Sukey is a known nickname for Susan, and, with never more than half a dozen slaves at the Washington house, it is always "Sukey" or "Susan" that is mentioned, never both. Sukey's fifth and youngest child, Ellen Stewart, was safe with her mother . . . for the time being.[21]

Sarah Stewart's December 1843 letter noted that Paul's family was well, but by the subsequent spring, Jennings had gotten word that his wife was not at all well. It may have been he who requested an exchange of servants between the city and the country, given that on 6 April Payne wrote to his mother that Ralph, Nicholas, and Becca were on the road to Washington and that once they reached her house and unloaded their provisions, Paul could return with the wagon to Orange. On 23 April Jennings updated his mistress from Orange. This is the first of his extant letters that are now at the Library of Congress because Dolley saved them with her private collection. It is written on fine paper with a second half sheet serving as envelope, a residue of sealing wax still affixed. Like other such household correspondence written by Montpelier's white or black residents, Jennings's letter is full of news and regards for individuals in the domestic circle, referencing not just Montpelier black and white denizens but those of neighboring farms as well. But foremost on Jennings's mind was the health of his wife: "I found faney very porley but she says she is better than she was in the winter." He added that his wife sends her love and is "very thankful to you for my Coming to see her."[22]

Between 6 April and 11 May, Paul and Fanny's first grandchild was born—a baby girl to their approximately sixteen-year-old daughter, Frances. The birth was announced in the letter of the latter date to Rebecca from her husband, Peter Walker ("Frances at Howard's [has had] a fine daughter . . . born since your departure for Washington"). Walker reported, too, on the declining condition of Fanny: "Paul's wife is nearly gone We expected last night any moment would be her last." Two days later Jennings penned a letter to Sukey. In an apparent religious frame of mind, given his wife's precarious hold on life, he addressed Sukey as "sister" and others mentioned in the letter as "brother" and "sister" likewise, and described how his wife had called him to her bedside and expressed herself in the tone of a repentant sinner. "Pore fanney," Jennings lamented, "I am looking every day to see the last of her." At the bottom of the paper he instructed Sukey to "Answer this letter as soon as you can," concluding "I come to a close By sayn no more." Dolley not only saved the letter but noted on the "envelope" that it was answered on 20 May, though that response is lost.[23]

In fact, Fanny Gordon Jennings lingered until the first week in August. Her son Franklin recalled the house where his family lived at Howard Place and that his father, even while residing in Washington, would come and stay with them there. Fanny's much younger brother, Edmund Spotsey, knew Paul Jennings from Howard Place and stated that Jennings and his sister were married for thirty years; "It was all done when I was raised and I lived in the house of my sister Fannie until I was very near a young man." Actually, the marriage came to a close, upon Fanny's death, after twenty-two years. Franklin, about seven when he lost his mother, and his little brother William only about two, confirmed that his father was with his mother when she died and had been for some time before that. Jennings's mistress generously allowed him to remain in Orange over the full period of his wife's final illness. But the day after her death, he was on the road back to the city. This is clear from a letter of Payne's to his mother dated 5 August 1844: "I shall send on the Carriage with Paul whose wife died last night if not requested otherwise." Before he left Howard Place, Jennings dictated a letter to Dolley, employing Charles Howard—the owner of his now-motherless children—as amanuensis. In it he referred to death as the "final change."[24]

Two life-changing events befell Paul Jennings the first week of August 1844 and intensified his already-divided loyalties. Not only had his wife succumbed to a fatal illness, but Dolley Madison, under severe financial strain, was selling Montpelier, his lifeline to his family.

Jennings must have been in a state of near shock driving the carriage back to Washington, his mind reeling with the implications of this one-two punch. At the moment that his children lost their only custodial parent, he learned that his mistress, with him as an integral part of her household, would now reside in Washington full time.

The date on the agreement selling Montpelier to Richmond merchant Henry Moncure was 8 August 1844, though a long string of legal maneuvers with the new owner followed (many of them rooted in Payne endlessly hassling Moncure, for whom he held a deep dislike). All told, an analysis of the historical evidence suggests that about half of Montpelier's one hundred enslaved individuals were sold off the plantation, with the remaining men, women, and children roughly divided by two again, one part sold to Henry Moncure and the other retained by Dolley and Payne. The last group of people included Ralph and Catharine Taylor, who joined Paul and Sukey as servants in Dolley's city household, bringing along their two young children. Like Ben Stewart, Ralph Taylor (whose given name often turns up with alternate spellings Ralf or Raif) had deep Montpelier roots. His grandfather appears in the Montpelier records as Ralf Senior.[25]

Most of the enslaved people retained by Dolley and her son after Moncure took over Montpelier lived at Payne's estate, Toddsberth, where log houses were erected for them. Before the sale of the mansion house with 1,050 acres entailed, Payne was deeded various parcels of Montpelier land, and on the tract called Toddsberth he built a strange and fanciful residence of multiple units, featuring a "rotunda." Dolley also deeded slaves to her son in July 1844. Sukey and daughters Becca and Ellen, and Ralph and Caty Taylor and their children were listed. Though the slaves deeded to Payne continued to be practicably considered as joint assets with his mother, it is noteworthy that Paul Jennings, alone among the house servants, was not listed in the transfer. Payne at this time was fooling with various get-rich-quick schemes, growing mulberry trees for silk and quarrying for gold and marble on his property. These exertions represented a sort of last hurrah but went nowhere. Payne had marinated in his bad habits and errant ways so long that every ambition turned stale. Dolley meanwhile was being dunned by his creditors.[26]

Not even the sale of Montpelier and many slaves saved Dolley Madison from continuing "pecuniary embarrassment," as her niece Mary Cutts described it. Dolley hired Jennings out to President Polk at the White House in 1845. Polk had begun his term in March of that year, on a day that rain fell steadily. Sarah Polk and Dolley Madison were frequently in one another's company. They enjoyed carriage rides together on pleasant afternoons, and Dolley was invited to every Cabinet dinner and all entertainments hosted at the executive mansion. As precedent-setting First Lady, Dolley coached Sarah Polk on her role in the White House, as she had the hostesses of the van Buren and Tyler administrations.[27]

James Polk was a major slave owner, holding people both at his home estate in Tennessee and at a cotton plantation in Mississippi, where he was absentee landlord. He derived an ample income from the latter enterprise, to add to his presidential salary. Polk inevitably defended the interests of the slave states. He maintained that the federal government had no authority to control slavery, not even in the District of Columbia or the territories, and he supported prohibition of antislavery sentiment in the nation's capital.

According to William Dusinberre, author of *Slavemaster President: The Double Career of James Polk,* the President took just one of his home slaves to work as a domestic in the White House, a young man named Henry Carter. A combination of slaves purchased or hired in Washington and local free blacks filled nearly all of the service roles in the Polk White House; for those who lived in, their quarters were in the cellar. The one white domestic staff member was steward Henry Bowman. His office/bedroom was the space right off the north entrance, called the porter's lodge during the Madison administration and later the chief usher's office.[28]

Jennings would have observed many changes at the White House from his first tour of duty there. Of course the east room had long been completed; one visitor during the Polk administration described it as a "spacious apartment splendidly furnished and brilliantly illuminated." And central heating and gas lighting were installed in the mansion during Polk's tenure. Jennings must have been gratified to study the George Washington portrait in place, in part thanks to his own actions over thirty years earlier. The enormous portrait hung in what was formerly Dolley Madison's yellow sitting room, known at this time as the Washington Parlor in honor of the first President's likeness.

While Jennings was employed at the Polk White House in 1845, there was an incident one evening in early May involving "Martin the porter" and a fellow who had brought two loaves of bread and as many bottles of wine to the executive mansion to share with Martin. This interloper "afterwards flaunt[ed] about the house with a knife in his hand, and when they were looking for him up stairs, he would be down, and *vice versa*." All this hullaballoo led to a rumor, reported in the newspapers the next morning, that there had been an assassination attempt on President Polk in the White House. If Jennings was not part of the chase scene in the mansion that evening, perhaps he heard the rumors even before he made his way up the street to report to work the next day. Guests attending White House receptions encountered black servants like Jennings throughout their visit—one in the entrance hall, for example, in charge of cloaks and hats, and another just outside of the oval drawing room who was described by a Washington correspondent as "a latch-string in the shape of a handsome negro." After President Polk received his guests in the drawing room, he entered the east room with Dolley Madison on his arm whenever she was present, with his wife contentedly following.[29]

Jennings's mind may not have been altogether on his work during this second White House experience. Separated from his family in Orange, Jennings struggled to keep up with his children. According to their uncle Edmund, the siblings' half sister Elizabeth (now Elizabeth Webb, having married a John Webb) "came home and took charge of her mother's house and children." A short undated letter from Jennings to Dolley reads:

> Dear Mistris thair is nothing doing and I wish if you pleas to let me go to
> see my children and my mother—if you pleas. Paul

This letter was probably written in 1845, since we know that Jennings received a pass from Dolley to visit his family in June that year.[30]

Dolley was having a tough summer herself. She anxiously wrote letters to Payne without receiving a single reply. Finally, she corresponded with the Orange postmaster to confirm that her mail had been delivered. As the weeks went by, Jennings stayed in Orange longer than Dolley had approved. Undoubtedly she had asked him to check up on Payne, but she had not heard back from either of them. She was perturbed and feeling disrespected. Not only was she nettled, she was hot, having "suffered from the heat too much [because] the Ther: has been above 90 for many days." On 8 July, in the midst of this heat wave, Dolley lifted a pen to draft two documents referencing Paul Jennings's future: One offered to emancipate him for the low price—"in consideration of the faithful services of my man servant Paul"—of $200; the other would sell him to Payne Todd for $____ (no price filled in). She described Jennings as forty-eight, "a man of a dark mulatto complexion, about five feet three & half inches high." Both of these documents look like no more than drafts. There are no witnesses, no known legal recordation, and yet they were saved with Dolley's other papers when she could have ripped them up once the mood passed.[31]

On 17 July, Dolley wrote to Payne, "I wish to say a few words on the subject of Paul." She went on to express displeasure with her servant. She noted that she had hired him to the President and that he was given the privilege of visiting his family for two or three weeks but should have since returned and resumed his duties. "But he has not appeared or written an apology," she concluded, "of course he will lose the best place and his mistress convenient resources."

Jennings's position was hazardous. For one, Dolley was looking for money wherever she could find it. For another, she was teeming with anger at Payne, and when she sent Jennings after him and did not hear from him either, she transferred her frustration with her son to her bondman. Worried that even he might not be immune to sale after all, Jennings determined to free himself by raising his purchase money, "whatever he might be."[32]

In contrast to Jennings's determination, feckless Payne, by the end of 1845, had taken the path of least resistance once more. At the end of November, he noted in his journal (a source as eccentric as its creator) that he had broken his abstinence from drink yet again and passed out in front of the fire. Reflecting on this, he ended the entry with a question: "Can I rise?" He never did.

Since Jennings was still enslaved a year after his mistress set his purchase price, he must have found it hard to raise the money. He was hired out, but his mistress received the payments. When Jennings's story later appeared in an abolitionist newspaper, the wording was harsh: "After [Mrs. Madison] brought him to this city he worked . . . on wages, which she took to the last red cent, leaving him to get his clothes by presents, night-work, or as he might." In 1846 Jennings decided to act. He would present his case to Daniel Webster.[33]

By then Webster was once again a senator. He leased a furnished house, more modest than his earlier Lafayette Square residence; it was located on D Street, closer to the Capitol than the White House. This is where Jennings went looking for him. He was familiar with the statesman's reputation as a friend to slaves in need. Webster began his association with a number of enslaved African Americans in Washington by purchasing and freeing them. Most of these individuals paid off their debt—that is, their purchase price—by working in his household, in some cases remaining in his employ afterward. Webster may have been big-hearted, but he was also impecunious.

One biographer claimed that Webster was indifferent to wealth: "He never coveted it as an end, but only as a means of doing good and of gratifying his peculiar tastes."

Reaching the Senator's house, Jennings likely entered on the cellar level, where the kitchen was located, and called for Monica McCarty, Webster's cook, who had a tale or two to tell.[34] She probably had shared her own backstory with Jennings years earlier when they both worked on Lafayette Square.

MONICA MCCARTY WAS BORN IN VIRGINIA about 1800 and started working as a hired cook for Daniel Webster in Washington when she was about twenty. McCarty was a slave belonging to Circuit Court judge William Cranch, and when Webster expressed his supreme satisfaction with her culinary skills, Cranch offered to sell her. Aghast, Webster told the judge he would never own a human being but that he would like to purchase McCarty's freedom and then employ her as a servant to work out the price. Webster set terms with the judge for his own payments ($100 down, with the rest of the $500 cost to follow in installments) and in turn arranged a liberal pay-back plan with his cook. Monica McCarty worked for Webster until the day he died. Newspaperman Benjamin Perley Poore wrote that when Webster moved into the house on D Street, "Monica, the old colored woman, continued to be his favorite cook, and her soft-shell crabs, terrapin, fried oysters, and roasted canvas-back ducks have never been surpassed at Washington."[35]

Henry Pleasants was an African American who had been a part of Webster's household since boyhood. Webster first encountered Henry as a young slave working at a Washington boardinghouse where the statesman roomed. Feeling that the boy was being cruelly misused, Webster purchased him for $500 and freed him. Born about 1817, Henry was just a few years older than Webster's son Edward, and the two became close as they grew up together. By 1846 Henry Pleasants had married Frances Posey, and the couple had a daughter.[36]

Another African-American domestic in Webster's household in the 1840s was Ann Bean. About thirty-six in 1846, she was free, but her husband was enslaved. Webster had helped him draw up an agreement with his owner that would allow him to earn occasional money "on the side" and deposit it into an interest-bearing account toward the purchase of his freedom, a sum set at $1,500. Peter Harvey, Webster's friend and biographer, described what happened next:

> In 1846, I think, I was in Mr. Webster's house in Washington . . . Mr. Webster said to me, "Let's go into the kitchen and see Monica." We went down, and found Monica cooking the dinner. This man Bean was also there; he had come over to see his wife. . . . Mr. Webster began a conversation with him in regard to the financial condition of his freedom fund. Bean told him that he had accumulated, I think, all but one hundred and seventy-five dollars (it was certainly less than two hundred dollars). . . . He said to Bean, smiling: "Go on; don't relax a muscle . . . and when the month of September arrives (this, perhaps, was June), whatever you lack of this two hundred dollars I will make up. I know . . . that you will not relax exertion in consequence of this promise of mine. You know that I am poor myself; but you shall be free in September."[37]

THE SUMMER OF 1846 WAS THE VERY TIME when Jennings approached Webster for aid. Jennings later told his story to the Washington correspondent for the New York *Albany Patriot;* the paper reported that Jennings had "induced a distinguished Northern Senator to advance for him the purchase money and give him time to work it out." Because Webster was chronically strapped for cash and perhaps also because he tended to keep his transactions involving slaves hushed, the process was drawn out and entailed a third party who acted both as intermediary and money lender.

In September 1846 Dolley accepted $200 from local insurance agent Pollard Webb as "full payment of the purchase money of my negro man named Paul Jennings." The Pollard Webb sale was not recorded until six months had passed, just before the next transaction, namely, Daniel Webster paying $120 for Paul Jennings. Since slaves did not depreciate in this fashion, it is likely that it was Webster who arranged for the $200 to be transferred from Webb, whose office was a few blocks from Webster's home, to Dolley Madison. In March 1847 Webster reimbursed Webb the $120 balance to add to the $80 Jennings evidently had worked off up to that point. Jennings himself always maintained that he bought his freedom from Dolley Madison, and Mary Cutts concurred: "[Mrs. Madison] allowed him to purchase [his freedom] for a very small sum."[38]

When Dolley got $200 from Pollard Webb on 28 September 1846, Webb, at least on paper, got Jennings: the document is written as a straightforward sale. However, less than three weeks later, Jennings was in Orange, so the understanding may have been that he had autonomy of movement, even as he was charged with working down the advance.

On 16 October Jennings wrote a letter from Orange to his former mistress (still addressing her by this title). He passed on greetings from Mr. and Mrs. Howard at Howard Place, where his children resided and where he was presumably staying. He noted that "your ole servants ar all well" and that they had made a good crop of corn and had plenty of bread though meat was scarce. And, with the wording relaying the distinct impression that Dolley had asked him to check up on her son, he reported that he told "mas payne" his mother wanted to hear from him but that he replied he was too busy to write. The April before, in a replay of the summer of 1845, Dolley had written to Payne: "What are you about that prevents your communicating with your Mother?" The closing gave away her state of mind: "Anxious Mother!"[39]

Ralph Taylor took over Jennings's houseman role at the Lafayette Square house. Dolley's great-niece Adele Cutts remembered attending a reception there as a young girl: "We were ushered in by Ralph the young negro, who had succeeded Paul so well known as Mr. Madison's body servant in old times." Now it was Taylor whom niece Mary Cutts borrowed from her aunt when arranging a dinner party: "I will ask the Spencers & that nice girl and you will lend me Ralph and a pot of cream."[40]

On Friday, 19 March 1847, Daniel Webster wrote on a flyleaf, "I have paid $120 for the freedom of Paul Jennings—he agrees to work out the same at $8 per month, to be furnished with board, clothes & washing—to begin when we return from the South—His freedom papers I gave to him; they are recorded in the District." Jennings was sold to Daniel Webster and freed by him in the span of a paragraph. It was an early spring day, just as when he had first arrived in the city in 1809. Paul Jennings walked down the road in possession of this all-important piece of paper. He still owed Senator Webster $120, but this he would pay off "with his own free hands."[41]

CHAPTER SIX

"His Own Free Hands"

*The night of Saturday, 15 April 1848, a landing
near the 7th Street wharf, Washington City*

It was a moonless night and that was an advantage, for the activity at the wharf was highly illegal. Paul Jennings played a role in the operations that led to this action and is thought to have been the black man silently observing the scene in the shadows noticed by ship captain Daniel Drayton. Drayton approached this witness, who told him that he knew what was going on but that the captain need have no apprehension on his account. Before the night was over, seventy-seven enslaved men, women, and children would board a schooner named Pearl anchored at the edge of the Potomac River and stow themselves under the hatch.[1] Before the new day dawned, they would be on their way to freedom in the North.

Among the individuals hidden in the hull that Saturday night was Dolley Madison's runaway slave Ellen Stewart, Sukey's youngest child. Jennings had likely escorted the fifteen-year-old girl to the dock (a mile or so south of Pennsylvania Avenue) and watched her board the fifty-four-ton baycraft schooner. It may well have been Ellen's desperate need for flight that precipitated Jennings's

own involvement in the slave escape venture, known by the schoo-
ner's name as the Pearl incident or affair. One day approximately
five months earlier, Dolley had called Ellen to the parlor of the
Lafayette Square house nominally for an errand "but really to
show her to a Georgian as the colored people call the slave drivers."
After Ellen was dismissed, Dolley arranged with the trader to pick
up the girl at the pump in the public square where she would send
her at a prearranged time under the ruse of fetching water. But
Ellen got wind of the maneuver, dashed across Lafayette Square,
and escaped into the bustle of the city.[2]

ONE OF THE FIRST THINGS THAT PAUL JENNINGS
seems to have done as a free man was take himself to a photographer's
studio and pose for his daguerreotype. The resultant image is of a handsome man with a certain Frederick Douglass–like fierceness. He looks
off to one side, clearly not in timidity because his light-colored eyes
are piercing. His face reveals all of his genetic heritage: Afro, Anglo,
and American Indian. He is holding a prop of his choosing: a book.
The first photography studio in Washington opened in 1840. Nine
years later, a young daguerreotypist named Mathew Brady set up shop
in the nation's capital, intent on taking portraits of all its distinguished
government men and other prominent Washingtonians. The latter
would include the eighty-one-year-old former First Lady Dolley Madison. Not many ordinary citizens could afford to have their pictures
taken, claimed Washington memoirist Sarah Vedder, remembering one
lady who paid $5 to sit motionless for up to ten minutes.[3]

Five dollars would represent a lot of money to Paul Jennings.
His agreement with Daniel Webster stated that he would pay off his
$120 purchase price at the rate of $8 a month. That would take fifteen

months, but it is not clear when in 1847 Jennings began working in Webster's household. His duties were to commence when Webster returned "from the South," but in fact the Senator's tour of the Southern states was postponed repeatedly. He did not get away until the very end of April. Moreover, between the late start and a bout of ill health, Webster bypassed Washington when his journey ended and went directly to Massachusetts, not returning to the capital until well into the fall.

When Jennings took on the role of butler and dining room servant in Webster's brick house on D Street Northwest (between 5th and 6th Streets), he did not reside there. The agreement the two men struck included Jennings's board, clothes, and washing but made no mention of "room." Federal census and city directory data show that Jennings lived in a house with three other people of color located just a couple blocks west of the White House. The head of this household was a Sarah Smith, presumably the same African-American woman of that name known to be one of Daniel Webster's domestic servants at this time.[4]

Webster's residence, originally built in 1831 as a two-story plus attic, was far from spacious. He wrote to George Ticknor in January 1846, "We have taken a house, called *ready* furnished, about as big as two pigeon-boxes, but pleasantly situated, and some little space and shrubbery about it. Our nearest neighbor is the Unitarian Church." The Unitarian Church bell served as the quasi-official timekeeper in this part of the city, and we can imagine Paul Jennings and Sarah Smith commuting to Webster's house together early each morning, hurrying on as the church bell rang out the hour.[5]

Daniel Webster was a true man of parts, and it must have taken some time for Jennings to fairly size him up. One observer thought the statesman owed half his fame to his sheer physical presence. Webster was not of giant size, but his great head and oratory made him appear majestic. During Fanny Kemble's stay in the capital, she went to the Senate specifically to hear him speak (as many visitors to Washington did) and reported, "Webster's face is very remarkable, particularly the

forehead and eyes. The former projects singularly, absolutely overhang-
ing the latter, which have a melancholy, and occasionally rather wild,
expression." As orator, he adapted his rhetoric to the audience and
his purpose, alternately appealing powerfully to the head or the heart.
With a disposition that varied from sunny to dark to explosive, he
lacked the even temperament that Jennings's earlier boss was known
for. Like James Madison, he tended to wear a singular costume, though
a showier one: blue coat with brass buttons, black pants, and a white
vest and tie (though at least once he substituted a blue vest embroi-
dered with gold flowers). According to one biographer, Webster's "capacity for drink entered into his capacity for grandeur, which was part
of his reputation."[6]

Webster reveled in rural life, and kept a cow and some fowl in the
city to remind him of it. He would come home from a day's work in
government, empty his wife's work basket, and use it to collect hens'
eggs. Sometimes during the workday Webster and his private secretary
would leave the office for an afternoon of fishing at the Great Falls
of the Potomac River. Webster would cast his line and, forgetting his
political and pecuniary cares, exult happily when he hooked a fish.
Fishing and keeping animals in his yard in Washington were interludes
to the rustic role Webster liked to assume at Marshfield, his treasured
country home in Massachusetts.

Webster entertained liberally at the D Street house, first as senator, and then—starting in July 1850—as President Millard Fillmore's
Secretary of State. Dinners featured the cream of culinary perfection
from Monica McCarty's kitchen. A guest detailed one menu: "pickled
pork, a quarter of a lamb, fried chicken and nice vegetables, and cool
wine." At the head of the table, Webster carved the principal meat dish
himself, peppering the act with anecdotes and quotations. Indeed, he
"talked like a book." The meals that McCarty cooked and Jennings
served were appreciated. "The table is capital," reported one diner,
"everything is given at the top of the heart." On a March morning
in 1851, Webster wrote a friend, "Mrs. Webster and I hope to see the

same company to-day [as at a dinner they attended the day before], at five o'clock, partaking of a Potomac shad, and some other *provant* or other *vivres* at our house."

Webster was his own purveyor. His contribution to his cook's repasts was shopping at the market. He decided if the Potomac shad looked good that morning. Center Market was just a few blocks southwest of Webster's house, and the busiest place in town from dawn to midmorning. There shoppers surveyed the provisions for sale, including game, seafood, fruit, vegetables, and fresh greens and flowers brought in from the surrounding countryside. In his soft felt hat with broad brim, Webster, in the company of Jennings or another servant, was a common sight on market days. Going from stall to stall, followed by his attendant carrying a roomy basket for the purchases, "he would joke with the butchers, fish-mongers, and green-grocers with a grave drollery."[7]

Some baskets were filled with goods for Dolley Madison. In her last years, reported Jennings, "she was in a state of absolute poverty, and I think sometimes suffered for the necessaries of life." Niece Mary Cutts described her as a now "powerless lady" and noted that those who knew her late in life "have seen the high and the low take from themselves to give to her." Webster regularly sent Jennings to Dolley's house with a market basket full of provisions and told him that if he noticed anything she was in need of, to take it to her. "I often did this, and occasionally gave her small sums from my own pocket," Jennings added.[8] In an ironic reversal of fortune, then, the ex-slave showed a generosity of spirit toward his former mistress.

◆

THE BID FOR FREEDOM OF SEVENTY-SEVEN PEOPLE—including Ellen Stewart—on the schooner *Pearl* in April 1848 was the largest-scale slave escape ever attempted in America. Paul Jennings was one of the local African-American leaders who organized this scheme with Northern abolitionists. Ellen had been in hiding for at least five months from the time she ran away until she entered the *Pearl*'s hold, and Jennings likely had been assisting her all along. The year 1848 was Jennings's first full year of freedom. He was rising, but he had not forgotten from whence he came, and he risked his own hard-won freedom to help others still enslaved reach the same status.

Following the 1835 "Snow Riot," the tendency of Washington authorities to cater to slaveholders' interests and oppress free African Americans led to expressions of countersentiments. One manifestation of this growing antislavery spirit was the petitions against slavery that poured in on Congress. (They came in even greater number after that body passed the gag rule in 1836 that tabled such petitions.) Another was the growth of Underground Railroad activity in Washington. Activists took one of two basic tactics in helping slaves in imminent danger of being sold: assistance with escape to a free state and freedom by purchase from the slave owner. Known associates of Jennings, including John Freeman and his sons, served as "managers" at fundraising events for slaves threatened by sale. These events were staged as "sitting parties" or "social suppers"; they included speeches and refreshments, but the main objective was to collect money to purchase the freedom of an enslaved individual in peril. Such fundraisers are an example of what historian James Horton referred to when he wrote: "The informal response to shared needs became central to black Washingtonians' role in the abolition movement and the Underground Railroad."[9]

Among the thirty-eight men, twenty-six women, and thirteen children stowed belowdecks on the *Pearl* the night of 15 April 1848 were four brothers and two sisters of the Edmonson family. These six enslaved siblings had been hired out as skilled servants to various city householders but were in danger of being sold following changes in their owner's circumstances. The freedom of the siblings' eldest sister, Elizabeth, had been purchased years before by her future husband, John Brent. Paul Jennings had grown close to this family. John and Elizabeth Edmonson Brent lived at L and 18th Streets in northwest Washington, and Paul may have met them through the Freemans, who lived just two blocks away, one of their few neighbors in this sparsely settled area. Jennings also got to know the Brents through the Methodist Church. John Brent, a prominent African-American religious leader, founded the John Wesley A.M.E. Zion Church, the only congregation with which Jennings is known to have associated, and held services in his own home before a church building was secured. It was within the protective walls of churches that issues of importance to the African-American community were debated and actions proposed. The Brent home was a haven for family and friends generally, especially the family members working in Washington or needing a place to gather when in the city from Maryland, where the Edmonson parents lived.[10]

The Underground Railroad operations in the District of Columbia were cross-racial, the work of local blacks and whites from free states who came to the capital to organize and agitate or who helped from a distance with funding and communications. Abolitionists on the national stage, such as William Lloyd Garrison, Frederick Douglass, and Gerrit Smith, recognized that the nation's capital was a uniquely important theater for antislavery action. It was one place where the federal government clearly held the authority to abolish slavery, and activists knew that if slavery—or at least the slave trade—was outlawed in the capital, the symbolic as well as practical value would be significant.

The germ of the *Pearl* episode has been traced to a free black man in Washington named Daniel Bell, who was seeking an opportunity to transport his enslaved wife and children, threatened with sale to the South, to freedom in the North by boat. The plan expanded from there to entail additional escapees and a complex collaboration among local black operatives and white abolitionists in the North and on the ground in Washington. The primary organizer among the latter was William L. Chaplin of the New York State Anti-Slavery Society. Chaplin was also Washington correspondent for the *Albany Patriot,* an abolitionist newspaper in upstate New York. He wrote to his patron, Gerrit Smith, on 25 March 1848, "The number of persons here, who are anxious to imigrate, is increasing on my hands daily. I believe there are not less than 75 now importunate for a passage." Among them, Chaplin referred to Ellen Stewart and the Edmonson siblings. He informed Smith that he was "every day expecting the arrival of a vessel from Philadelphia on purpose to take off 50 or more."[11] A sea captain named Daniel Drayton had been hired to secure a boat. Chaplin was responsible for pulling funding together and for logistical elements in Washington. He was the liaison with local black leaders and relied on them to coordinate operations among members of the African-American community.

According to author John H. Paynter, a great-nephew of the Edmonson siblings, the three most active community leaders in this regard were Paul Jennings, Samuel Edmonson, and Daniel Bell. Paynter's book, *Fugitives of the Pearl,* was published in 1930 by the Associated Publishers, a press founded by Carter Woodson's Association for the Study of Negro Life and History to publish research on African-American history. The Brents' daughter Catharine married James Paynter in 1861, and they lived first at the Brent house, then a block away in their own home. Their son John Paynter, born in 1862, grew up in the neighborhood and interviewed his great-uncle Samuel Edmonson and other "old citizens" who had been close to the escape event before he wrote an article by the same name in 1916, published in the *Journal of Negro History.* The journal article covered the same material as the book but implicated only his great-uncle as a conspirator, not mentioning Jennings and Bell as in the full-length treatment—told as a dramatization—wherein the three men comprised what he termed the "Black Triumvirate."[12]

Paynter's work represents one of two lines of evidence for Jennings's involvement in the *Pearl* episode. The second, described by Mary Kay Ricks in her 2007 book, *Escape on the Pearl,* is Jennings's association with William Chaplin. Chaplin's dispatches for the *Albany Patriot* provide evidence of his communications with Jennings, who, though never named, is clearly the source for details on his own story as well as information on Dolley Madison and on Ellen Stewart and her mother. The first two articles, headlined "Mrs. Madison's Slaves" and "Mrs. Madison's Slaves Again," were filed, respectively, on 19 February and 8 March 1848; the second included corrections for slight inaccuracies in the first, obviously supplied by Jennings. Chaplin engaged with Washington's African Americans on a daily basis, and, once his reputation for trust and sincerity was known, they drew him in, confiding in and consulting with him. Historian Stanley Harrold, who has researched Chaplin's activism extensively, concluded, "No white person active against slavery in Washington during these years more willingly exposed himself to physical, mental, and emotional stress than Chaplin."[13]

The *Pearl* arrived at Washington's 7th Street wharf on Thursday, 13 April, with a crew of three: Drayton, the supercargo responsible for the escapees, plus the schooner's captain, Edward Sayres, and a young mate named Chester English. By coincidence, that same day there were celebrations in the city in honor of the recent restoration of democracy in France. As Drayton saw to preparations for the trip, Sayres and English listened to some of the speeches. Senator Henry Foote of Mississippi was effusive in his comments, holding out "to the whole family of man a bright promise of the universal establishment of civil and religious liberty." Foote declared that "the age of tyrants and of slavery was rapidly drawing to a close, and that the happy period to be signalized by the *universal emancipation* of man from the fetters of civic oppression, and the recognition in all countries of the great principles of popular sovereignty, equality and brotherhood, was at this moment visibly commencing." At the edge of the crowd, Paul Jennings, Samuel Edmonson, and Daniel Bell listened, too. Afterward, they reviewed the escape plan scheduled for Saturday night. They liked the sentiments they heard in the speeches, especially the forecast of universal liberty. They would do their part to further this goal. Paynter claimed that "The Edmonson boys actively promoted the scheme and, rightly in so just a cause, abused the privileges which their integrity and unusual intelligence had won for them." This described Jennings's attitude as well. James Madison taught that the exercise of conscience—"the most sacred of all property"—was a natural and inalienable right.[14]

Paynter's book-length treatment of the *Pearl* affair is a dramatization; notwithstanding an allowance for poetic license, two episodes in the book concerning Jennings are not only unverifiable but unlikely. One is his meeting with Drayton in Baltimore to arrange for the schooner. The other is his intention to sail on the *Pearl* himself followed by a change of mind because he did not want to run out on his remaining debt to Webster. There is no evidence that Drayton knew Jennings (and there is evidence against it if Jennings was the black man Drayton noticed at the dock the night the *Pearl* set sail); moreover, the known details on securing and funding the schooner and crew involved other conspirators. As for Jennings going along, there is no reason to think that he would take that risk when he was already free and would be leaving behind his children enslaved in Virginia. Daniel Bell never considered sailing with the *Pearl;* he apparently planned to meet his family at the trip's termination point.[15]

With the human cargo belowdecks, the schooner cast off at approximately ten o'clock on Saturday night only to be stranded soon in a dead calm. Finally the wind picked up, but the *Pearl* had lost precious time as it sailed down the Potomac for about 100 miles, reaching Point Lookout, where the river flowed into the Chesapeake Bay, as the sun set on Sunday. The plan was to head north up the Chesapeake for 120 miles to a landing at the top of the bay where the fugitives would be met and led to Philadelphia. But a stiff north wind prevented their entering the bay. They dropped anchor in a sheltered cove called Cornfield Harbor just inside the mouth of the river, and Captain Drayton suggested that everyone rest. Contrary winds—first too light to move down the Potomac rapidly, then too strong to move out to the Chesapeake Bay—had conspired against the hopes of those who now sought sleep in the hold. Theirs was a daring plot in detail and scope, destined to be foiled by those contrary winds and a turncoat of their own color.

Meanwhile, certain white people in Washington City, in George-town, and in Alexandria had discovered that morning—even if gradu-ally, given it was a Sunday—that some black servants were missing. They were alerted to the servants' whereabouts when a local African American named Judson Diggs, who held a grudge against one or more of the runaways, turned informant. A posse of about thirty men was formed. In his *Journal of Negro History* article, John Paynter offered a poignant analysis of the owners' reaction to their slaves' mass bid for freedom:

> The action of the masters in this emergency is eloquent testimony that the
> fine oration of two days before concerning the spread of liberty and uni-
> versal brotherhood had been nothing more than so many meaningless con-
> versations. When confronted on Sunday morning with the fact that their
> and their neighbors' slaves, in so great numbers, had disappeared during
> the night, the realization of the difference between popular enthusiasm for
> a sentiment and a real sacrifice for a principle was borne in upon them and
> they found that while they enjoyed the former they were not at all ready to
> espouse the latter.[16]

In a small steamboat, the posse caught up with the *Pearl* about two o'clock Monday morning. The still-sleeping fugitives belowdecks awoke to the noise of tramping feet and fiery male voices as, weapons in hand, the men boarded the boat. When they raised the hatch, one of their mem-bers exclaimed, as recorded in Drayton's memoir, "Niggers, by G_d!" Samuel Edmonson's brother Richard climbed on deck and cautioned, "Do yourselves no harm, gentlemen, for we are all here." The black men had considered a fight but, unarmed as they were, gave up the idea as futile. Within seconds the runaways' emotions fell from a joyous sense of freedom in the offing to the bitter taste of defeat, not to mention dread at the gloomy prospects now facing them. Not only would they not make it to liberty in the North, but their worst nightmare might well become reality: sale by slave traffickers to the Deep South market and permanent separation from family.

The captives disembarked from the *Pearl* after it was towed back to Washington early Tuesday morning. On being paraded through the city—the men bound in pairs, the women and children following— they were jeered by onlookers. Ellen Stewart, the same age as Mary and two years older than Emily, probably walked alongside the Edmonson sisters. One observer shouted out as the girls went by and asked if they were not ashamed of their actions. When young Emily bravely replied to the contrary, the observer remarked, "Han't she got good spunk?" The owners came to the jail the next day to claim their human property, and most immediately struck deals to sell their slaves to traders on the scene. Resale by these local traders to the South was the final fate of many, if not most, of the African Americans who had boarded the *Pearl* four days before. Such was Ellen Stewart's prospect, sitting in a prison cell a few blocks northeast of Paul Jennings's workplace, the Webster house.[17]

Many in Washington, officials and citizens at large, saved special scorn for the three white men who comprised the *Pearl*'s crew. Daniel Drayton actually had his ear cut by an outraged onlooker who pulled a knife during the forced march from dock to jail. Certainly, the thinking went, mischief-making whites had to have led otherwise-contented slaves astray, and those whites must have been backed by Northern abolitionists with, as Senator Foote of Mississippi pointed out, a blatant disregard for property rights. The attack on Drayton was just the start of three days of angry, sometimes violent, demonstrations known to historians as the Washington Riot. Once the *Pearl*'s crew and passengers were (relatively) safe behind bars, the mob targeted the office and editor of the *National Era,* the city's antislavery newspaper.

Authorities were able to implicate only the three crew members in the scheme, and Drayton and Sayres convinced them that the young mate, Chester English, had no prior knowledge of the *Pearl*'s true mission, so eventually he was released. There is not more evidence on the other conspirators because the plot was secret and well constructed, with intelligence dispensed on a need-to-know basis. The identity of the other conspirators remained unknown to the authorities. Drayton could get away with not revealing their names because Sayres had no knowledge of them; he had been recruited and paid by Drayton.[18]

Meanwhile, the devastating news of the *Pearl*'s capture reached the fugitives' loved ones. Two days after the schooner was towed back to Washington, the Edmonson brothers and sisters were sold for $4,500 to an Alexandria slave trader who hoped to double his money by reselling the siblings in New Orleans. They were transported to that city in the hold of a brig, arriving after twenty days at sea in mid-June, even as family and friends were making efforts to generate funds for their purchase. Held in a slave pen on the edge of the French Quarter, Mary and Emily were marketed as "fancy girls" with sexual implications and were repeatedly displayed in a showroom. When a yellow fever epidemic befell the city, the valuable Edmonson sisters were transported northward. By August, they found themselves again held in Alexandria, Virginia. Three of their brothers remained in New Orleans, where Samuel had already been sold; Richard traveled with his sisters and was the first of the siblings freed through purchase. Money was frantically being raised for the release of Mary and Emily before they could be returned to New Orleans. "None did more valiant service, both by advice and actual soliciting for funds than their true friend and sympathizer, Paul Jennings," according to the Edmonson family. To realize the asking price of $2,250, a large net was cast. The girls' father traveled with William Chaplin to New York, where the Anti-Slavery Society connected him with the Reverend Henry Ward Beecher. The sisters were finally freed in November. Their connection with nationally prominent abolitionists—they influenced Harriet Beecher Stowe's writing and attended antislavery events with Frederick Douglass and Gerrit Smith—led to a certain celebrity for Mary and Emily Edmonson.[19]

If the Edmonson sisters were the public face of the *Pearl* fugitives, Daniel Drayton was the public face of the conspirators, both because of

the trial and because he later wrote a memoir. Drayton and Sayres were
charged with stealing slaves and illegally transporting them out of the
city. In the end, prosecution lawyer Philip Barton Key, son of Francis
Scott Key, got a conviction on the latter charge. The two sea captains
served four years and four months in prison before a presidential par-
don from Millard Fillmore in 1852 released them. Drayton had been
hired for his role in the *Pearl* escape venture, but he also undertook the
dangerous assignment on principle. As he wrote in his memoir:

> Nobody in this country will admit, for a moment, that there can be any such
> thing as a right of property in a white man. The institution of slavery could
> not last for a day, if the slaves were all white. But I do not see that because
> their complexions are different they are any the less men on that account.
> The doctrine I hold to, and which I desired to preach in a practical way,
> is the doctrine of Jefferson and Madison, that there cannot be property in
> man,—no, not even in black men.[20]

But there was property in man, legally speaking, and Dolley Madison exercised her legal prerogative when she first arranged to sell Ellen
Stewart to a slave trader. She exercised that prerogative again when,
shortly after Ellen gave that trader the slip, she sold her mother, Sukey.
William Chaplin's *Albany Patriot* article, dispatched on 19 February
1848, noted that a number of slaves resided with Dolley Madison in
Washington, including a mother, fifty-odd years of age, and her daughter of fifteen. Chaplin described how directly after Ellen ran away some
three months before the article dateline, "Mrs. Madison, either piqued
a little at the loss of her daughter, or from her necessities, offered the
mother for sale. By great good luck, she found a family in the city in
want of a capable woman like herself. The price was paid to her mistress, and she is now at work with the prospect of freedom *some time*."
Further evidence that the mother referred to was indeed Sukey is the
timing of the sale with the disappearance of "Sukey" and "Susan" from
the Montpelier records; her last mention is in a September 1847 letter

from Payne to his mother.[21] After the sale, Sukey's trail goes cold. (The federal census of 1860 lists a Susan Stewart as a free black servant living in Washington who was born in Virginia; this may be Sukey but, if so, the birth date of 1805 is off by some years.)

As to the fate of Sukey's daughter Ellen, one Washington journalist, upon discovery of the mass exodus aboard the *Pearl*, mused, "I believe Mrs. Madison misses one of her girls today, who is probably gone with the party." Mrs. Madison had been missing her girl for months, of course. Perhaps the newspaperman got the former First Lady's name from among the slaveholders who were asked to come forward and identify their runaway property. Like most of the owners of the *Pearl* fugitives, Dolley had no interest in taking her slave back. She sold Ellen Stewart for $400 to a Baltimore dealer hovering at the city jail to take advantage of such transactions. Ellen was among the slaves destined for the buyer's Baltimore slave pen who departed the city by train on Friday, almost a week since boarding the *Pearl*. An observer passing by the railroad depot noticed "a large number of colored people gathered round one of the cars." Their manifestations of grief caused him to draw nearer, and he found in one of the cars "about fifty colored people . . . a majority of them were of the number who attempted to gain their liberty last week. About half of them were females. . . . The men were ironed together, and the whole group looked sad and dejected."[22]

Meanwhile, Dolley penned Payne:

If you can wait for a few days I hope to send you $100 which will put your clothes in order—by the sale of Ellen at $400—who is kept quietly in jail until she recovers from her 6 months dissipation—You have seen perhaps in the N. papers that she was taken in the vessel freighted for the North by Abolitionists—I have not seen her, but hear a bad acct. of her morals & conduct—I wait as you suggest a quieter time for the Bill & sale of the girl.

On 24 May 1848, a month after Dolley's letter to her son, an article written by William Chaplin ran in the *Albany Patriot* that noted:

"Ellen Steward, sold by Mrs. Madison, can be redeemed for four hundred and seventy-five dollars, although removed from the District to Baltimore. She is a sprightly, active girl, of fifteen." Chaplin added: "Her mother is overwhelmed with grief at the fate of this, the last child of five that slavery has snatched from her arms." Perhaps Jennings had supplied Chaplin with this last piece of information. The $75 price differential was the pen-keeper's compensation. Efforts were under way to raise the money to purchase Ellen. Congressman John G. Palfrey of Massachusetts contributed. Dolley Madison, unaware of his efforts on Ellen's behalf, invited the Congressman to tea; he declined, writing a friend, "The thought of the poor fugitive child, whom she had been selling and buying, was in the way, and Mrs. M. had to take her tea without me." Others who contributed to the fund included Joseph E. Snodgrass, a Baltimore physician and abolitionist, who went to the Baltimore slave pen when the required total was reached in June 1848 and paid out the money for Ellen Stewart's freedom. Two months later, Chaplin mentioned the young woman in an article one last time: "Ellen is in the vicinity of Boston, where her friends have provided a good situation for her."

After it was all over—Sukey sold, Ellen living up North—Dolley Madison received a letter from Ben Stewart, now in his mid-twenties and still a slave in Georgia. Ben was in the dark as to what had happened to his family members. In his July 1848 letter, he asked his former mistress to buy him back because he longed to return to "my Relatives, who are very near & very dear to me."²³ Ben's request fell on deaf ears. He would have to wait until after the Civil War for his freedom.

◆

BY THE NEXT SUMMER, PAUL JENNINGS, now at the half century mark in age, had been working for Daniel Webster as a dining room servant for two years and was courting a woman who lived in Alexandria. The Virginia port town was reached by the Long Bridge at the

base of 14th Street. A bridge over the Potomac River here was first constructed during the Madison administration. It was just a partial bridge
when Jennings first arrived in Washington in 1809; one diarist remembered descending the temporary stairs built from the bridge's truncated
termination to the water and continuing to the opposite bank by boat
or, in winter, by walking on ice. Alexandria was part of the original
District of Columbia, but in 1846 the town had been ceded back to
Virginia. How Paul met Desdemona, nicknamed Desday, is unknown,
but he must have crossed the bridge regularly to romance her. On 12
June 1849, Paul Jennings and Desdemona Brooks were married in Alexandria County. The bride was about the same age as the groom and,
like him, a single parent with five children. Desdemona, again like
Paul, was the offspring of one black parent and one white parent, but
in her case, it was her mother who was white and free. That meant that
Desdemona and her children were always free.

Desdemona Brooks was described in the Alexandria Free Negro
Register in 1835 as a thirty-year-old mulatto woman, 5 feet 4 inches
tall, with a freckled face and "only one point per tooth." Later census
records established her birth date closer to 1800. Paul Jennings was
characterized by family tradition as a "Jim Dandy" and a "dresser,"
someone who cared about his appearance and spent some of his dis-
posable income on fine suits and kidskin shoes.[24] This leads one to
suppose that, despite the confounding image of "only one point per
tooth," Desdemona Jennings, formerly Brooks, was likely an attractive
June bride.

No sooner had the couple married then they were off on a trip, but
not necessarily one accurately described as a honeymoon. The same day
as the wedding, the newlyweds boarded a train in Baltimore, final destination Boston, along with Webster's cook, Monica McCarty. Webster
had prepared a memorandum, presumably carried by the threesome,
so that as African Americans traveling to places where they would not
be known, they would not be troubled or abused. One is left simply
to match the date on the memorandum and the date of the marriage,

painting a picture of Paul and Monica meeting Desdemona in Alexandria for a simple wedding ceremony and the three of them then going on to catch a train north. The memorandum reads:

Washington June 12th. 1849

Paul Jennings, & Monica McCarty, are free colored persons, belonging to my Family, and are now bound for my residence, in Marshfield. They are entitled to Free passage, from Baltimore to Philadelphia: & New York to Boston, by the Stonington Line, or the Fall River Line. Vid: Capt Swifts pass—to Philadelphia. Desday Jennings, the other colored woman, is the wife of Paul Jennings, & is a free person. But she is not a member of my Family. I will thank Mr. Guy, (United States Hotel, Baltimore) to speak to the Conductor, & be responsible for them as free persons; viz. three in all.

Danl Webster

In a letter written the next day, Webster alerted his wife in Massachusetts that Paul Jennings and Monica McCarty had left Washington for Marshfield and that he was "getting along as fast as I possibly can."[25] Jennings's ken was expanded by this, at least limited, exposure to major cities like Philadelphia, New York, and Boston over a trip that would have taken several days. Perhaps Monica prepared a wedding dinner for the newlyweds once they arrived at their destination of Marshfield.

Strolling about Marshfield with his new wife, Jennings surveyed a farm of some twelve hundred acres where hay was a major crop. Marshfield, also called Green Harbor, looked out to Cape Cod Bay, a mile off. The estate was dotted with small houses, barns, and other buildings. The main house included a great library room of over one thousand volumes. True to form, Webster poured money into Marshfield when he could, as careless in farm management as in all his financial accounting. He employed a foreman and boatman along with laborers at Marshfield, and when he was in residence, several of his African-American servants from Washington would be there, too. Mornings when Webster was not fishing, he might be hunting for marsh birds, duck, or woodcock. Jennings observed Webster at Marshfield in pastoral mode—a fisherman in loose coat and tall boots, a farmer in work pants and slouched hat. Dinner was usually at four. Monica's clam chowder was Webster's favorite.[26]

Walking about the property now, Paul and Desdemona paused when they came to the two weeping elm trees that Webster planted on the front lawn a year earlier as a memorial to his son Edward and daughter Julia. He named the trees "the Brother and the Sister." Even while Jennings had been preoccupied with the *Pearl* venture and the trial that followed, Webster was mourning the passing of his two children. Edward had died from typhoid fever in the Mexican War on 23 January, but Webster did not receive the news in Washington for a full month. Meantime, his daughter Julia was very ill with tuberculosis. Webster was at her side in Massachusetts by the end of March. She died a month later. Edward's body and effects arrived in Boston on 1 May 1848, the day Julia was buried.

Monica, for Desdemona's sake if Paul already knew it, might have told the story of Edward's service and death and the role played by Henry Pleasants, her former coworker whom Webster had purchased and freed when he was a young slave. When Edward enlisted in the Mexican War, he asked his boyhood companion Henry, now a husband and father, to accompany him as servant. Pleasants, who had remained close to the Webster family, agreed. Edward contracted a severe case of typhoid fever in Mexico; Pleasants nursed him through his final day and accompanied Edward's body home to Webster in Massachusetts. He also brought Edward's horse, which Edward had watched and fed through a window near his bed during his illness.

George Ticknor recalled that when Webster related this same story to him, the Senator "became very much agitated, and, as he ended, saying: 'I paid five hundred dollars for Henry, and it was the best spent money I ever laid out in my life,' the tears flowed freely over his face, and his whole person was convulsed."[27] Of Webster's five children (all by his first wife, who died in 1828, the year before he married Caroline LeRoy), only one son would survive his father. The memorial of weeping elm trees for Webster's son and daughter must have made Paul Jennings reflect on his own children still enslaved in Virginia, his youngest, William, just seven years old.

◆

DOLLEY MADISON DIED ON 12 JULY 1849. Her last days were filled with angst and confusion. Instead of holding her hand, her son was anxious to secure one last handout from the assets she would leave behind. On her deathbed, she cried out for her long-deceased husband: "Oh, for my counselor." Paul Jennings and Daniel Webster missed the funeral held at St. John's Church on 16 July. Though Webster implied in the mid-June letter to his wife that he was traveling right behind his servants, he reached Massachusetts only the day before the former First Lady died. Surviving nearly into the second half of the nineteenth century, Dolley Madison had become a living icon of the generation of the Founding Fathers. At her passing, she was honored with the largest state funeral the nation's capital had ever staged. The many dignitaries present were headed by President Zachary Taylor. One newspaper account noted that the galleries of St. John's Church were "densely filled with spectators including no small number of the colored race." It continued: "There were forty-eight carriages, public and private, and the occupants took their places in accordance with the programme. One hack was appropriated to the colored domestics of the household of the deceased." The mourners, wearing black stars and badges, followed the beplumed catafalque to the Congressional Cemetery located half a mile southeast of the Capitol. Paul Jennings waited until his memoir to eulogize Dolley Madison, stating that she was "beloved by every body in Washington, white and colored." Though this may be the kind of platitude one would expect Jennings to express publicly, such a genuine feeling on his part is the family tradition down to the present.[28]

Dolley loved her son to the end. "My poor boy, forgive his eccentricities," she would implore, "his heart is right." But Payne—though he received the Lafayette Square house and $10,000—resented his mother's bequests to Annie Payne and attempted to break her final will, making little effort to conceal his leechlike tendencies. Debauchery and insolvency lay ahead for Payne Todd. And an early death.

Payne's thoughtless ways had repercussions for the servants at the Lafayette Square house. Clueless as to his master's plans, Ralph Taylor wrote to Payne in November 1849 and again five months later: Might he go ahead and hire himself out? May his wife be baptized? And when are you coming to Washington? Payne finally showed up and, in April 1851, sold the Lafayette Square house for $11,000, though this barely eased his financial predicament, in part because the house had been mortgaged.[29]

In 1851 Payne sustained an injury from a fall and by the close of the year he had developed typhoid fever. He died in January of the new year in the rooming house on Pennsylvania Avenue where he spent his last months, attended by the Taylors. He drank to feel better than he did when he refrained. Payne Todd grew from boyhood on a slave-tilled estate but died in a boardinghouse bed, a broken profligate. His last words were "I have been my own worst enemy."

If Dolley Madison's death signaled the close of a political era, Payne Todd's represented the demise of a particular errant type. District of Columbia chronicler George Townsend wrote sharply of the scions of Upper South plantations "where the land was so exhausted that it hardly gave sustenance, while meantime the proprietors hunted, fed, and frollicked just as in better days and found the most spontaneous and reliable of their resources to be the increase and marketableness of dusky human nature. It was not uncommon [for some members of the] gentry of Washington to so embarrass themselves at the gaming tables as to be obliged to sell their body servants."[30]

Payne Todd's funeral was attended by two carriages; one held a single friend, more likely a creditor, and the other, the servants with him at the end. His will was prepared less than a month before he died. Payne was well aware of his lack of assets, so it seemed a bit of a hollow gesture that, by the terms of the will, the slaves still remaining among those his mother had deeded him were to be freed and fifteen of them granted $200 each. Payne had staked some of these same individuals as "collateral" on more than one occasion when the sheriff came around with a summons for his indebtedness. Now at least one family member thought it highly improbable that the slaves would be freed because Payne's estate was insufficient to meet the outstanding debts. Clara Payne wrote to her husband John in February 1852 that even their nephew's effects were seized for delinquent rent and scheduled to be sold at public auction. As Clara predicted, Payne Todd's creditors did not want to honor the instruction in his will to free the slaves attached to his estate. Some, including Ralph and Catharine Taylor and their four children, sued the estate administrator to attain their freedom.[31] Hardly surprising, none of the individuals bequeathed $200 in Payne's will received a check.

◆

WHEN PAUL AND DESDEMONA JENNINGS RETURNED from Marshfield to the Washington area, they did not live together right away. As previously described, in the 1850 census, Paul Jennings, fifty, is found living in the same house as his coworker Sarah Smith. The city directory of 1853 lists Mrs. Smith, probably a widow, as head of this household, located on 17th Street, just a couple blocks west of the White House. The same census shows Desdemona, fifty-five, listed with the Brooks surname, residing in the town of Alexandria with three of her children: Elizabeth, twenty-five; Georgianna, seventeen; and Gouvenour, ten. Her other daughters, Ellen and Sarah, both in their twenties, must have been out on their own at this time. Desdemona was living with her husband by 1854, but how much earlier than that is not known. They might have roomed together at Sarah Smith's any-time after the census data was gathered in 1850, or Desdemona might have had a job—her occupation was later given as ladies' nurse—that kept her in Alexandria.[32]

Paul Jennings was ready to move on in his working life. On 23 June 1851, Daniel Webster penned a recommendation for him: "Paul Jennings was a servant in our house, for a considerable time. We think him very honest, faithful and sober; and a competent dining room servant. Formerly he was body servant to Mr. Madison." This original document with its envelope labeled "Paul Jennings" rests with the Alfred Chapman Papers at the University of North Carolina. As noted earlier, Chapman was the son of James Madison's niece Rebecca and active in community affairs in Orange County, Virginia. Since 1850, Chapman had been living in Washington, a clerk first in the pension office, then the bureau of Indian affairs, both under the Department of the Interior. He and Jennings would have been perfectly familiar with one another and probably both were happy to talk Orange County news together. We can visualize Daniel Webster handing Jennings the envelope with his name on it, and Jennings—still working those connections—handing it over to Alfred Chapman in turn. This kind of patronage often made all the difference: Jennings landed a low-level but steady government job in the pension office.[33]

Exactly when Jennings started his new job is not clear. The official register of federal employees came out every other year; Jennings missed the 1851 edition but was listed as "laborer" in the pension office in the next one. The designation "laborer" in government offices at this time was often a catchall term applied to black workers. It did not refer to ditch digging or even necessarily to janitorial duties but usually to message running, door keeping, and other such assignments. Even where African Americans performed higher-level roles—copyist or clerk—they usually retained the laborer or messenger designation. The opposite held true as well: Alfred Chapman groused that he held the title of clerk but was charged with opening the mail. In May 1849, the Washington correspondent for the *Georgia Telegraph* filed a story, replete with indignant sarcasm, on the appointment of black men to government posts. He referred to Daniel Webster procuring a messenger position for a "buck negro" when "fifty poor white men would have been delighted to receive it" as the "coolest piece of impudence" in that week's news. "Emboldened by the success of their brother nigger, two 'colored gentlemen,' as they were called, came to Washington all the way from Massachusetts . . . seeking *clerkships!*" The correspondent noted that a pair of black men had recently been appointed messengers or laborers in each of three federal departments. "And I have myself seen negroes writing in the passages of the Departments, directing packages, while white men were scrubbing the floors," the writer fumed, concluding, "it is enough to make the blood boil to think of these things."[34]

The Department of the Interior was created in 1849; before that, the pension office was under the jurisdiction of the Secretary of War. The new department, designed to take charge of the nation's internal matters, combined the pension office with the patent office and the bureaus of Indian affairs and public lands (additional functions like the census were added later). In 1851 the pension office was located in the Winder Building, which was on the same block as the house where Jennings boarded, on 17th Street Northwest between F and G Streets, a three-minute "commute." At five stories, the Winder Building was Washington's first "high-rise." It was built in 1848 by William Winder, who accurately predicted that the government would need to lease more and more office space.

In 1841, the pension office was run by four clerks and one messenger; six years later, there was a total staff of sixteen. In 1853, Paul Jennings was one of fifty-nine employees in the pension office. His annual salary was $400. Clerks made from $900 to $1,800 while the top salary of $3,000 went to the commissioner. Work in government offices began at eight o'clock. Each day at ten minutes before twelve a large black ball was hoisted to the summit of a pole on the National Observatory roof, and exactly at noon it dropped, giving all the city's residents a chance to regulate their watches. At three o'clock federal employees were released for the day, and hundreds of them poured onto Pennsylvania Avenue and the other thoroughfares. Dinnertime followed rush hour directly.[35]

Jennings lost his easy commute in 1854 when the pension office relocated to the just-completed east wing of the Patent Office Building. A masterpiece of Greek Revival architecture, the building's history went back to 1836, when its construction was authorized by President Jackson. Located halfway between the White House and the Capitol on a site set aside for a monumental structure by the original city planners, it was built in stages. The patent office moved in when the south wing was ready in 1840. Upon the building's final completion in 1868—four wings around an inner courtyard—the marble and granite edifice occupied the entire square from F to G Streets and 7th to 9th Streets. Today the building houses the Smithsonian's American Art Museum and National Portrait Gallery; the east wing, where the pension office was located, is the only part of the interior that still exists as originally built.

"Business at the Pension Office in Washington is rapidly accumulating. The applications for bounty lands are pouring in," an April 1855 newspaper noted. The pension office occupied the southeast corner on the first floor of the Patent Office Building's east wing. The new wing boasted modern conveniences like gas lighting, forced-air heat from furnaces in the basement, hot and cold running water piped to marble basins, and even a facility for sterilizing cuspidors.

The patent office took up more space in the building than any other bureau, the model room alone occupying the entire third floor, a soaring space with masonry vaulting and large skylights. Surely Jennings occasionally climbed to the third floor during his break time to view the models of inventions being considered for patents. Historical, art, and scientific collections were displayed there, too, including the Declaration of Independence. Among the exhibits were locks of hair of the early Presidents, James Madison's included. His former barber must have paused at this.[36]

◆

WHEN PAUL JENNINGS LEFT DANIEL WEBSTER'S EMPLOY-
MENT in 1851, Webster was in the throes of dealing with the after-
math of the Compromise of 1850, the series of resolutions enacted by
Congress in September 1850 in an effort to settle the sectional strife
over slavery. In 1844, once John Quincy Adams led the way in over-
turning the gag rule that had allowed Congress to ignore the thousands
of antislavery petitions that sat on their collective desk (a clear violation
of the constitutional right of citizens to petition the government for
redress of grievances), the slavery debate again raged in both the House
of Representatives and the Senate. The *Pearl* affair of 1848 hastened
the Compromise of 1850 by intensifying the call to quell the animos-
ity between North and South. The most contentious measure of the
Compromise of 1850 was the fugitive slave bill, which mandated the
return of escaped slaves to their masters; it included provisions for en-
forcement that the earlier (1793) fugitive slave act lacked and subjected
persons who assisted runaway slaves to criminal sanctions. A counter-
measure designed to fit the "compromise" descriptor was the abolish-
ment of slave trading in Washington.[37]

Paul Jennings may well have answered the door to Henry Clay's
knock the evening he procured Daniel Webster's support for the nature of the compromise. The Senator from Kentucky came to Webster's
house about seven o'clock on 21 January 1850. "In state of the weather
which rendered it very unfit for Mr. Clay to be abroad, his name was
announced at Mr. Webster's house without previous intimation of his
visit"; he wanted to talk about the "sectional controversy." The two
Senators held a long discussion "concerning the best mode of action to
settle the difficulties growing out of slavery."

Clay introduced his series of compromise resolutions to the Senate
and debate followed. Webster was scheduled to address that body on 7
March. His friend Philip Hone wrote in his diary: "Mr. Webster is to
speak on Thursday. His position is extremely delicate and embarrass-

ing, even to a man like him, of iron nerves. I apprehend some disappointment amongst the anti-slavery spirits of the North and his own state of Massachusetts. Union is his paramount motive, the Constitution the star by which he steers; to preserve these he will probably concede more to the South than the fiery politicians (Whigs even) of the North may think expedient." When the day came, the chamber was swelled with listeners as Webster began what was probably his most famous speech: "I wish to speak today, not as a Massachusetts man, nor as a Northern man, but as an American . . ."[38]

Webster's support for the end of the slave trade in Washington was not new. In a presentation made to the Senate on 16 March 1836, James Madison's last birthday, Webster had held that Congress had full control over slavery in the District of Columbia. Efforts to outlaw slave trading in the capital went back to the fourth President's own administration: Virginia congressman John Randolph had recommended consideration of such a ban in 1816. As in the past, the proposal at hand focused not on the enslaved victims (or why not abolish slavery in Washington outright?) but on the sensibilities of whites who objected to the nation's capital being "a great slave mart." As one judicial official put it, "The frequency with which the streets of the city had been crowded with manacled captives, sometimes on the Sabbath, could not fail to shock the feelings of all humane persons." If this resolution passed through Congress, slaves would remain in the District, but at least slave coffles, auction blocks, and holding pens would disappear.

It was Webster's support for the most contentious resolution— the fugitive slave bill—that was controversial. When Webster gave his speech in March, he was a Senator, but by the time the measures were voted on in September, he was President Millard Fillmore's Secretary of State. Fillmore was in office only a few months when he signed the bill, having received the opinion of his Attorney General that it was constitutional. When the fugitive slave law was entered in the statute book, the bill's supporters from the House of Representatives organized a serenade to President Fillmore and his Secretary of State. "The

President bowed his acknowledgements from a window of the Executive Mansion, but Mr. Webster came out on the broad doorstep of his home, with a friend on either side of him holding a candle, and attired in a dressing gown, he commenced a brief speech."

The approbation of those present that evening was far from universal. The fugitive slave law brought down a torrent of objection from abolitionists and other citizens. It cost Fillmore the renomination in 1852, and Webster was roundly condemned by many for his efforts to enforce the new law. Historian Merrill Peterson, analyzing Webster's political "conservatism," has written that "what was to be conserved, fundamentally, was the heritage of the Founding Fathers, the Constitution, the Union, and the Anglo-American law."[39]

Such a refrain was familiar to Paul Jennings. He was bearing witness again to the concept of union first and always, keeping indeed with the heritage of the Founding Father he knew so well: union trumps slavery. While the infamous fugitive slave law brought an erosion of already-limited black rights and heartbreak to many individuals and families, African Americans and other abolitionists confronted these developments with renewed antislavery efforts. In contrast, Webster epitomized those bent on sacrificing moral justice and principle to political expediency and appeasement. Even given Webster's "sacrifice," the sectional issues in contention were hardly "settled"; the Compromise of 1850 only deferred a civil war. Webster's stance lowered his reputation among most African Americans and perhaps influenced the timing of Jennings's exit in 1851 after four years in Webster's employ.

Between the personal losses of his children Edward and Julia and the political backlash from the fugitive slave law, Daniel Webster suddenly appeared old. His constitution was breaking down. Still, when the Secretary of State left Washington for Marshfield in early September 1852, he could not have guessed that he would never return. In residence with the Squire of Marshfield—providing sympathetic service to him in his last illness—were Monica McCarty, Sarah Smith, Ann Bean, and Webster's final manservant, William Johnson. Johnson, according to George Ticknor, had been "bought and emancipated" some time before and now "seemed to claim the exclusive right to serve Mr. Webster, but he hardly ate or drank anything." Webster called Monica to his sick chamber; she moved about the room in agitation, approaching the bed, holding up her hands, uttering bits of prayers. Daniel Webster died on 24 October 1852 at age seventy. He had signed his last will and testament just three days earlier. In it, he declared Monica McCarty, Sarah Smith, and Ann Bean "all free" (a simple clarification since all were free), and he directed that William Johnson not repay any portion of the $600 that he had loaned him for his freedom.[40]

◆

PAUL JENNINGS'S SERVICE TO WHITE POWER HOLDERS was past. He had a new wife and a government job. But there were pieces missing in his pursuit of the right to rise. It was time to go back to Virginia for his children, still living in slavery. And it was time to see if owning property of one's own—land and a house—was all it was cracked up to be.

CHAPTER SEVEN

First Families of Color

31 October 1854, L at 18th Streets,
Northwest Washington

Paul and Desdemona Jennings appreciated their new home. It was a small house on a small piece of ground but of great significance to them. Carpenter John S. James had owned lot 23 in square 107. Beginning in the early spring of 1854, having divided the land into three parcels, he built three wood-frame houses facing L Street. Each parcel had about 13 feet 4 inches fronting L Street and ran from 84 to 115 feet back to a diagonal alley. Jennings purchased the easternmost house, closest to 18th Street, from James on the twenty-eighth of September for $1,000. He had saved $400 of the purchase price, a substantial down payment. Earlier on this last day of October, a month after the sale, husband and wife had been at the Washington clerk's office, where each signed a document borrowing the $600 balance. That is, Paul signed; Desdemona, who was not literate, applied her mark. She acknowledged the same as her husband ("willingly and freely and without being induced thereto by fear or threats of, or ill usage by, her husband or fear of his displeasure")—namely, that if their payments were not made, the property would be forfeited.

The arrangement specified quarterly installments of $100 plus interest. Accumulating the down payment could not have been easy; nor would coming up with $100 every three months. Washington was one of the most expensive cities in the world. Government clerks earning $900 to $1,800 annually in the pension office were hard pressed to support their families. Jennings's salary was $400. Given the payment schedule, the debt would be satisfied in May of 1856. At that time, Paul Jennings, a man legally held as property for forty-eight years, would own his piece of land and modest house free and clear, for himself and his heirs and assigns forever.[1]

In choosing this particular house-buying opportunity, Jennings had the support and friendship of two families well known to him who were already living in the neighborhood. On K Street, a matter of about twenty yards from the alley at the back end of Jennings's property, was the Freeman family. John Freeman had died in 1839, but Melinda and some of the children were still at home. At the corner of 18th and L Streets were Jennings's closest neighbors, the Brents—John and Elizabeth, and their eight children. There was just a scattering of houses in the area in 1854. The city's established, finer residences and legations ran from the vicinity of Capitol Hill to the White House and a small section north and west from there. Though it was only a few blocks farther northwest, Paul and Desdemona's new neighborhood was in the midst of marsh and cow pasture, countryside where rabbits could be shot and where blackberries and huckleberries grew in season.[2]

ON 1 AUGUST 1853, PAUL JENNINGS'S YOUNGEST SON, William, was emancipated. "I Charles P. Howard," the document read,

"for divers good causes and considerations . . . also in further consideration of one dollar currant money of the Unites States to me in hand
paid, have released from slavery . . . my negro boy named William Jennings, being of the age of thirteen years and able to work and gain a
sufficient livelihood and maintenance." According to later records, the
adolescent was a year or two younger than Howard indicated. The source
for the dollar bill—as well as an element of special consideration—may
well have been William's father.

When Paul Jennings visited his family in Orange as a free man in
the 1850s, he could observe various changes. By the end of the decade,
Orange County would have 6,299 blacks (6,111 enslaved and 188
free) and 4,407 whites, and his old home, Montpelier, had changed
hands four times. At Howard Place, Charles Howard plied his dual
roles as farmer and merchant, though he was getting on—eighty-five
according to the 1850 federal census—owning real estate valued at
$19,000. He was a widower now. Jane Taylor Howard's decline had
started in 1844. She injured her hip with a fall from a carriage the same
summer that she lost the help of her maid when Fanny Jennings died;
her recovery was very slow. If Paul Jennings had picked up a *National
Intelligencer* in Washington on 20 January 1849, he might have noticed
Jane Howard's obituary notice.[3]

The 1850 slave schedule listed thirty enslaved men, women, and
children at Howard Place. Once William was free, three of Jennings's
children remained there. (Felix seems not to have survived slavery; he
is not mentioned in Howard Place records, and no other known source
discloses any trace of him.) Son John (or Jack) was about nineteen and
Franklin seventeen in 1853. Paul's only daughter, Frances, who never
married, was about twenty-six. The baby girl born to her in 1844 did
not survive, but she had a son, Taylor, born a year or so later. Frances
was "of unsound mind," as her brother Franklin described it. Whether
she had an inborn condition or an affliction that developed over time
is not known.

Some of Franklin's experiences as a Howard Place slave were passed down to his descendants. His granddaughter Sylvia was told of an occasion when a white man came on the property and threw up a handful of coins for the enslaved children to scramble after as the shiny metal hit the ground. Later, Franklin's master sent him to Richmond to learn the candy-making trade. While no details of Franklin being hired to a Richmond confectioner have been located, evidence of other Howard Place slaves being hired out in the Virginia capital has survived. A letter that Howard Place slave Quintus Barber wrote to Howard in 1840 shows that he was being hired out, working at Boshers Dam near Richmond. Quintus Barber mentioned a second slave with him, and another record named these two men and two others, all hired out in the state capital.[4]

These same four men were freed by Howard in 1854. They were among the twenty-three slaves that Orange County court house records show Charles Howard emancipated over the period from 1834 to 1856. The last person Howard freed in his lifetime was Franklin Jennings. Two and a half years after William's release, Franklin was freed on 16 January 1856. "I do manumit, emancipate and set free a young negro male slave named Franklin, sometimes called Franklin Jennings, a bright mulatto, and about twenty years of age" affirmed the document.[5]

Howard died two months after freeing Franklin. In his will, he manumitted his remaining slaves and provided $5,000 for their settlement in one of the states or territories in which slavery was illegal. Any of that sum not used for relocation was to be divided among those families "declining to emigrate." Some of the people freed by Howard's will went to Highland County or Fayette County, Ohio, and a few went to Allegany County, Pennsylvania; in both cases, they followed individuals already living there who had been freed in Howard's lifetime.

The final inventory of Howard Place slaves took place on 27 October 1856. There were twenty-six slaves named plus three very young ones not named. The list included Fanny's mother, Old Kate, with a

$300 charge to the estate; Edmund, worth $900 (Fanny's forty-one-year-old brother, one of two uncles Franklin said relocated to Ohio without naming the other); and Paul's son Jack, valued at $1,100, daughter Frances, at $500, and grandson Taylor, at $500. Though none of the three young children unnamed in the inventory were associated with Frances, later records reveal that she had a new baby boy, Hayward, born two months before the October accounting. Hayward (whose full name was Felix Hayward, presumably after his lost uncle) was either the last Jennings born in slavery or the first born free. In reuniting with his children in the 1850s, Paul Jennings was fortunate in two ways: Howard's apparent discomfort at being a slave owner, given his Quaker background, and the fact that the Howards were childless.[6]

When William first went to live with his father and stepmother in Washington, he and his father had two and a half years to reconnect before they were joined by William's siblings. As the youngest, William was most in need of a parent, and we can imagine his father taking the opportunity to teach his adolescent son how to read and write over this period. William was the only one among Jennings's children who ever picked up these skills. Before 1856 was out, William's brothers and his sister and her sons joined the city household on L Street.

Jennings had a special plan for his needy daughter and his grandsons. On 15 May 1856, the deed of release stating that Paul and Desdemona Jennings had paid off their $600 debt was recorded in the Washington clerk's office, and Jennings was ready to take on a new commitment. On 23 November 1856, he purchased the house similar to his own on the piece of land next to him and had the tenant occupying it removed. He bought this property in his and his daughter's names, and three days later, Frances appeared with her father at the Washington clerk's office and made her mark on the same document that her father signed, borrowing the money necessary to pay for the second house, which, like the first, cost $1,000.[7]

The community that Paul Jennings and his family lived in was integrated, as were most neighborhoods where free blacks lived in antebellum Washington. Relations between black and white in this northwest neighborhood were not markedly antagonistic, not ostensibly anyway; yet free African Americans operated under restrictive laws. These included ones that limited their employment opportunities. Many occupations in Washington required a license, and one of the few licenses available to blacks was for hack or cart driving. However, the black code was not always strictly enforced, and, in fact, Washington blacks worked as cooks, waiters, blacksmiths, carpenters, teachers, preachers, and barbers. (One Englishman noted with irony that in this latter capacity, a black man "might even enjoy the privilege of taking the President of the United States by the nose.") Some blacks ran profitable businesses of their own, including shops and restaurants. A small number secured coveted government jobs.[8]

Among the substantial subset of African Americans who prospered in the District were several of Jennings's new neighbors. Like him, these men headed families, owned their own homes, held government jobs, and were church, community, or race activists. Three families illustrate the theme (in addition to the Freeman family, which also fits the pattern, as John Freeman had worked a low-rung job in the State Department and bequeathed his wife a brick house on K Street).

John Brent owned a large piece of land on the corner of 18th and L Streets, his front door facing 18th. Like Jennings, Brent had purchased his own freedom. He and his wife, Elizabeth, raised five daughters and three sons, enlarging their house as the family grew. John Brent's occupation for a period of years was messenger to the second auditor in the Treasury Department. He owned property assessed at $4,660 by the close of the 1850s, with his house valued at $800. Insulted by the denigrating treatment black worshippers were shown at white-controlled Methodist churches, Brent led a breakaway group and founded John Wesley A.M.E. Zion Church. Services were conducted in the Brents' parlor until the church building on nearby Connecticut Avenue was ready.

William B. Ingraham was brother-in-law to John and Elizabeth Brent, having married Elizabeth's sister, Emeline Edmonson. Parents to five children, their home, too, was on 18th Street between K and L. By the end of the 1850s, Ingraham owned property valued at $1,500. He was a messenger for the government enterprise known as the United States Coast Survey, its objective to survey the country's Atlantic, Gulf, and Pacific shorelines. The Ingrahams were as involved as the Brents at John Wesley A.M.E. Zion Church, with William serving as a trustee of the new church.[9]

Lindsay Muse lived a block south of the Ingrahams on 18th Street and worked under the Secretary of the Navy beginning in 1828. Levi Woodbury, while Navy Secretary in 1831, was informed by an anonymous citizen that his messenger "who is a colored man," an apparent reference to Muse, "is the receiver and one of the agents for . . . 'The Liberator.'" Though the letter writer thought any association with the abolitionist cause dangerous and advised Woodbury to replace this messenger with a white man, Woodbury simply filed the letter. Muse was assistant messenger/doorkeeper at the Secretary's office for decades. Although he patiently waited to take over as chief messenger/doorkeeper, he was not satisfied with his $400 annual pay and in August 1856 petitioned the United States Senate for an increase in compensation. Muse received pay raises, but not until about 1869, when the French-born white man directly over him left the department, did he assume primary responsibility for access to the Secretary and receive $840 per year. Though a widower with nine children, Muse managed to steadily acquire real estate and by the end of the 1850s was paying taxes on almost $6,000 assessed property value. A leader in another African-American church in the area, the 19th Street Baptist Church, Muse was a deacon there and founder of the Sunday School Union.[10]

The number of Washington's free blacks had increased by 70 percent in the 1840s, but restrictive laws in the following decade, including the Fugitive Slave Act, which kept runaway slaves from using Washington as a safe harbor, lowered their growth rate relative to that of the white population. Despite this, there were substantial gains in the number of African-American property owners and the value of their holdings. The 413 black property owners paying taxes on $529,654 assessed value of land and improvements listed in the Washington City tax books by the end of the 1850s represented a striking jump of 60 percent. At the close of the decade, Paul Jennings was one of 179 free blacks in the city of Washington—along with John Brent, William Ingraham, and Lindsay Muse—who held property valued at $1,000 or more.[11]

Church was important to most of Washington's African Americans, not just for religious sustenance but for solidarity on a host of issues, both political and personal. Another way that a sense of community among African Americans was manifested at this time was the formation of mutual aid societies, such as the Colored Union Benevolent Association that Lindsay Muse helped found. Individuals paid into these organizations, and this was the source of funding when assistance was extended to members in times of sickness or accident and to cover funeral costs at their deaths. Paul Jennings's friend (and former Montpelier slave) Catharine Taylor, for instance, referred in her will to burial expenses being paid by "the Society to which I belong."

Education, viewed as key to elevation, was as important as church and community to Washington's free blacks. Those African Americans who could afford it educated their children at their own expense even while they paid taxes for public education of white children. Some basic schooling was conducted in churches; John Wesley A.M.E. Zion Church, for example, had two teachers and 150 students in the mid-1850s. Twelve percent of Washington's free black children were getting some form of instruction by the end of the decade, but not until the 1860s would public funding be directed to their education.

Contending with legal disabilities and the power and prejudices of whites, Paul Jennings and other energetic and enterprising African Americans in his neighborhood made remarkable progress in the nation's capital. They provided economic security and schooling for their offspring and created a viable, vigorous community. The good fight was ongoing, but meanwhile good times were reflected in social occasions in the neighborhood, such as the marriage of the Brents' twenty-one-year-old daughter Catharine to James Paynter. It was even covered in the newspaper: "A brilliant wedding took place in this city. Miss Kate Brent . . . was married to Mr. James Painter. . . . The marriage took place at the house of the bride's father. The company enjoyed themselves until the wee hours of the morning on the delicacies of the season."[12]

◆

THE FIRST FULL YEAR THAT PAUL JENNINGS SPENT reunited with his four children was 1857. The year began with a great snow. Flakes started falling on Saturday, 17 January, as Michael Shiner noted in his diary, and continued without letup for three days. Shiner, who said he was as cold as he had ever been in his life, reported snow-drifts of ten and twelve feet in the city's valleys and ditches. Ice was the dominant winter element in February, thick enough to freeze up the Potomac and Eastern Branch rivers.

But extremes of weather were as nothing compared to the devastating news that issued from the Supreme Court on 6 March, just two days after James Buchanan became the nation's fifteenth President. That morning Chief Justice Roger Taney handed down the Dred Scott decision against the enslaved man who had sued for his freedom eleven years earlier on the basis of his having resided with his master in a free territory. The court's opinion, which the Chief Justice had written himself and read aloud and which has been described as "a breathtaking example of judicial activism," found that slaves could be held in free territories and that not only slaves but even free persons descended from them were entitled to none of the rights, privileges, and immunities guaranteed by the Constitution. Taney rendered his interpretation of the country's founding documents plainly enough: members of the "negro African race," characterized as "a subordinate and inferior class of beings," could never rise to the rank of citizen; indeed, "they had no rights which the white man was bound to respect." For Jennings and his neighbors, life the day after this announcement was much the same as the day before it—there were meals to cook and work to do—but this kind of psychological battering, even setting aside the legal implications, added immeasurably to the challenge of being black in 1857 America.[13]

When Franklin Jennings recalled living with his siblings and their father and his second wife on L Street, he did not mention any of his stepmother's children living with them, though one or more of them surely resided there, given that Desdemona's youngest child was just seventeen at this time and that two of her children were living with her and her husband by the 1860 census. Franklin did describe the extended family being increased by one in 1857 with the arrival from Virginia of his half sister, Elizabeth Webb.

Elizabeth, the daughter of Fanny Gordon Jennings by a first husband, is rather a mysterious figure for whom both Paul Jennings and his son Franklin seemed not to feel much warmth. She married a Virginia-born John Webb, and they had a son born about 1835, who lived in Fayette County, Ohio, by 1860 at least. How Elizabeth achieved her freedom and when she was widowed has not been uncovered. Her uncle Edmund stated that when his sister Fanny died, Elizabeth "came home" to care for her stepsiblings at Howard Place. In 1857 Paul Jennings "placed" Elizabeth in the second house on L Street in order to help care for Frances and her two sons, Taylor, then about twelve, and little Hayward. Though Frances was "not of sound mind and was incapable of taking care of herself or attending to business," she took in work and earned some money washing and ironing. Elizabeth and Frances were expected to pay the taxes due on the property by renting rooms and other earnings, though Frances's father helped with this, at one time giving them $100. For easy access between the two dwellings, Jennings had facing doors cut along the area partition between them.

The two houses then, which eventually came to be designated as 1804 and 1806 L Street, were "practically used as one."[14]

On 15 May 1857, Paul Jennings witnessed the will of Melinda Colbert Freeman. Melinda Freeman had lived in the neighborhood for almost four decades and watched it develop, slowly for much of that period but at a quicker pace over recent years. In 1857, the neighborhood became home to two young associates of Paul Jennings who worked as laborers in the pension office with him. Charles Syphax's house was to the northeast of Jennings's, on M Street near 15th, while Edward M. Thomas lived on the opposite side of Jennings, at the corner of K and 17th Streets.

Charles Syphax, like the Jenningses and the Freemans, had a connection to a United States President and his Virginia plantation. Syphax was descended from Mount Vernon slaves on both his mother's and father's sides. His mother was Maria Carter, the daughter of Mount Vernon slave Arianna Carter and George Washington Parke Custis, the grandson of Martha Washington. His father was Charles S. Syphax Sr., born into slavery at Mount Vernon, the son of Eloisa, and thus brother to the Nancy Syphax who was an enslaved member of John Gadsby's household on Lafayette Square while Jennings served in the same capacity at Dolley Madison's house.[15]

Edward M. Thomas was born in Philadelphia but settled in the District after marrying a native Washingtonian in 1846. Literate, learned, and community-minded, Thomas pursued an array of interests outside of his work in the pension office. He was an official with a number of black fraternal organizations. Especially devoted to Freemasonry, he had been active in the African Supreme Council in Philadelphia and established a council in Washington. His personal library of nearly six hundred volumes included many titles on Masonic literature. Thomas also collected paintings, rare coins and medals, autographs of famous people, and historic documents. He must have been delighted by the anecdotes that certain of his neighbors, especially coworker Paul Jennings, could tell of their experiences with presidents and other notables.[16]

For all the snow and ice of January and February, a sultry hot summer had set in by June 1857. "Our city is a vast furnace . . . few have courage to venture out of doors; and even then, if one escapes the *sun,* the *dust* is inevitable," complained one society lady, adding, "The better half of the population is already off to the watering-places. . . . In a few weeks the city will be what is called empty; nothing will be left but 'P.P.C.s' and ice-carts moving in the dusty streets." Heat and dust or no, Paul Jennings—and Charles Syphax and Edward Thomas—set off for the pension office at the southeast corner of the Patent Office Building each workday. For Jennings, the walk was about eleven blocks to the east and another five blocks south, though surely he had long ago found a diagonal route that shortened the distance.

So-called public transportation was available along Pennsylvania Avenue. As one city chronicler noted, "If a man wished to ride from the Capitol to the White House he could take the omnibus at a cost of only twelve and a half cents." But not a black man. The use of the horse-drawn buses was confined strictly to whites, except for a "colored woman who had somebody's white baby on her lap." A Pennsylvania Avenue route did not suit Jennings's workday needs anyway, and besides, riding over the corrugated surface of Pennsylvania Avenue was an uncomfortable trip. It was the heavy, horse-drawn omnibuses themselves, along with poor drainage, that had broken up the pavement and made the broad avenue, as in the past, either a bed of dust or sea of mud.[17]

When Jennings did venture into the part of the city that held the landmarks he was so familiar with, he would note similar cases of stop-and-go progress. The Washington Monument, whose cornerstone had been laid on the Fourth of July 1848 with Dolley Madison as one of the dignitaries in attendance, had risen to a third of its planned height and then been abandoned due to indecision and lack of funds. Building blocks lay strewn around the aborted obelisk. The Capitol was in the midst of yet another enlargement. Two prominent wings—one for the House of Representatives and one for the Senate—were being added, and the dome was being made taller and grander. In 1857 the new House chamber was ready for the congressmen to occupy it, while construction on the flanking wing continued. Jennings picked up a sample of stone from the site and kept it as a souvenir (the artifact descended in his family). The rotunda of the Capitol was a great yawning space above which workmen were laboriously building the redesigned dome. Crated on the grounds below them was the sixteen-ton bronze Statue of Freedom that would top the dome when it was completed. The statue's original design had a cap like those worn by emancipated Greek slaves, but Senator Jefferson Davis objected that this might give American slaves dangerous ideas and insisted on an eagle-feather helmet.

Jennings was scheduled to make three payments on the house at 1806 L Street in 1857: $100 plus interest due at the end of May, August, and November. By the time he furnished the November installment, the cold and ice of the winter before had returned. On the twenty-fifth of November, the Potomac River was frozen across. A month later, it snowed on Christmas.[18]

◆

IT IS NOT CLEAR HOW LONG THE EXTENDED HOUSEHOLD described by Franklin persisted on L Street. Paul Jennings was widowed a second time. Franklin said that for about three years after the death of Desdemona Jennings, his father slept in the house at 1804 L Street and took his meals in the one at 1806 (where Elizabeth and Frances undoubtedly prepared them). Franklin also noted that his father resided for some time on 14th Street between I and H Streets. There is confusion of timing in reconciling Franklin's statements with federal census and city directory data. The date of Desdemona's death is unknown, but she was still alive in 1860, living with her husband and two of her children at the 14th Street address. Elizabeth and Frances were at 1806

L Street along with Taylor and Hayward in the census of 1860, but the three Jennings brothers made no appearance in the census. That they might have moved on from their father's direct care is not surprising. John, Franklin, and William would be about twenty-six, twenty-four, and eighteen, respectively, that year. John and Franklin joined relatives in Ohio. Perhaps William did too, though when he next turned up, in early 1865, it would be in Philadelphia. The picture that emerges, whatever the precise timing, is that while the household at 1806 L Street remained intact, the one at 1804 broke up. Paul Jennings's sons left Washington to pursue new adventures, and Jennings himself, first with Desdemona and then as a widower again, resided on 14th Street. It may be that Jennings lived at the 14th Street address because it was financially advantageous for him to board there and rent out his L Street house. It would be a closer location to his workplace as well.[19]

In 1861 a new clerk, a native of Massachusetts, began work in the pension office. His name was John Brooks Russell, and he and Jennings would form a unique association. About the same age as Jennings, Russell had been a voracious reader of history and biography as a young student. While still a teenager, he went to Boston to learn the printer's trade. He published a weekly gazette devoted to agriculture and domestic economy, ran a seed store, and, in 1829, was one of the founders of the Massachusetts Horticultural Society. He was responsible for the society's library as well as its collection of seeds, scions, drawings, and models. Russell became a husband and father and relocated his family first to Cincinnati, where he worked as a newspaper editor, and then to Louisville, Kentucky. One more move took the family to Washington, D.C., where Russell was appointed clerk in the Department of the Interior's pension office, earning $1,400 a year. Jennings had received a pay increase himself by now; he made $600 in 1861. Russell had retained his interest in history over the years and occasionally contributed pieces to the *Historical Magazine and Notes and Queries Concerning the Antiquities, History and Biography of America*. At some point, he became aware of his coworker Paul Jennings and his background. Intrigued by Jennings's experiences with James and Dolley Madison, the two men eventually talked at length. Russell recorded Jennings's story in "almost his own language" and submitted it to the historical magazine. The piece ran in the January 1863 issue under the title *A Colored Man's Reminiscences of James Madison.* The first-person narrative was preceded by a paragraph on Jennings himself with the attribution "J.B.R., Washington, D.C." The events surrounding the War of 1812 were a highlight of the narrative, which was about 2,640 words in length.[20]

The country was focused on another war now. There was just a parenthetical reference to the Civil War in Jennings's reminiscences, a mention that the old brick Capitol was being used to confine "secesh prisoners." South Carolina had seceded shortly after Abraham Lincoln was elected President, and other Southern states followed suit. The tension and fear were such that for security's sake, the President-elect had to steal into Washington unannounced ten days before his inauguration of 4 March 1861. When the day came—the weather cold, cloudy, morose—the carriage taking Lincoln to the ceremony was surrounded by cavalry with drawn sabers, and there were riflemen on the roofs along the route to the Capitol. In April, the bloody battles between North and South began. The capital was in for a true sea change. Southern office holders left town, followed by clerks and other ordinary citizens who, like Alfred Chapman from Orange, "went with their state."

By September 1861, Paul Jennings's workplace was receiving casualties from the war front, as the Patent Office Building doubled as a military hospital and morgue. One thousand cots were set up in the building's exhibition galleries, and wounded soldiers lay among the glass cases holding models of inventions. President Lincoln and the First Lady came to visit the sick and wounded there, as did a young poet named Walt Whitman (subsequently a clerk in the Department of the Interior), who read to the men and wrote letters for them.[21]

Abraham Lincoln clearly stated that his objective as commander in chief was to preserve the Union, even if it meant preserving slavery. But as the war raged on and Lincoln considered emancipation as a war tactic, he decided to make a test case of abolition in Washington, D.C. The numbers were not overwhelming: in 1860, there were 1,774 slaves in Washington City, 577 in Georgetown, and 834 in Washington County. All were freed once Lincoln signed the bill for compensated emancipation on 16 April 1862. "Thanks be to the almighty," wrote Michael Shiner in his diary. Congress had appropriated $1 million to compensate the owners ($300 per slave on average) and additional funds to colonize the former slaves. Lincoln thought colonization would help win white support for general emancipation, and in an effort to sell the idea to blacks, he met at the White House with prominent African Americans from the District in mid-August. The contingent was headed by Paul Jennings's neighbor and coworker Edward M. Thomas. Lincoln attempted to make colonization appealing with the pessimistic reminder that even when free, "not a single man of your race is made the equal of a single man of ours." As chairman, Thomas replied that the delegation would consult, then communicate their deliberations to the President.[22]

Though Lincoln did not succeed at generating enthusiasm among African Americans for colonization, he still included the concept in his strategizing. In September, he issued a preliminary Emancipation Proclamation. Designed to preclude recognition of the Confederacy by European powers and to appease slaveholders in the loyal border regions, it threatened those states in rebellion with the liberation of their slaves effective 1 January 1863 if they did not return to the Union and allowed slave owners in loyal states to retain their slaves while offering compensation and colonization as inducements to give them up voluntarily.

Some blacks in the District of Columbia kept vigil through the night on New Year's Eve, waiting for the Emancipation Proclamation to take effect. It may have been a war measure to Lincoln, but it was an event of great jubilation for people of color. Henry McNeal Turner, pastor of an A.M.E. church in Washington, recalled rushing to the of-

fices of the *Evening Star* and squeezing through a crowd to grab a copy
of the printed text. He ran down Pennsylvania Avenue . . .

> When the people saw me coming with the paper in my hand they raised a
> shouting cheer that was almost deafening. As many as could get around me
> lifted me to a great platform, and I started to read the proclamation. . . . I
> was out of breath, and could not read. Mr. Hinton, to whom I handed the
> paper, read it with great force and clearness. While he was reading every kind
> of demonstration and gesticulation was going on. Men squealed, women
> fainted, dogs barked, white and colored shook hands.

"It was indeed a time of times," concluded Turner.[23]

The course of the war and the nation's future were profoundly altered by the Emancipation Proclamation. African Americans had been
trying to volunteer for service from the beginning of the war, reason-
ing that if black men participated in the fighting, they could not be
denied the rights of citizenship. Once they were permitted to enlist in
early 1863, Frederick Douglass issued a challenge to men of color: "I
urge you to fly to arms and smite to death the power that would bury
the Government and your liberty in the same hopeless grave." About
180,000 black men took up the call to arms, forming more than 10
percent of Union forces by the end of the war. All three of Paul Jennings's sons responded. To former slaves like John, Franklin, and William Jennings, this was a crusade to end generations of bondage as well
as to prove their manhood and fitness for citizenship. Black soldiers
joined the fight to impact how their race would fare after the war.[24]

John Jennings was the first of the brothers to enlist. A laborer residing in the town of Greenfield in Highland County, Ohio, he joined
the 127th Ohio Volunteer Infantry, the first African-American regiment recruited in the state, on 7 July 1863. About twenty-nine at the
time, he had gray eyes and was five feet eight inches in height, an inch
taller than the regiment average. Mustered into Company E, Private

Jennings reported for training at Camp Delaware, twenty miles north of Columbus. He had enlisted for a term of three years, knowing he would serve under white officers and be paid $10 a month, $3 less than his white counterparts. In November, after four months of drilling, the regiment—renamed the 5th United States Colored Troops—was deployed. The 5th USCT would do its fighting in Virginia and North Carolina, and it was in the latter state, at Sandy Swamp, in December, that the men first engaged Confederate forces. By May 1864, the unit was at City Point, Virginia, one of the six African-American regiments that comprised the Third Division of the XVIII Corps of the Army of the James. Another of the six regiments in the all-black division was the 5th Massachusetts Colored Cavalry, which included in its Company B none other than Franklin Jennings.[25]

Franklin had enlisted earlier that same month, having returned to Washington from Ohio. The 5th Massachusetts Colored Cavalry, after training at Readville, Massachusetts, had been ordered to Washington in early May, where the troopers received the demoralizing news that they were to be deprived of their horses and sabers because they were needed for infantry duty to chip away at the front and rear of Robert E. Lee's Army of Northern Virginia. The regiment enlisted forty-nine fresh recruits in Washington, including Franklin Jennings and John S. Brent, son of John and Elizabeth Brent. Franklin, now twenty-eight, was described as a five-foot-six-inch-tall laborer with brown eyes and a copper complexion; he enlisted for a three-year term starting on 12 May 1864. About one thousand men strong, the 5th Massachusetts Colored Cavalry was transported to City Point, Virginia, eight miles north of Petersburg.[26]

Camped in a wheat field, the first month of Franklin's war experience consisted of musketry drill, picket duty, and reconnaissance marches. The soldiers in his brother's regiment, which arrived at City Point about the same time, likewise undertook these often-tedious routines. Not that picket duty was not dangerous. On one occasion, for example, pickets from John's regiment were ambushed and men wounded or taken prisoner. Still, it was on the battlefield that black soldiers wanted to prove their service. A major assault against the Confederates at Petersburg was brewing, and they would get their chance.

The Jennings brothers were part of the famous Black Phalanx that saw action and glory on 15 June 1864. That Wednesday morning, the regiments of the Third Division moved toward Petersburg. The sun was setting when they saw the stars and bars of the Confederate flag waving over the imposing breastworks that would need to be overcome before Petersburg's inner fortifications could be attacked. Sweeping from the woods onto the open field, the men charged the defensive line, exchanging fire with the entrenched opposition. The solid lines of black soldiers kept coming. They drove off the rebel gunners and captured their cannons. The sight of the panicked enemy abandoning their artillery positions was a joyful one. Shouting and dancing, the men in Franklin's regiment gleefully loaded one twelve-pound howitzer onto a cart and wheeled it back to camp like a trophy. The success of the Black Phalanx was duly noted in newspapers and field reports. "The troops were all untried in battle, and by many it was still a problem whether the Negro would fight. The events of the day justify the most sanguine expectations for the future," wrote one of the commanders.[27]

Franklin's regiment was sent to Point Lookout, Maryland, in July 1864 to guard the Confederate prisoners of war there. This camp was very close to Cornfield Harbor, where the *Pearl* had hunkered down with its cargo of runaway slaves some sixteen years earlier. Franklin was the designated company cook for some of his time at Point Lookout. In September, after four months of service, the 5th Massachusetts Colored Cavalry was issued horses, and the troopers spent considerable effort while at Point Lookout training with their mounts and sabers. Franklin Jennings's descendants still own the two swords he was issued, a much-nicked field sword and a smooth dress sword. It is true that Civil War African-American servicemen were used extensively for fatigue and garrison duty, but, as we have seen, many also had an opportunity to prove themselves in combat. John Jennings's regiment certainly amassed an impressive combat record. One of the highlights was the Battle of New Market Heights, Virginia, in late September. Sixteen Medals of Honor were awarded to African-American armymen during the Civil War, and four of them went to noncommissioned officers of the 5th USCT for taking command of companies that had lost their white officers in the fighting at New Market Heights. (Although only white men were eligible to receive commissions as officers, regimental commanders could appoint black soldiers as noncommissioned officers.)[28]

With the start of 1865, Franklin was still at Point Lookout. John's regiment had moved on to the Campaign of the Carolinas, though John, wounded and ill, spent the first two months of the year recovering. On 25 February, the youngest Jennings brother enlisted in the war effort. William F. Jennings was a twenty-two-year-old Philadelphia waiter when he signed up with the 24th USCT for a one-year term; he was the shortest of the brothers at five foot five and a half inches. William was mustered into Company F of the 24th USCT, the last of eleven African-American Philadelphia regiments to be trained at Camp Penn and dispatched to the front. William's regiment was sent to Camp Casey near Washington, but that was not until 5 May, after the astounding events of April 1865 had occurred.[29]

Washington was a much different city on 4 March 1865, when Abraham Lincoln rode to his second inauguration and African-American troops marched in an inaugural parade for the first time, from what it had been four years earlier. The capital had become dense with people, many of them soldiers and, in the last two years, many so-called black contraband (the term applied to former slaves who fled to Union lines or to Northern cities). The political center of the city was denser with more government and more buildings, too, including temporary or retrofitted structures, though Paul Jennings's workplace was no longer used as a military hospital. Lincoln's second inaugural ball was held in the same arched hall of the Patent Office Building where the soldiers' cots had been. The pension business had exploded, on its way to becoming a full-scale data-processing bureaucracy. In many ways, Washington City was at last growing into its original plan. But livestock still grazed in the city, and down by the canal, goats and pigs roamed free.[30]

The end of the war was in sight. Petersburg had finally been taken, and the Confederate capital, Richmond, was doomed. President Jefferson Davis accepted the inevitable and ordered the city evacuated on 2 April. Many Federal forces were camped outside of Richmond that evening, including Franklin Jennings's regiment, which General Grant himself had ordered to the scene. The next morning, the 5th Massachusetts Colored Cavalry had the great honor to be the first Union regiment to enter the fallen capital on the heels of the retreating enemy. "I looked down the street," a female Confederate copying clerk remembered, "and to my horror beheld a Negro cavalryman yelling: 'Richmond at last!'" That evening one of the troopers wrote in a letter to his sister: "Today is the most glorious in the history both of the country and our regiment. . . . It will be an event in history that colored troops were the first into the city." It certainly was a major event in the life of Franklin Jennings. Riding into Richmond as conquering heroes mounted four abreast: that was a tale to tell your grandchildren, and Franklin did, many times. His granddaughter Sylvia told the story in Franklin's first-person voice in 2008. Franklin credited himself with assisting his commanders in choosing the best route to Richmond from the spot in the pines where they had bivouacked the night before. Franklin knew the way because he was familiar with Richmond from his days learning the candy-making trade there.[31]

Washingtonians were jubilant when they received news of the fall of Richmond. Paul Jennings would have cause for particular pride if he knew the role his son's regiment had played. The public buildings were illuminated with gaslights. At the Patent Office Building, the gaslights actually spelled out "UNION." There was more rejoicing in the nation's capital when word of General Lee's surrender came. Another illumination took place in celebration on Thursday, 13 April. This time, six thousand candles lit the Patent Office Building. President

Lincoln addressed a great crowd of people from a White House window. Watching the celebrating throngs from the window of his hotel room was a Confederate sympathizer named John Wilkes Booth. The President went to a play the following evening, riding down Pennsylvania Avenue to Ford's Theater. The next time he rode down the avenue would be in a coffin.

Abraham Lincoln's assassination was a profound blow to most African Americans. Wednesday, 19 April, the day Lincoln's body was carried in an elaborate funeral procession from the White House to the Capitol, was clear and sunny. Bells tolled, guns sounded, and solemn dirges played as the procession began at two o'clock. An African-American infantry, as it turned out, led the way. Arriving late, the troop came in from a side street and marched right onto Pennsylvania Avenue, heading off the funeral cortege. Thirty thousand participants followed Lincoln's catafalque, including four thousand African-American civilians in high silk hats, holding hands as they marched in columns of forty. Government offices, draped in black crepe, were closed for the day. Paul Jennings may well have been among the solidly packed mourners, many in tears, who witnessed the procession.[32]

Once the war was concluded, Jennings's thoughts turned to his sons' safe return. One by one, the Jennings brothers were mustered out of service. Most of William's abbreviated tour had been spent in patrol and provost duty at Richmond. Though William never experienced the combat his older brothers did, only he was promoted from private rank, having been appointed corporal on 18 August 1865, undoubtedly due to his ability to read and write. On 1 October he was mustered out, as his brother John had been ten days earlier. Franklin, whose regiment had gone on to Texas to keep still-active Confederates from escaping across the Mexican border, was discharged the last day of October. Franklin returned to his family in Washington with a war injury. He had sustained a serious blade wound in a skirmish. Much of the muscle was cut from his right arm, and he would never again have full use of it.[33]

◆

BEFORE 1865 WAS OVER, *A Colored Man's Reminiscences of James Madison* by Paul Jennings was published in book form. The start of this coming about was the untimely death of Edward M. Thomas. The future promise of Thomas's leadership was cut short when he died in March 1863 at the young age of forty-two. As president of the Anglo-African Institute for the Encouragement of Industry and Art, he was in the midst of organizing a national exposition of black talent. Almost two years after Thomas's death, the remarkable collection he left behind—described as a "Rare and Valuable Collection of Coins, Autographs, and Books" in a *Daily National Intelligencer* advertisement headline—was auctioned for the benefit of his widow. The auction was held the evening of 10 January 1865 at the downtown auction room of James C. McGuire and Company (McGuire was an art collector who had served as executor of the wills of both Dolley Madison and Payne Todd).[34]

The *Historical Magazine and Notes and Queries Concerning the Antiquities, History and Biography of America* featured the auction in its April 1865 issue. This important collection "belonged to the estate of the late Edward M. Thomas, *a colored man,*" the article emphasized, adding, "Surmounting the prejudices of caste and the disadvantages of a want of early education, he devoted his leisure hours and limited means, to artistic and literary objects." The prices the items fetched were considered high. Autographs sold included those of Napoleon, John Brown, John Hancock, Robert Fulton, Toussaint L'Ouverture, Talleyrand, George III, Benjamin Rush, Aaron Burr, Thomas Jefferson, and James Madison. An autograph of the fourth President went for $1.05, while a four-page letter from Lafayette to Madison on the subject of slavery ("Their plan is founded upon a purchase and employment of slaves, a thing I *detest,* and shall never do . . .") sold for $16.50, more than any of the autographs or letters listed in the magazine piece. One of the items sold at the event (though its price was not given in the article) was a flyleaf, signed by Daniel Webster, emancipating Paul Jennings and setting the terms of Jennings's reimbursement of the $120 Webster advanced for his freedom. It is easy to imagine Jennings having given or sold this document to Thomas, perhaps along with other of the historic items that found a home in his neighbor and coworker's unique collection.[35]

The editor of the *Historical Magazine and Notes and Queries Concerning the Antiquities, History and Biography of America* from 1859 through 1865 was historian John Gilmary Shea. Shea now ordered seventy-five copies of *A Colored Man's Reminiscences of James Madison* privately printed, each one containing an inlaid facsimile of the Webster document on Paul Jennings's freedom. Shea conceived of this publication as forming the second work in the "Bladensburg Series." Earlier in 1865, the printer Shea worked with, Joel Munsell of Albany, had issued a reprint of an 1816 work called *The Bladensburg Races* in a limited edition of seventy-five quarto, or large paper, copies. This was a satirical tale in verse of the flight of President Madison from Washington and of the militia from the Battle of Bladensburg during the War of 1812. Jennings's *Reminiscences* was the second in the series. Each of the seventy-five large paper copies, measuring about nine by twelve inches, bore the inscriptions "Bladensburg Series, Number Two" and "Seventy-five copies, No. ___." Intended as a collector's edition, some of the extant copies have inserted illustrations. According to one source, Shea, instead of selling the books, distributed them as presentation copies. Smaller octavo versions were also run off the same print setup; they, too, bore the inlaid Webster flyleaf facsimile but no Bladensburg series designation or reference to number of copies. The production run of the octavo seems to have been limited as well. Both versions are very rare today, but one is as likely to find the quarto as the octavo in library special collections (sometimes with the facsimile removed).[36]

Other than the inclusion of the Webster document, the book version of the *Reminiscences* differed from the 1863 magazine text by the addition of a second paragraph to the preface. This paragraph described the auction of Edward Thomas's collection (and misidentified Thomas as an employee in the House of Representatives rather than the Department of the Interior). The initials J.B.R. followed the lengthened preface though the "Washington, D.C." descriptor from the magazine version was dropped. The book was published in New York, with "By Paul Jennings" prominently displayed on the title page.[37]

Jennings must have been proud when a book with his byline came out. Before 1865 was over, he had another reason to be proud, for himself and for his former master, James Madison, Father of the Constitution: in December, the Thirteenth Amendment forever forbidding slavery was added to the United States Constitution.

◆

THE LAST YEAR JENNINGS WAS EMPLOYED at the pension office was 1866. He had worked his way up to an annual salary of $720, but such an income hardly allowed for a cushy retirement. The year before, the *Daily National Intelligencer* announced that the chief clerk at the pension office had resigned his position "due to the utter inadequacy of the salary," and he made $2,200 a year. Jennings worked for six more years after he left the pension office, part of that time as a bookbinder. He returned to his L Street house by 1868. Sons John and Franklin lived in Washington after the war, but William returned to Pennsylvania. Settling in Carlisle in Cumberland County, William married a Virginia-born woman named Fannie and raised a family, his first child born in 1867. Franklin was the next son to marry. He had been courting a young woman in the neighborhood named Ella Logan. The Logan family lived on K Street near 21st and had since the 1840s. Somewhere along the way, romantic sparks flashed between Franklin and Ella's younger sister, Mary. On 16 May 1868, Franklin and Mary married in the city but—having caused the Logans, Ella in particular, acute embarrassment—the couple left for Ohio almost immediately, where they would reside for a dozen years before returning to the Washington area. John Jennings, meanwhile, moved in with his father.[38]

According to the 1870 census, Paul Jennings owned real estate valued at $1,200, and $100 more in personal property. He and son John, now about thirty-six, shared quarters at 1804 L Street. Next door were half sisters Elizabeth and Frances, along with fourteen-year-old Hayward. Frances's older son had moved on and may well be the Taylor Jennings described in the census as a Virginia-born, twenty-six-year-old black farm laborer living in Fayette County, Ohio, where he would have relatives. Both Jennings households on L Street had an additional member in 1870, presumably boarders taking up single rooms, a common way for families to economize. At 1804 L Street was a hundred-year-old woman named Matilda Church, and next door was a young man named Eli Jackson, who later that year would become John Jennings's brother-in-law (a family of three shared Frances's house at 1806 L Street when the census was enumerated ten years earlier).

The 1870 federal census form had a column for "Constitutional Relations." Male citizens twenty-one years or older were asked if there was any reason besides "rebellion or other crime" for which his right to vote was denied. Paul Jennings and his sons and every American black man had reason to draw satisfaction from this query, which was a reflection of the brand-new Fifteenth Amendment, stating that a citizen's right to vote could not be denied "on account of race, color, or previous condition of servitude." Amendment Fourteen, the other so-called Reconstruction Amendment, had been added to the Constitution two years earlier. Among its provisions was a definition of citizenship that overruled the Dred Scott decision.[39]

The neighborhood by this time included other former Montpelier slaves. On L Street, just a block east of Paul Jennings, lived Ralph and Catharine Taylor and their two daughters and Benjamin Stewart and his Georgia-born wife, Juno. These two families resided together at 1726 L Street in 1870. Ben Stewart had spent twenty-two years in Georgia. When he returned to Washington after the war, he worked first as a waiter, then as a messenger. Afterward, he secured a position as a guide at the Capitol, where visitors enjoyed being shown about by James Madison's former slave. "I have done very well here," claimed Stewart. "I am proud of having been connected with the Madison family. I have some pictures of Dolley Madison and her husband which were given to me by the family." The Taylors had lived in Washington continuously since the mid-1840s. Once free, Ralph Taylor found work as a hotel waiter. He and Catharine and their four children lived at various locations in the city, including an earlier residence in the northwest neighborhood, very close to the Edward Thomas family on K Street. When the Taylors moved to 1726 L Street in 1870, Ben and Juno Stewart had already been living there for three years. However, it was the Taylors who came to own the house while by 1876 the Stewarts relocated to 1821 L Street, on the same block as the two Jennings houses. Stewart referred to "own[ing] a good house in the city which I built myself," so that must be this second home on L Street where he and Juno, who had no children, lived into the 1890s.[40]

The prevalence of black families with presidential connections in the neighborhood was augmented by the families of Charles Syphax's brothers, Colbert and William, settling in. Colbert's house was two blocks east of Jennings's on L Street while, by 1872, oldest brother William (who would witness Catharine Taylor's will) resided just a few houses away from brother Charles on M Street, having earlier lived on 15th Street near K. Like his brother Charles and Paul Jennings, William Syphax was employed by the Department of the Interior for many years. He started as a messenger in the office of the Secretary and was eventually promoted to a clerkship at $1,000 a year. An energetic community leader, William Syphax was one of the founders of the Civil and Statistical Association, formed in 1850 to further the moral, educational, and financial advancement of Washington's people of color. He made notable contributions to the cause of public education for the District's black children, becoming the first president of the board of trustees of the Colored Schools of Washington in 1868.

That was the same year the new neighborhood school on 21st Street between L and K was completed. William Syphax suggested the name, Thaddeus Stevens School, in honor of the Pennsylvania congressman who had taken a firm abolitionist stance. One of Washington's first publicly funded schools for African-American youngsters, the brick structure was poorly heated and ventilated, but its four floors provided twelve classrooms and six hundred desks. Paul Jennings's grandson Hayward might have been among the first students. He was twelve when Stevens School opened and was described as being "at school" in the census two years later. (The first of the Jennings descendants whose attendance at Stevens School can be confirmed was Hayward's son and namesake, Hayward Taylor Jennings, a first grader there in 1889.)[41]

When Paul Jennings settled back into his home on L Street in 1868, he was just a year from turning seventy. His history was well-enough known in the capital that newspaperwoman Mary Clemmer Ames, writing a book on Washington society, sought him out for a quote on the former First Lady. He was "'Uncle Paul,' her colored servant, who had lived with her from boyhood, and who still lives." Jennings obliged the author, describing Dolley's dresses and turbans, and remarking on her fabled Drawing Rooms ("We always had our Wednesday-evening receptions in the Old Madison House, and we had them in style"). The friends and associates from his days with the Madisons with whom Jennings kept up, in addition to the Freemans, the Taylors, and Ben Stewart, included former White House steward John Sioussat. Until Sioussat died in 1864, he and Jennings occasionally got together and recalled old times. To Sioussat's children and grandchildren, Paul Jennings was "the old colored coachman." Jennings's own descendants described him in a way that harkened back to his last position with the Madisons. He was "Dolley Madison's coachman" who drove her anywhere in the city she wanted to go (as he had earlier been "James Madison's valet").

One of the favorite topics from their days at the President's mansion that Jennings and Sioussat regularly returned to was the rescue of the portrait of George Washington in 1814. One or the other told the tale while children and grandchildren listened. Though direct participants in the rescue, they were not above a little embellishment of their own roles. Sioussat's descendants were assured that he had cut the canvass from its frame with a penknife, while Jennings's great-granddaughter shared the tradition in his line that he had kept the portrait safely hidden under the old Key Bridge. In the spirit of such folklore, Ben Stewart credited his mother, Sukey, with slicing the picture out of the frame with a carving knife. Modern conservation studies proved that the portrait was never cut out by anyone; rather, the frame was broken and the picture carted away as a stretched canvass.[42]

◆

PAUL JENNINGS PREPARED HIS WILL in September 1870. It was witnessed by three of his friends from the neighborhood, John Brent, William Ingraham, and Lindsay Muse. He bequeathed the house at 1804 L Street to sons John and Franklin and charged them with supplying their sister, Frances, with $5 every month for five years following his death. Jennings referred to a future wife named Amelia Dorsey and further instructed his sons to make available to her, over the same five-year period, "one good room" in the house, free of rent or other demands. On 14 September, a day after the date on his will, Paul Jennings, seventy-one, a bridegroom for the third time, and Amelia Dorsey, about fifty-three and originally from Maryland, were married at John Wesley A.M.E. Zion Church.[43]

Son John married later the same year. His bride was Louise Jackson, nicknamed Lulu, at least a dozen years his junior. She was the daughter of Presley Jackson, head of a family that had resided in the neighborhood for decades. The wedding took place at the 19th Street Baptist Church on 15 December 1870. In 1871 and 1872 Paul Jennings worked as a bookbinder, and for these two years—presumably for reasons connected with the workplace or with his (or his son's) newlywed status—he and his wife lived away from the L Street house. He finally retired in 1873. Back home, Jennings spent the remainder of his days living with Amelia and with John and Louise and their little ones as they came along. Fannie was a toddler and John still a baby (and the only other grandchild in Washington, Hayward, an eighteen-year-old butler), when their grandfather passed away.

Paul Jennings died at home on the 20th of May 1874. He had outlived two of three wives. His son William had died about two years before, leaving a wife and three daughters. Franklin and his wife, Mary, were the parents of three children born in Ohio between 1869 and 1873. Paul Jennings, then, had ten grandchildren at his death.[44] The world they inhabited was very much different from the one he had been born into three quarters of a century earlier.

The Right to Rise

24 August 2009, the White House, Washington, DC

It was nowhere near as hot or steamy an afternoon as one would expect for late August in Washington, and that added to the happy anticipation the two dozen group members felt and the lightness in their step. They were expected for a private tour of the White House. Why not savor the stroll along the curved walkway from the iron gate to the east portico? Curator William Allman came out to meet them before they reached the double doors and welcomed the descendants of Paul Jennings to the executive mansion.

Some in the group lived in the capital metropolitan area. Others had traveled from the remaining corners of the country— New York, California, Texas—to be part of this special occasion. It was on this day in history, 195 years earlier, that their ancestor helped Dolley Madison save a national treasure. Once in the entrance hall, the curator explained that the portrait of George Washington was the only piece of fine art in the mansion in 1814, although the painting was most highly prized as the iconic image of the Father of the Country. Its symbolic value had only grown in the years since it was rescued from the torches of the invading British army. The portrait hung in the east room now (its home from 1873 to 1903 and again from 1929 through the present).

The Jennings descendants crossed the room's threshold and ambled along the long stretch of the rectangular space in twos and threes until all came to stand facing the portrait. Ah! The sheer size of it! What a difficult job it must have been to remove the bigger-than-life-size painting from the wall under intense pressure and carry it safely away.

The descendants arranged themselves in front of the portrait for an official photograph.[1] The sense of pride knowing that this national icon might not grace the east room today without the actions of their ancestor was strong, but stronger still was the satisfaction of being honored with a private tour of the White House in recognition of Paul Jennings's role within its walls just seven months after an African American had commenced service as President of the United States.

FROM *A Colored Man's Reminiscences of James Madison,* ONE LEARNS that Paul Jennings was touched by history. Jennings's own story shows how he *touched* history. He did not grab it by the shirt front as James Madison did, yet—in the face of relentless legal, social, and psychological impediments—it took as much strength, application, and courage just to touch it.

First to bestow the "Father of the Constitution" epithet on Madison and his last visitor of prominence, Charles Jared Ingersoll wrote: "No mind has stamped more of its impressions on American Institutions than Madison's." What about the American institution of slavery? Here, unlike the issue of religious liberty, just as contentious in its day, Madison's legacy is one of failure by omission. He refused to consider any plan for emancipation that was not coupled with colonization. "The impression remains, and it seems to be indelible that the two

races cannot co-exist, both being free & equal," Madison apprised Lafayette, "The great *sine qua non* therefore is some external asylum for
the colored race." Madison and other whites thought free blacks lazy,
depraved, vicious, and likely to rise up in rebellion.[2] And this was even
before Nat Turner's instance of bloody revenge. As the historical record
suggests, most blacks wanted only to rise, not rise up, and were less
prejudiced and enraged against whites than whites were against them.

The "right to rise" phrase has been applied to Abraham Lincoln's
sense of fair economic opportunity.[3] If one had the right to rise as an
American—that is, the right to *pursue* rising—a reasonably level playing field without insurmountable economic or legal roadblocks was
implied. As if extending this concept to include color, Paul Jennings
proceeded deliberately in pursuit of his American birthright. There was
no a priori reason to accept color as a limiting factor in the right to
rise. Here he had knowledge to fortify and inspire him. As the constant
servant in Madison's study, Jennings listened to many discussions on
freedom of conscience, individual rights doctrine, and the Constitution and Bill of Rights. He absorbed the arguments and philosophy
that supported his innate yearning for freedom and allowed him to
identify it as an inherent right of man. He acted in ways that were
courageous, even audacious, interpreting what he learned based on his
own worldview and applying it to all Americans, including those enslaved. Not only did he secure his own freedom and his family's future,
but as an intrepid antislavery activist, he forged passes and free papers,
aided runaway slaves, helped organize a major slave escape attempt,
and raised funds for slaves in peril.

"Liberty & Learning lean on each other for their mutual and sur-
est support," Madison asserted.[4] The connection between liberty and
learning was a major theme in the lives of both James Madison and
Paul Jennings. Madison was always the statesman with a book under
one arm. Jennings struck a similar pose when he sat for his daguerreotype. Both men, each by his own lights and in theaters of different
scale, applied his learning in the service of freedom.

◆

SIX YEARS AFTER JAMES MADISON DIED, a visitor arrived at Montpelier to find the mistress away from home. An elderly slave showed the man around the place, and, when they reached the grave-yard, pointed out Madison's burial site, marked only with a short wooden stake. The visitor was shocked that the grave of the illustri-ous Madison was identified by nothing more than "a white oak stake or the word of an octogenarian negro." When Paul Jennings died in 1874, he was buried in Harmony Cemetery, an African Ameri-can burial ground in northeast Washington. With the turn of the new century, a magazine article reported that while "the former slave sleeps in a well marked spot in the capital of his country, Madison, the mighty man he served, lies neglected there at what was formerly the beautiful Montpelier." Madison's grave was marked with a stone obelisk by this date, but the old family graveyard was dilapidated and overgrown with weeds. The contrast is now reversed. By 1959, Har-mony Cemetery was decayed, unkempt, and encroached by a Metro train station. The following year, the graves were reinterred in the new National Harmony Memorial Park in Maryland, but Paul Jen-nings's remains were somehow misplaced. Sylvia Jennings Alexander remembered hearing her cousin Pauline exclaim, "They lost Grandpa Paul! They lost Grandpa Paul!" James Madison's grave is carefully tended in the manicured graveyard at Montpelier, now owned by the National Trust for Historic Preservation. The Montpelier mansion has been architecturally restored and is a popular historic attraction.[5] Nearby Howard Place is known as Mayhurst today and is a bed-and-breakfast establishment. Fanny Gordon Jennings presumably is buried somewhere on the grounds.

Paul Jennings's third wife, Amelia Dorsey Jennings, availed her-self of a room in the house at 1804 L Street for five years after her husband's death, just as he provided for in his will. In April 1879, she relinquished all claim to Jennings's estate in exchange for the room's furniture. The bed, wardrobe, rocking chair, and other items listed in the inventory must have been the furnishings she had shared with Jennings, especially given that they included a bookcase, and Amelia was illiterate. In September of that year, an indigent Amelia Jennings was admitted to St. Elizabeths, the government "hospital for the insane" located in southeast Washington. Suffering from "acute melancholia" brought on by "disappointed affections," she recovered and was released fifteen months later.[6]

As their family grew, John and Louise Jennings continued to reside at 1804 L Street until 1881, when they moved to a house across the street. John died two years later, survived by his wife and five children. At 1806 L Street, a pronounced unpleasantness developed between Frances and Elizabeth. Frances was "put out" of the house by Elizabeth, and a year or two later, about 1888, she died in the Washington Asylum (also known as the poorhouse or almshouse) located in the city's southeast quadrant.[7] Apparently neither brother Franklin, who had returned to the Washington area with his wife and three children in 1880, nor son Hayward, living in the neighborhood with a family of his own, came to Frances's rescue.

In the mid-1890s, Franklin brought suit against his half sister Elizabeth in an effort to eject her from 1806 L Street, claiming that since the house was in his father's and sister's names, he was heir to the property. Elizabeth's lawyer countered that Franklin, born to slaves, was the offspring of a union that had no legal standing so therefore he could not be considered the legal heir of Paul Jennings. The circuit court agreed. The case, with its potential for setting a significant precedent, was covered by the *Washington Post*. The court of appeals reversed the lower court's decision based on evidence that Franklin and his lawyer produced (including the deposition of Franklin's maternal uncle Edmund Spotsey, mailed from Ohio) showing that the marriage followed the traditions of the day for enslaved persons and thus qualified as a marriage equivalent to that between free people for the purposes of legal inheritance by the children of such unions.[8]

Franklin, who lived until 1926, did well for himself. He farmed in Dumfries, Virginia, and alternated living there and in the city house on K Street that his wife, Mary Logan Jennings, inherited. The couple acquired other properties in the neighborhood, properties that as the years went by became prime city real estate. The old neighborhood is a fully commercial corridor today, with only Stevens School, which operated as a public elementary school until 2008, to give away its former life as a vibrant residential community.[9] Paul Jennings's two houses occupied land now covered by retail establishments. Yet many of the structures where Jennings lived or worked in Washington are extant, including the Dolley Madison house, the Octagon, the Winder Building, the Patent Office Building, and, of course, the White House.

Paul Jennings's legacy as the author of the first White House memoir lives on, though *A Colored Man's Reminiscences of James Madison* might easily have fallen into total obscurity. John Brooks Russell deserves credit for getting Jennings's recollections into print and John Gilmary Shea for their publication in book form, but the limited number of copies produced made the volume a rarity. By contrast, Simon Northup's narrative, *Twelve Years a Slave,* published in 1853, had a first printing of eight thousand copies, which sold within a month, and by 1856, over thirty thousand copies had been sold. One factor in Jennings's book not being entirely lost was its promotion by Daniel Murray, the first African-American Assistant Librarian of Congress. He included it, for example, in the exhibit of works by African-American authors that he prepared for the Paris Exposition of 1900. The limited availability of the book was featured in a 1909 *Colored American* magazine article titled "The Negro behind President Madison." The author, George W. Forbes (who cofounded the *Boston Guardian* with William Monroe Trotter), began the article with a description of the vigorous bidding that ensued when a rare copy of Jennings's *Reminiscences* was offered at a Boston book auction.[10]

◆

THE RIGHT TO RISE REVERBERATES THROUGH the generations of Paul Jennings's descendants. As with any African-American family, following the growth rings of the Jennings family tree traces the historical experiences and challenges of being black in America. But that does not mean that every black family shares the same development pattern. Paul Jennings's descendants, by and large, have been light-complexioned African Americans of means who, like him, value family, education, community leadership, and achievement.

Among the many accomplished descendants of Paul Jennings, Dr. C. Herbert Marshall is one whose story exemplifies his ancestor's legacy of both advancement and race activism. Herbert Marshall, born in 1898, was the son of Jennings's granddaughter and namesake Pauline, whose father, John, was enslaved until about age twenty-two. She married Charles Marshall, also the child of a slave. Charles Marshall earned an M.D. from Howard University and became a practicing physician in Georgetown, where he and Pauline purchased a house: a remarkable achievement the first generation out of slavery. Their son became a physician as well. Dr. C. Herbert Marshall inherited his parents' home in Georgetown and acquired the house next door, where he set up his doctor's office. As president of the historically black National Medical Association, he agitated for full access to all-white medical schools, hospitals, and professional societies. Dr. Marshall was not just active in issues of equality for black doctors but was an all-round "Jim Crow buster." As president of his local citizens' association, he spearheaded a petition drive against segregation of the neighborhood playground and tennis courts. A lifetime member, and officer, of the National Association for the Advancement of Colored People, he contributed bold editorials on race issues to various publications. Today, Dr. Marshall's grandson Raleigh, who graduated from James Madison

University, lives in the same house in Georgetown that his father, grandfather, and great-grandparents before him did.[11]

Until the 1960s, grandchildren of Frances, John, and Franklin and their families occasionally got together, but with these individual lines spreading on their own after the births of the next generation, get-togethers with extended kin fell off. Then in February 2009, more than two dozen descendants of Paul Jennings gathered at the meaningful locus of their ancestor's plantation home, Montpelier. Direct descendants of Frances, John, and Franklin attended, and "new" cousins met one another for the first time. Present at the Montpelier reunion was Paul Jennings's great-granddaughter, Sylvia Jennings Alexander, the only survivor of her generation and keeper of the family's oral traditions. She was too ill to attend the White House event that August, and two months later, at the age of ninety-four, she passed away. The Jennings surname, as far as is known, went with her.

◆

THE YEAR THAT JAMES MADISON SWORE to protect and defend the Constitution as the fourth President of the United States was 1809. Two hundred years later, the forty-fourth President took the same oath. He was a "colored man"—one black parent, one white parent—the same as Paul Jennings. America progressed from a liveried footman like Jennings being the only allowable role for a black man in the White House to the first African-American chief executive and his family making their home in that historic structure. President Barack Obama would be the first to acknowledge that his own rapidly rising star was hitched to Paul Jennings's and to those of untold numbers of other African Americans who overcame a barrage of obstacles, and rose.

A Colored Man's Reminiscences of James Madison

by Paul Jennings

PREFACE

Among the laborers at the Department of Interior is an intelligent colored man, Paul Jennings, who was born a slave on President Madison's estate, in Montpelier, Va, in 1799. His reputed father was Benj. Jennings, an English trader there; his mother, a slave of Mr. Madison, and the granddaughter of an Indian. Paul was a "body servant" of Mr. Madison, till his death, and afterwards of Daniel Webster, having purchased his freedom of Mrs. Madison. His character for sobriety, truth, and fidelity, is unquestioned; and as he was a daily witness of interesting events, I have thought some of his recollections were worth writing down in almost his own language.

On the 10th of January, 1865, at a curious sale of books, coins and autographs belonging to Edward M. Thomas, a colored man, for many years Messenger to the House of Representatives, was sold, among other curious lots, an autograph of Daniel Webster, containing these words: "I have paid $120 for the freedom of Paul Jennings; he agrees to work out the same at $8 per month, to be furnished with board, clothes, washing," &c.

—*J.B.R.*

REMINISCENCES OF MADISON

About ten years before Mr. Madison was President, he and Colonel Monroe were rival candidates for the Legislature. Mr. Madison was anxious to be elected, and sent his chariot to bring up a Scotchman to the polls, who lived in the neighborhood. But when brought up, he cried out: "Put me down for Colonel Monroe, for he was the first man that took me by the hand in this country." Colonel Monroe was elected, and his friends joked Mr. Madison pretty hard about his Scotch friend, and I have heard Mr. Madison and Colonel Monroe have many a hearty laugh over the subject, for years after.

When Mr. Madison was chosen President, we came on and moved into the White House; the east room was not finished, and Pennsylvania Avenue was not paved, but was always in an awful condition from either mud or dust. The city was a dreary place.

Mr. Robert Smith was then Secretary of State, but as he and Mr. Madison could not agree, he was removed, and Colonel Monroe appointed in his place. Dr. Eustis was Secretary of War—rather a rough, blustering man; Mr. Gallatin, a tip-top man, was Secretary of the Treasury; and Mr. Hamilton, of South Carolina, a pleasant gentleman, who thought Mr. Madison could do nothing wrong, and who always concurred in every thing he said, was Secretary of the Navy.

Before the war of 1812 was declared, there were frequent consultations at the White House as to the expediency of doing it. Colonel Monroe was always fierce for it, so were Messrs. Lowndes, Giles, Poydrass, and Pope—all Southerners; all his Secretaries were likewise in favor of it.

Soon after war was declared, Mr. Madison made his regular summer visit to his farm in Virginia. We had not been there long before an express reached us one evening, informing Mr. M. of Gen. Hull's surrender. He was astounded at the news, and started back to Washington the next morning.

After the war had been going on for a couple of years, the people of Washington began to be alarmed for the safety of the city, as the British held Chesapeake Bay with a powerful fleet and army. Every thing seemed be left to General Armstrong, then Secretary of war, who ridiculed the idea that there was any danger. But, in August, 1814, the enemy had got so near, there could be no doubt of their intentions. Great alarm existed, and some feeble preparations for defence were made. Com. Barney's flotilla was stripped of men, who were placed in battery, at Bladensburg, where they fought splendidly. A large part of his men were tall, strapping negroes, mixed with white sailors and marines. Mr. Madison reviewed them just before the fight, and asked Com. Barney if his "negroes would not run on the approach of the British?" "No sir," said Barney, "they don't know how to run; they will die by their guns first." They fought till a large part of them were killed or wounded; and Barney himself wounded and taken prisoner. One or two of these negroes are still living here.

Well, on the 12th of August, sure enough, the British reached Bladensburg, and the fight began between 11 and 12. Even that very morning General Armstrong assured Mrs. Madison there was no danger. The President, with General Armstrong, General Winder, Colonel Monroe, Richard Rush, Mr. Graham, Tench Ringgold, and Mr. Duvall, rode out on horseback to Bladensburg to see how things looked. Mrs. Madison ordered dinner to be ready at 3, as usual; I set the table myself, and brought up the ale, cider, and wine, and placed them in the coolers, as all the Cabinet and several military gentlemen and strangers were expected. While waiting, at just about 3, as Sukey, the house-servant, was lolling out of a chamber window, James Smith, a free colored man who had accompanied Mr. Madison to Bladensburg, gallopped up to the house, waving his hat, and cried out, "Clear out, clear out! General Armstrong has ordered a retreat!" All then was confusion. Mrs. Madison ordered her carriage, and passing through the dining-room, caught up what silver she could crowd into her old-fashioned reticule, and then jumped into the chariot with her servant girl, Sukey, and Daniel Carroll, who took charge of them; Jo. Bolin drove them over to Georgetown Heights; the British were expected in a few minutes. Mr. Cutts, her brother-in-law, sent me to a stable on 14th street, for his carriage. People were running in every direction. John Freeman (the colored butler) drove off in the coachee with his wife, child, and servant; also a feather bed lashed on behind the coachee, which was all the furniture saved, except part of the silver and the portrait of Washington (of which I will tell you by-and-by).

I will here mention that although the British were expected every minute, they did not arrive for some hours; in the mean time, a rabble, taking advantage of the confusion, ran all over the White House, and stole lots of silver and whatever they could lay their hands on.

About sundown I walked over to the Georgetown ferry, and found the President and all hands (the gentlemen named before, who acted as a sort of body-guard for him) waiting for the boat. It soon returned, and we all crossed over, and passed up the road about a mile; they then left us servants to wander about. In a short time several wagons from Bladensburg, drawn by Barney's artillery horses, passed up the road, having crossed the Long Bridge before it was set on fire. As we were cutting up some pranks a white wagoner ordered us away, and told his boy Tommy to reach out his gun, and he would shoot us. I told him "he had better have used it at Bladensburg." Just then we came up with Mr. Madison and his friends, who had been wandering about for some hours, consulting what to do. I walked on to a Methodist minister's, and in the evening, while he was at prayer, I heard a tremendous explosion, and, rushing out, saw that the public buildings, navy yard, ropewalks, &c., were on fire.

Mrs. Madison slept that night at Mrs. Love's, two or three miles over the river. After leaving that place she called in at a house, and went up stairs. The lady of the house learning who she was, became furious, and went to the stairs and screamed out, "Miss Madison! if that's you, come down and go out! Your husband has got mine out fighting, and d___ you, you shan't stay in my house; so get out!" Mrs. Madison complied, and went to Mrs. Minor's, a few miles further, where she stayed a day or two, and then returned to Washington, where she found Mr. Madison at her brother-in-law's, Richard Cutts, on F street. All the facts about Mrs. M. I learned from her servant Sukey. We moved into the house of Colonel John B. Taylor, corner of 18th street and New York Avenue, where we lived till the news of peace arrived.

In two or three weeks, after we returned, Congress met in extra session, at Blodgett's old shell of a house on 7th street (where the General Post Office now stands). It was three stories high, and had been used for a theatre, a tavern, an Irish boarding house, &c.; but both Houses of Congress managed to get along in it very well, notwithstanding it had to accommodate the Patent-office, City and General Post-office, committee-rooms, and what was left of the Congressional Library, at the same time. Things are very different now.

The next summer, Mr. John Law, a large property-holder about the Capitol, fearing it would not be rebuilt, got up a subscription and built a large brick building (now called the Old Capitol, where the secesh prisoners are confined), and offered it to Congress for their use, till the Capitol could be rebuilt. This coaxed them back, though strong efforts were made to remove the seat of government north; but the southern members kept it here.

It has often been stated in print, that when Mrs. Madison escaped from the White House, she cut out from the frame the large portrait of Washington (now in one of the parlors there), and carried it off. This is totally false. She had no time for doing it. It would have required a ladder to get it down. All she carried off was the silver in her reticule, as the British were thought to be but a few squares off, and were expected every moment. John Susé (a Frenchman, then door-keeper, and still living) and Magraw, the President's gardener, took it down and sent it off on a wagon, with some large silver urns and such other valuables as could be hastily got hold of. When the British did arrive, they ate up the very dinner, and drank the wines, &c., that I had prepared for the President's party.

When the news of peace arrived, we were crazy with joy. Miss Sally Coles, a cousin of Mrs. Madison, and afterwards wife of Andrew Stevenson, since minister to England, came to the head of the stairs, crying out, "Peace! peace!" and told John Freeman (the butler) to serve out wine liberally to the servants and others. I played the President's March on the violin, John Susé and some others were drunk for two days, and such another joyful time was never seen in Washington. Mr. Madison and all his Cabinet were as pleased as any, but did not show their joy in this manner.

Mrs. Madison was a remarkably fine woman. She was beloved by every body in Washington, white and colored. Whenever soldiers marched by, during the war, she always sent out and invited them in to take wine and refreshments, giving them liberally of the best in the house. Madeira wine was better in those days than now, and more freely drank. In the last days of her life, before Congress purchased her husband's papers, she was in a state of absolute poverty, and I think sometimes suffered for the necessaries of life. While I was a servant to Mr. Webster, he often sent me to her with a market-basket full of provisions, and told me whenever I saw anything in the house that I thought she was in need of, to take it to her. I often did this, and occasionally gave her small sums from my own pocket, though I had years before bought my freedom of her.

Mr. Madison, I think, was one of the best men that ever lived. I never saw him in a passion, and never knew him to strike a slave, although he had over one hundred; neither would he allow an overseer to do it. Whenever any slaves were reported to him as stealing or "cutting up" badly, he would send for them and admonish them privately, and never mortify them by doing it before others. They generally served him very faithfully. He was temperate in his habits. I don't think he drank a quart of brandy in his whole life. He ate light breakfasts and no suppers, but rather a hearty dinner, with which he took invariably but one glass of wine. When he had hard drinkers at the table, who had put away his choice Madeira pretty freely, in response to their numerous toasts, he would just touch the glass to his lips, or dilute it with water, as they pushed about the decanters. For the last fifteen years of his life he drank no wine at all.

After he retired from the presidency, he amused himself chiefly on his farm. At the election for members of the Virginia Legislature, in 1829 or '30, just after General Jackson's accession, he voted for James Barbour, who had been a strong Adams man. He also presided, I think, over the Convention for amending the Constitution, in 1832.

After the news of peace, and of General Jackson's victory at New Orleans, which reached here about the same time, there were great illuminations. We moved to the Seven Buildings, corner of 19th-street and Pennsylvania Avenue, and while there, General Jackson came on with his wife, to whom numerous dinner-parties and levees were given. Mr. Madison also held levees every Wednesday evening, at which wine, punch, coffee, ice-cream, &c., were liberally served, unlike the present custom.

While Mr. Jefferson was President, he and Mr. Madison (then his Secretary of State) were extremely intimate; in fact, two brothers could not have been more so. Mr. Jefferson always stopped over night at Mr. Madison's, in going and returning from Washington.

I have heard Mr. Madison say, that when he went to school, he cut his own wood for exercise. He often did it also when at his farm in Virginia. He was very neat, but never extravagant, in his clothes. He always dressed wholly in black—coat, breeches, and silk stockings, with buckles in his shoes and breeches. He never had but one suit at a time. He had some poor relatives that he had to help, and wished to set them an example of economy in the matter of dress. He was very fond of horses, and an excellent judge of them, and no jockey ever cheated him. He never had less than seven horses in his Washington stables while President.

He often told the story, that one day riding home from court with old Tom Barbour (father of Governor Barbour), they met a colored man, who took off his hat. Mr. M. raised his, to the surprise of old Tom; to whom Mr. M. replied, "I never allow a negro to exceed me in politeness." Though a similar story is told of General Washington, I have often heard this, as above, from Mr. Madison's own lips.

After Mr. Madison retired from the presidency, in 1817, he invariably made a visit twice a year to Mr. Jefferson—sometimes stopping two or three weeks—till Mr. Jefferson's death, in 1826.

I was always with Mr. Madison till he died, and shaved him every other day for sixteen years. For six months before his death, he was unable to walk, and spent most of his time reclined on a couch; but his mind was bright, and with his numerous visitors he talked with as much animation and strength of voice as I ever heard him in his best days. I was present when he died. That morning Sukey bought him his breakfast, as usual. He could not swallow. His niece, Mrs. Willis, said, "What is the matter, Uncle Jeames?" "Nothing more than a change of *mind,* my dear." His head instantly dropped, and he ceased breathing as quietly as the snuff of a candle goes out. He was about eighty-four years old, and was followed to the grave by an immense procession of white and colored people. The pall-bearers were Governor Barbour, Philip B. Barbour, Charles P. Howard, and Reuben Conway; the two last were neighboring farmers.

Jennings Family Genealogy

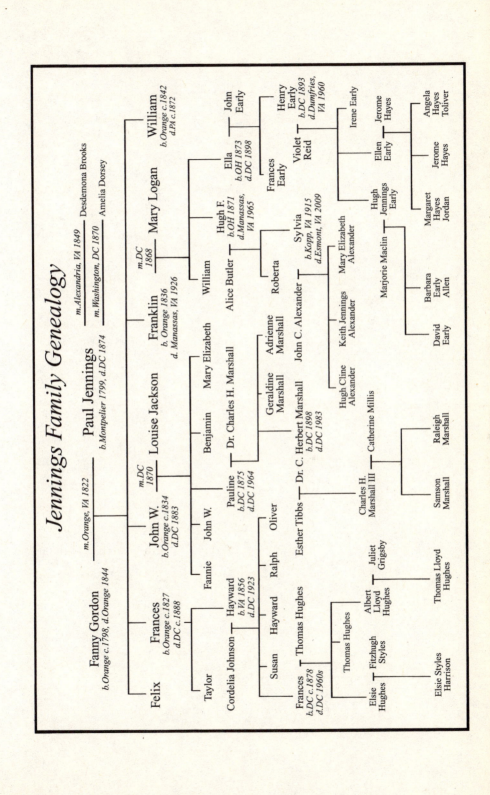

NOTES

SINCE THE DECISION IN THE EJECTMENT SUIT THAT
Franklin Jennings brought against his half sister, Elizabeth Webb, in the 1890s
hinged on Franklin's paternity, the court case documents provide a relative
wealth of information on Paul Jennings and his family. The case documents,
which are housed at the National Archives and Records Administration
(NARA) in Washington, DC, are cited here as *Franklin Jennings v. Elizabeth
Webb, 1896,* case file #470, Records of the United States Court of Appeals,
District of Columbia, Record Group 276, NARA.

Franklin Jennings was also the source for information on Paul Jennings,
his first wife, Fanny (including her Gordon surname), and their children (including the only mention of a son named Felix) contained in the papers of
Daniel Murray, Assistant Librarian of Congress beginning in 1881. In the
course of researching a biographical entry on Paul Jennings for his monumental but unpublished work *Biographical Encyclopedia of the Colored Race,*
Murray interviewed Franklin Jennings in 1901. The Daniel Murray Papers are
available on microfilm in the Manuscript Division of the Library of Congress
in Washington, DC. The material on Paul Jennings therein is cited here as
Notes on Paul Jennings, Daniel Murray Papers, Reel Five, Library of Con-
gress. Murray prepared a typewritten manuscript titled *Paul Jennings and His
Times, President Madison's Biographer and Valet* and presented a bound copy to
President Theodore Roosevelt. It was transferred from the White House to the
Manuscript Division of the Library of Congress in 1913. Cited here as Daniel
Murray, *Paul Jennings and His Times, President Madison's Biographer and Valet,*
Miscellaneous Manuscripts Collection 1970, Library of Congress, this manu-
script incorporates Murray's biographical sketch of Jennings, though many of
its twenty-nine pages are taken directly from *A Colored Man's Reminiscences of
James Madison.*

According to Daniel Murray, Franklin Jennings claimed that his father was born in 1790; nevertheless, the birth year for Paul Jennings of 1799 provided in the *Reminiscences* has been used in this book, since it is confirmed by the federal censuses of 1850, 1860, and 1870. Consistency in age/birth year among census or other nineteenth-century records is as likely to be the exception as the rule. For persons highlighted in this narrative for whom the records give multiple birth years, the most likely year considering all available evidence has been used, often along with a "circa" designation. A similar approach has been taken where the records offer variant spelling of names, as they sometimes do (even Janning or Jannings for Jennings). The spelling used consistently for a given person's name in this work is that which is the most reliable or prevalent. The exception would be in the case of direct quotation. The original spelling and grammar for direct quotations generally have been retained, except for rare silent corrections made for the sake of clarity.

ABBREVIATIONS

DMDE   Dolley Madison Digital Edition. This online collection of the papers of Dolley Madison is edited by Holly C. Shulman at the University of Virginia. Accessed at http://rotunda.upress.virginia.edu:8080/dmde, most of the known letters and other papers of Dolley Madison through 1840 are covered to date. This is the preferred citation used here for Dolley Madison letters; those not yet included in DMDE are cited elsewhere, if not in a published source, then usually the Dolley Madison Papers at the Manuscript Division of the Library of Congress.

PJM-CS   *The Papers of James Madison, Congressional Series.* Edited by William T. Hutchinson et al. Chicago: University of Chicago Press, 1962–1977; Charlottesville: University of Virginia Press, 1977-1991. The only one of the four series of *The Papers of James Madison* that has been completed, volumes 1 through 17, cover March 1751 to March 1801.

PJM-SS   *The Papers of James Madison, Secretary of State Series.* Edited by Robert J. Brugger et al. Charlottesville: University of Virginia Press, 1986–2011. Nine volumes to date, covering March 1801 to June 1805.

PJM-PS   *The Papers of James Madison, Presidential Series.* Edited by Robert A. Rutland et al. Charlottesville: University of Virginia Press, 1984–2008. Six volumes to date, covering March 1809 to October 1813.

PJM-RS   *The Papers of James Madison, Retirement Series.* Edited by David B. Mattern et al. Charlottesville: University of Virginia Press, 2009. One volume to date, covering March 1817 to January 1820.

JMP-LC   James Madison Papers, Library of Congress. Most of the James Madison letters not yet published in *The Papers of James Madison* can be accessed in digitized form at the Library of Congress Web site, http://memory.loc.gov/ammem/collections/madison _papers.

CM I   Cutts Memoir I. Schlesinger Library, Radcliffe Institute for Advanced Study, Cambridge, MA.

CM II   Cutts Memoir II. Cutts Family Papers, Manuscript Division, Library of Congress, Washington, DC. Dolley Madison's niece, Mary Estelle Elizabeth Cutts, wrote two overlapping memoirs on the life of her aunt in the early 1850s. They will be published for the first time in *The Queen of America: Mary Cutts's Life of Dolley Madison,* edited by Catherine Allgor, Charlottesville: University of Virginia Press, 2012.

AUTHOR'S NOTE

1. *A Colored Man's Reminiscences of James Madison* is the first White House memoir according to the White House Historical Association, http://www.whitehousehistory.org/whha_publications/publications_documents/whitehousehistory_01-jennings.pdf, and William Seale, *The President's House,* vol. 1 (Washington, DC: The White House Historical Association, 1986), 122; G. Franklin Edwards and Michael R. Winston, "Commentary: The Washington of Paul Jennings—White House Slave, Free Man, and Conspirator for Freedom," *White House History* 1 (1983).

2. "Letters of a Convalescent, No. XIII, Montpelier—Residence of the Late President Madison," *The Madisonian,* Washington, DC, 26 October 1839. For the identity of the "convalescent" as Thomas Allen, see "Thomas Allen, President of the Pacific Railroad," *The Western Journal and Civilian* 9 (1852-1853): 425.

3. John H. Paynter, *Fugitives of the Pearl* (Washington, DC: Associated Publishers, 1930), 25.

CHAPTER ONE: "RAISED AND NURTURED"

1. For the Madisons and their slaves during this early period, see Douglas B. Chambers, *Murder at Montpelier: Igbo Africans in Virginia* (Jackson:

University Press of Mississippi, 2005), and Ann L. Miller, *The Short Life and Strange Death of Ambrose Madison* (Orange, VA: Orange County Historical Society, 2001).

2. Ann L. Miller, *Antebellum Orange: The Pre–Civil War Homes, Public Buildings and Historic Sites of Orange County, Virginia* (Orange, VA: Orange County Historical Society, 1988), 113–115, 119–121.

3. Paul Jennings, *A Colored Man's Reminiscences of James Madison* (Brooklyn: George C. Beadle, 1865), preface.

4. W. W. Scott, *A History of Orange County, Virginia* (Richmond, VA: Everett Waddey Co., 1907), 208.

5. Ralph Ketcham, *James Madison: A Biography* (Charlottesville: University of Virginia Press, 1990), 25; Cutts Memoir II, Cutts Family Papers, Manuscript Division, Library of Congress, Washington, DC, 36 (hereafter CM II).

6. Robert Rutland, *James Madison: The Founding Father* (Columbia: University of Missouri Press, 1986), 10; Douglass Adair, ed., "James Madison's Autobiography," *William and Mary Quarterly* 2 (1945): 198; Ketcham, *Biography,* 72–76.

7. Thomas Jefferson to James Monroe, 18 December 1786, *Papers of Thomas Jefferson,* edited by Julian P. Boyd (Princeton, NJ: Princeton University Press, 1954), vol. 10: 612; Thomas Jefferson to James Madison, 20 February 1784, *The Papers of James Madison, Congressional Series,* edited by William T. Hutchinson et al. (Chicago: University of Chicago Press, 1962–1977; Charlottesville: University of Virginia Press, 1977-1991), 7: 428 (hereafter PJM-CS); James Madison to Thomas Jefferson, 16 March 1784, PJM-CS 8: 13; Ketcham, *Biography,* 144–149; James Madison to Edmund Randolph, 26 July 1785, PJM-CS 8: 328; James Madison to Thomas Jefferson, 27 April 1785, PJM-CS 8: 270; Will of James Madison Sr., 17 September 1787, James Madison Papers, Manuscript Division, Library of Congress; Instructions for the Montpelier Overseer and Laborers, November 1790, PJM-CS 13: 302–304.

8. Jennings, *Reminiscences,* 17; "Madison's Body-Servant," *Milwaukee Sentinel,* 18 May 1884, for identification of Ben Stewart as Sukey's son, see chapter 5; Paul Jennings to Dolley Payne Madison, 23 April 1844, in David B. Mattern and Holly C. Shulman, eds., *The Selected Letters of Dolley Payne Madison* (Charlottesville: University of Virginia Press, 2003), 370.

9. James Morton Smith, ed., *The Republic of Letters: The Correspondence between Thomas Jefferson and James Madison* (New York: W. W. Norton,

1995), vol. 2: 1139–1141; James Madison to Thomas Jefferson, 28 February 1801, PJM-CS 17: 475.

10. Mattern and Shulman, *Selected Letters,* 38–40; John Cotton Smith quoted in "Washington, DC," *Harper's Weekly,* 13 March 1869, 170.

11. For background on Dolley Madison, see Catherine Allgor, *A Perfect Union: Dolley Madison and the Creation of the American Nation* (New York: Henry Holt and Company, 2006); Ketcham, *Biography,* 377, 378 for "dear husband and little babe" quote; Cutts Memoir I, Schlesinger Library, Radcliffe Institute for Advanced Study, Cambridge, MA, 8 (hereafter CM I).

12. "Rising young man" quoted in Ketcham, *Biography,* 159; Charles Jared Ingersoll was the first to refer to Madison as "Father of the Constitution."

13. CM I, 14; Dolley Payne Madison to Eliza Collins Lee, 15 September 1794, Dolley Madison Digital Edition, online collection of the papers of Dolley Madison edited by Holly C. Shulman, University of Virginia, accessed at http://rotunda.upress.virginia.edu:8080/dmde (hereafter DMDE); Catherine Coles to Dolley Payne Madison, 1 June 1794, DMDE.

14. CM II, 26; CM I, 6.

15. For construction of Montpelier, see Bryan Clark Green and Ann L. Miller, *Building a President's House: The Construction of James Madison's Montpelier* (Orange, VA: Montpelier Foundation, 2007); James Madison to James Monroe, 11 December 1798, PJM-CS 17: 184, and 30 January 1799, PJM-CS 17: 222.

16. Diary of Francis Taylor, 1786–1799, Virginia State Library, Richmond, VA.

17. Ibid.

18. 1800 division of the slaves of Erasmus Taylor, Deed Book 22: 59, Orange County Courthouse Records, Orange, VA.

19. Diary of Francis Taylor, 1786–1799, Virginia State Library. For background on slavery, see Peter Kolchin, *American Slavery, 1619–1877* (New York: Hill and Wang, 1993); "future increase forever" from James Madison Sr.'s will in conjunction with the female slaves he bequeathed to son James; "Mrs. Madison's Slaves," article filed 19 February for *Albany Patriot,* reprinted in the *Liberator* (Boston), 31 March 1848.

20. Edmund Berkeley Jr., "Prophet without Honor: Christopher McPherson, Free Person of Color," *Virginia Magazine of History and Biography* 77 (1969): 180–190; J. Robert Maguire, ed., *The Tour to the Northern Lakes of James Madison & Thomas Jefferson, May–June 1791* (Ticonderoga, NY: Fort Ticonderoga, 1995), 20.

21. Ketcham, *Biography,* 374–375

22. Jack N. Rakove, ed., *James Madison Writings* (New York: Library of America, 1999), 903; CM II, 35.

23. Thomas Jefferson to George Hay, 20 June 1807, Thomas Jefferson Papers, Library of Congress, online at http://memory.loc.gov/ammem/mtjquery.html; Thomas Jefferson to James Madison, 1 September 1807, Smith, ed., *Republic of Letters,* vol. 3: 1494.

24. Richard Beale Davis, ed., *Jeffersonian America: Notes on the United States of America Collected in the Years 1805–6–7 and 11–12 by Sir Augustus John Foster* (San Mateo, CA: Huntington Library, 1954), 145; Thomas Paine, *Common Sense* (Cambridge, MA: Belknap Press of Harvard University Press, 2010), 57.

25. Davis, *Foster,* 144, 307. Harriet Martineau, *Retrospect of Western Travel* (London: Saunders and Otley, 1838), 214.

26. James Madison to Thomas Jefferson, 8 August 1807; James Madison to Thomas Jefferson, 15 August 1807; Thomas Jefferson to James Madison, 16 August 1807; James Madison to Thomas Jefferson, 19 August 1807. Smith, ed., *Republic of Letters,* vol. 3: 1482, 1484, 1486, 1489.

27. Davis, *Foster,* 137–144.

28. Ibid., 141; Baron de Montlezun, "A Frenchman Visits Norfolk, Fredericksburg and Orange County, 1816, Part II: A Frenchman Visits President Madison, 1816," edited by L. G. Moffatt and J. M. Carriere, *Virginia Magazine of History and Biography* 53 (1945): 208–209.

29. Davis, *Foster,* 140–142; Thomas Allen, "Letters of a Convalescent, No. XIII, Montpelier—Residence of the Late President Madison," *Madisonian,* Washington, DC, 26 October 1839; Instructions for the Montpelier Overseer and Laborers, November 1790, PJM-CS 13:302.

30. John Finch, *Travels in the United States of America and* Canada (London: Longman, Rees, Orme, Brown, Green, and Longman, 1833), 240, 255.

31. Finch, *Travels,* 238; Dolley Madison to James Madison 5 December 1826, DMDE; Davis, *Foster,* 141–142; Lucia Stanton, *Slavery at Monticello* (Charlottesville, VA: Thomas Jefferson Memorial Foundation, 1996), 17.

32. Instructions for the Montpelier Overseer and Laborers, November 1790, PJM-CS 13: 302; Finch, *Travels,* 235; Allen, "Letters of a Convalescent"; Ralph Ketcham, ed., "An Unpublished Sketch of James Madison by James K. Paulding," *Virginia Magazine of History and Biography* 67 (1959): 436.

33. Allen, "Letters of a Convalescent"; CM II, 35; Henry Gilpin, "A Tour of Virginia in 1827: Letters of Henry D. Gilpin to his Father," edited by

Ralph D. Gray, *Virginia Magazine of History and Biography* 76 (1968): 468–469.

34. Finch, *Travels,* 239; James Madison to Dolley Payne Madison, 31 October 1805, DMDE.

35. Sylvia Jennings Alexander interviews, 2008–2009, on file with the Montpelier Foundation. This would not be dissimilar from the situation that historian Constance Green described where a slave owner "might give the slave children of his household a smattering of education by letting them sit in at lessons with his own white children" in *The Secret City: A History of Race Relations in the Nation's Capital* (Princeton, NJ: Princeton University Press, 1967), 21; Ketcham, *Biography,* 512; Ralph Ketcham, "Uncle James Madison and Dickinson College," in *Early Dickinsoniana: The Boyd Lee Spahr Lectures* (Carlisle, PA: Library of Dickinson College, 1961), 173, 189; Isabella Strange Trotter, *First Impressions of the New World on Two Travellers from the Old* (London: Longman, Brown Green, Longmans, and Roberts, 1859), 116; Jennings, *Reminiscences,* 5.

36. One gentry woman remembered going to the wedding of her mammy Maria's brother as a girl; when Mammy Maria referred to her brother as Mr. Ferguson, she asked her why she did not call him Henry, and the indignant response was: "Do you think 'cause we are black that we cyarn't have no names?" Susan Dabney Smedes, *Memorials of a Southern Planter* (Baltimore, MD: Cushings & Bailey, 1887), 86; Draft deed on the emancipation for $200 of Paul Jennings, 8 July 1845, Dolley Madison Papers, Library of Congress; John C. Fitzpatrick, ed., *The Last Will and Testament of George Washington and Schedule of his Property* (Mount Vernon, VA: Mount Vernon Ladies' Association of the Union, 1939), 4; Thomas Jefferson to James Madison, 4 April 1800, PJM-CS 17: 378.

37. James Madison Jr. to James Madison Sr., 8 September 1783, PJM-CS 7: 304 and fn. 4; Robert Rutland, ed., *James Madison and the American Nation: An Encyclopedia* (New York: Simon and Schuster, 1994), 163; James A. Bear Jr. and Lucia Stanton, *Jefferson's Memorandum Books: Accounts, with Legal Records and Miscellany, 1767–1826* (Princeton, NJ: Princeton University Press, 1997), vol. 2: 808, fn.; full quotation starts with "Knowledge will forever govern ignorance, and a people who mean . . .," James Madison to W. T. Barry, 4 August 1822, James Madison Papers, Library of Congress (hereafter JMP-LC).

38. James Madison Jr. to James Madison Sr., 8 September 1783, PJM-CS 7: 304; James Madison Jr. to James Madison Sr., 27 December 1795, PJM-CS 16: 174.

39. Thomas Jefferson's prescription for slave "education": "Children till 10. years to serve as nurses. From 10. to 16. boys make nails, girls spin. At 16. go into the ground or learn trades," quoted in Stanton, *Slavery at Monticello,* 25; Davis, *Foster,* 142.

40. Thomas Hamilton, *Men and Manners in America* (Philadelphia: Carey, Lea & Blanchard, 1833), vol. 2, 14.

CHAPTER TWO: PRESIDENTIAL HOUSEHOLD

1. Jennings is often inaccurately identified as valet to James Madison during his presidency, but Jennings states in the *Reminiscences* that he held that position for the last sixteen years of Madison's life (i.e., 1820-1836); during the White House years, given the description of Jennings's duties, footman is the appropriate designation. On wearing livery: even in the Jefferson presidential household, notable for its relaxed adherence to formality, footmen wore livery; see Lucia Stanton, "'A Well-Ordered Household': Domestic Servants in Jefferson's White House," *White House History* 17 (2006): 8. Assuming that tradition continued in Madison's White House is one rationale for describing Jennings in livery; also note that Augustus John Foster reported that black servants in Washington dressed in livery; see Richard Beale Davis, ed., *Jeffersonian America: Notes on the United States of America Collected in the Years 1805–6–7 and 11–12 by Sir Augustus John Foster* (San Mateo, CA: Huntington Library, 1954), 22. Gaillard Hunt, "Mrs. Madison's First Drawing Room," *Harpers Monthly Magazine* (June 1910): 141–148; CM I, 37; "Recollections of Matilda Lee Love," in Cazenove Gardner Lee Jr., *Lee Chronicle: Studies of the Early Generations of the Lees of Virginia,* edited by Dorothy Mills Parker (New York: New York University Press, 1957), 289.

2. Margaret Klaptor, "Benjamin Latrobe and Dolley Madison Decorate the White House," *Contributions from the Museum of History and Technology* 49 (1965): 153–164; William Seale, *The President's House,* vol. 1 (Washington, DC: White House Historical Association, 1986), 122–126 (but also see fn. 12 on p. 125); Elbridge Gerry Jr., *The Diary of Elbridge Gerry, Jr.,* preface and footnotes by Claude G. Bowers (New York: Brentano's, 1927), 181. On First Lady title, see Catherine Allgor, *A Perfect Union: Dolley Madison and the Creation of the American Nation* (New York: Henry Holt and Company, 2006), 417, n. 13; "The Drawing Room," *Weekly Visitor and Ladies' Museum,* 3 January 1818, 154; Edmund Quincy, *Life of Josiah Quincy of Massachusetts* (Boston: Fields, Osgood & Company, 1869), 198.

3. Jennings quoted in Mary Clemmer Ames, *Ten Years in Washington: Life and Scenes in the National Capital as a Woman Sees Them* (Hartford, CT: A. D. Worthington & Company, 1874), 568; Benjamin Ogle Tayloe, *Our Neighbors on La Fayette Square* (Washington, DC: Junior League of Washington reprinted 1982, first published 1872), 14; "Mrs. Madison's Slaves," article filed 19 February 1848 for *Albany Patriot,* reprinted in the *Liberator* (Boston, MA), 31 March 1848.

4. Paul Jennings, *A Colored Man's Reminiscences of James Madison* (Brooklyn: George C. Beadle, 1865), 16; Ames, *Ten Years in Washington,* 195.

5. Esther Singleton, *The Story of the White House,* vol. 1 (New York: McClure Company, 1907), 56; Sarah Ridg, 1809 Diary, Sarah Ridg Papers, Manuscript Division, Library of Congress; Margaret Bayard Smith, *The First Forty Years of Washington Society,* edited by Gaillard Hunt (New York: Charles Scribner's Sons, 1906), 59; for Madison carriage with liveried black coachman and footman, see Gaillard Hunt, "The First Inauguration Ball," *Century Illustrated Magazine* (March 1905): 757, and Seale, *President's House,* vol. 1: 131; Jennings, *Reminiscences,* 6.

6. Singleton, *Story of the White House,* 55–56 (includes Adams diary entry quoted); Christian Hines, *Early Recollections of Washington City* (Washington, DC: Junior League of Washington, reprinted 1981, first published 1866), 14–15; Smith, *First Forty Years,* 58.

7. Anna Thornton quoted in Conover Hunt-Jones, *Dolley and the Great Little Madison* (Washington, DC: American Institute of Architects Foundation, 1977), 29; Ralph Ketcham, *James Madison: A Biography* (Charlottesville: University of Virginia Press, 1990), 477; Jennings, *Reminiscences,* 5; Gerry Jr., *Diary,* 178–182; Seale, *President's House,* vol. 1: 122–126, 131; CM I, 35–36; Benjamin Henry Latrobe to Dolley Payne Madison, 21 April 1809, DMDE; for more on Stuart's Lansdowne portraits of Washington, see Betty C. Monkman, "Reminders of 1814," *White House History* 1 (1983): 35.

8. Dolley Payne Madison to John C. Payne, 21 September 1809, DMDE; CM II, 15; Joseph Dougherty to Thomas Jefferson, 15 May 1809, *Papers of Thomas Jefferson, Retirement Series,* edited by J. Jefferson Looney (Princeton, NJ: Princeton University Press, 2004), vol. 1: 199.

9. Seale, *President's House,* vol. 1: 102, 114–115, 194; Wilhelmus Bryan, *A History of the National Capital* (New York: Macmillan Company, 1914), vol. 1: 459; Jennings, *Reminiscences,* 17.

10. Paul Jennings gives the coachman's name as Bolin and Mary Cutts gives it as Bolen, but Bolden is the spelling used in documents in the DC Archives; there is no evidence that he was a Montpelier slave; CM I, 43;

Francis Scott Key to Dolley Payne Madison, 30 June 1810, DMDE; Stanton, "Well-Ordered Household," 8, 11–12, 19; John Freeman to Thomas Jefferson, 2 March 1809, Thomas Jefferson Papers, Library of Congress; Deed of John Freeman's Indenture to James Madison, 19 April 1809, *Papers of Thomas Jefferson, Retirement Series,* vol. 1: 156; Melinda Freeman, 10 October 1815, RG 217, Miscellaneous Treasury Accounts, Account 28634, National Archives and Records Administration (NARA); John H. McCormick, "The First Master of Ceremonies of the White House," *Records of the Columbia Historical Society of Washington, DC* 7 (1904): 170-194; CM I, 42; Seale, *President's House,* vol. 1: 122.

11. CM I, 42, 43; Jennings, *Reminiscences,* 9, 13; Gerry Jr., *Diary,* 181–182; for Sioussat identified as porter, see "Scenes of the Last War—Mrs. Madison's Flight from Washington," *Cleveland (Ohio) Herald,* 22 May 1849; for floor plan drawn by Benjamin Latrobe in 1803 with "porter's lodge" labeled, see Hunt-Jones, *Dolley and the Great Little Madison,* 32; Betty Monkman, former White House curator, e-mail message to author, 30 September 2010.

12. Stanton, "Well-Ordered Household," 10; Benjamin Grayson Orr to James Madison, 25 July 1801, *The Papers of James Madison, Secretary of State Series,* edited by Robert J. Brugger et al. (Charlottesville: University of Virginia Press, 1986–2011), 1: 482 (hereafter PJM-SS); and Benjamin Grayson Orr to James Madison, 25 June 1802, PJM-SS 3: 340; Francis H. Rozer to James Madison, 25 October 1801, PJM-SS 2: 203, and Francis H. Rozer to James Madison, 26 October 1802, PJM-SS 4: 59; Dolley Payne Madison to Eliza Custis Law, 17 October 1804, DMDE; Katherine Anthony, *Dolley Madison: Her Life and Times* (Garden City, NY: Doubleday and Company, 1949), 113; one example of a free person employed by the job was upholsterer Mary Sweeny, see Conover Hunt-Jones, *Dolley and the Great Little Madison,* 37.

13. Benjamin Henry Latrobe to Dolley Payne Madison, 8 September 1809, DMDE. There is no evidence that Sioussat was a chef, although later steward Henry Doyhar had cooking skills (see Benjamin Latrobe to Dolley Madison, 27 August 1813, DMDE, and Henry Doyhar to James Madison, 19 May 1814 letter, Papers of James Madison, Manuscript Division, Library of Congress). There are references to other White House cooks during Madison's second term in addition to Doyhar, including Pierre Roux (Pierre Roux to James Madison, 20 November 1816, JMP-LC) and an unnamed Montpelier slave, "a young fellow who was educated in Washington a cook" (James Madison to James Monroe, 19 November 1820, JMP-LC); Stanton, "Well-Ordered Household," 19;

Josephine Seaton, *William Winston Seaton of the "National Intelligencer," a Biographical Sketch* (Boston: J. R. Osgood and Company, 1871), 84–85.

14. William C. Preston, *Reminiscences of William C. Preston,* edited by Minnie Clare Yarborough (Chapel Hill: University of North Carolina Press, 1933), 9; Helen Duprey Bullock, "A View from the Square," *Historic Preservation* 19 (1967): 53; Frances F. Donaldson, *The President's Square* (New York: Vantage Press, 1968), 13; Seale, *President's House,* vol. 1: 38.

15. Edmund Bacon in James A. Bear Jr., ed., *Jefferson at Monticello: Recollections of a Monticello Slave and a Monticello Overseer* (Charlottesville: University of Virginia Press, 1967), 105; Jennings, *Reminiscences,* 5–6; Thomas Hamilton, *Men and Manners in America* (Philadelphia: Carey, Lea & Blanchard, 1833), vol. 2: 17.

16. Henry Cogswell Knight (published under the pseudonym of Arthur Singeleton), *Letters from the South and West* (Boston: Richardson and Lord, 1824), 40; Pierre M. Irving, *The Life and Letters of Washington Irving* (New York: G. P. Putnam, 1863), vol. 1: 269, 273; Hamilton, *Men and Manners,* vol. 2: 73; Henry Fearon, *Narrative of a Journey of Five Thousand Miles through the Eastern and Western States of America* (London: Longman, Hurst, Rees, Orme, and Brown, 1818), 290; Gerry Jr., *Diary,* 149.

17. Constance Green, *The Secret City: A History of Race Relations in the Nation's Capital* (Princeton, NJ: Princeton University Press, 1967), 33, 43; Constance Green, *Washington: Village and Capital, 1800–1878* (Princeton, NJ: Princeton University Press, 1962), 54; Henry S. Robinson, "Some Aspects of the Free Negro Population of Washington, DC, 1800–1862," *Maryland Historical Magazine* 64 (1969): 44–46.

18. Michael Shiner, *The Diary of Michael Shiner Relating to the History of the Washington Navy Yard 1813–1869,* edited by John G. Sharp (Navy Department Library online, 2007), www.history.navy.mil/library/online/shinerdiary.html; Thomas Howard will, http://genealogytrails.com/washdc/howard_will.html; T. Stephen Whitman, *The Price of Freedom: Slavery and Manumission in Baltimore and Early National Maryland* (Lexington: University Press of Kentucky, 1997), 51; Charles Ball, *Slavery in the United States: A Narrative of the Life and Adventures of Charles Ball, a Black Man* (New York: John S. Taylor, Brick Church Chapel, 1837), 27–28.

19. James Oliver Horton, "The Genesis of Washington's African American Community," in *Urban Odyssey: A Multicultural History of Washington, DC,* edited by Francine Curro Cary (Washington, DC: Smithsonian

Institution Press, 1996), 26. For overview on Edward Coles, see Kurt E. Leichtie and Bruce Garveth, *Crusade Against Slavery: Edward Cole, Pioneer of Freedom* (Carbondale: Southern Illinois University Press, 2011); Ralph L. Ketcham, "The Dictates of Conscience: Edward Coles and Slavery," *Virginia Quarterly Review* 36 (1960): 52; Thomas Jefferson to Richard Price, 7 August 1785, *Papers of Thomas Jefferson,* edited by Julian P. Boyd et al. (Princeton, NJ: Princeton University Press, 1953), vol. 8: 357.

20. Hamilton, *Men and Manners,* vol. 2: 73–74.

21. Baron de Montlezun, "A Frenchman Visits Norfolk, Fredericksburg and Orange County, 1816, Part II: A Frenchman Visits President Madison, 1816," edited by L. G. Moffatt and J. M. Carriere, *The Virginia Magazine of History and Biography* 53 (1945): 201.

22. Smith, *First Forty Years,* 81–83.

23. Bryan Clark Green and Ann L. Miller, *Building a President's House: The Construction of James Madison's Montpelier* (Orange, VA: Montpelier Foundation, 2007), 18, 24, 27–28; James Dinsmore to James Madison, 29 October 1809, *The Papers of James Madison, Presidential Series,* edited by Robert A. Rutland et al. (Charlottesville: University of Virginia Press, 1984–2008), vol. 2: 44–45 (hereafter PJM-PS); for a full analysis of Montpelier room use see chapter 4.

24. Ketcham, *Biography,* 496; George Jackson, *The Bath Archives: A Further Selection from the Diaries and Letters of Sir George Jackson from 1809 to 1816* (London: Richard Bentley and Son), vol. 1: 20; Davis, *Foster,* 84.

25. Jennings, *Reminiscences,* 6. Dolley Madison left a somewhat different version from Jennings: see Dolley Madison to Edward Coles, 31 August 1812, DMDE, where she describes President Madison getting the news of Hull's surrender en route to Montpelier and turning back to Washington.

26. Jennings, *Reminiscences,* 6; Mary Latrobe quoted in John E. Semmes, *John H. B. Latrobe and His Times* (Baltimore, MD: Norman Remington Co., 1917), 15, 17; Seaton, *William Winston Seaton,* 99.

27. Jennings, *Reminiscences,* 7; Gerry Jr., *Diary,* 188–189, 193–195; CM I, 67; on Gerry Jr. visiting the public baths, *Diary,* 155, 184, see Bryan, *History of the National Capital,* vol. 1: 517, fn. 5 on public baths in Washington; Gerry Jr. and soda water quotation is *Diary,* 154; there are more than half a dozen additional references to this penchant for carbonated water in the diary, for example, 168–169: "They were all *high* and their eyes showed they were *half-seasoned.*"

28. Gerry Jr., *Diary*, 203, 179–181, 178, 167–168; James Madison to
     Thomas Jefferson, 15 January 1823, in James Morton Smith, ed., *The
     Republic of Letters: The Correspondence between Thomas Jefferson and
     James Madison* (New York: W. W. Norton, 1995), 3: 1854.

29. Jennings, *Reminiscences*, 7–8; Irving Brant, *James Madison, Volume Six:
     Commander in Chief* (Indianapolis, IN: Bobbs-Merrill Company, 1961),
     317; Ball, *Slavery in the United States*, 467–468, 482–483.

30. Smith, *First Forty Years*, 91, 113; Gerry Jr., *Diary*, 199; Jennings,
     Reminiscences, 8–9; Anna Thornton, "Diary of Mrs. William Thorn-
     ton, Capture of Washington by the British," edited by W. B. Bryan,
     Records of the Columbia Historical Society of Washington, DC 19
     (1916): 175.

31. Jennings, *Reminiscences*, 9, 12–13. Jennings does not mention the "two
     gentlemen of New York," Jacob Barker and Robert DePeyster; the quota-
     tion referring to them is in Dolley Madison to Lucy Payne Washington
     Todd, 23–24 August 1814, DMDE; also see David B. Mattern, "Dolley
     Madison Has the Last Word: The Famous Letter," *White House History* 1
     (1983): 38–43. For Sioussat's crediting Jennings with holding the ladder,
     see McCormick, "First Master of Ceremonies," 181–83; Jennings cred-
     ited Sioussat and the gardener Thomas McGraw with actually removing
     the portrait from the wall; McGraw is also mentioned (though Jennings
     is not) in "Scenes of the Last War—Mrs. Madison's Flight from Wash-
     ington," *Cleveland (Ohio) Herald*, 22 May 1849, for which Sioussat was
     a source; this newspaper article also confirms Jennings's statement that
     Dolley Madison left in a carriage with Sukey (referred to as "little black
     girl" in the article) before the portrait was removed from the mansion.
     Reference to "two colored boys" is Jacob Barker letter of 8 February 1848
     reproduced in *Incidents in the Life of Jacob Barker* (originally published
     in Washington, 1855, reprinted Ann Arbor: University of Michigan Li-
     brary, 2006), 114. For the wealth of false information connected with
     this episode, see chapter 7.

32. Jennings, *Reminiscences*, 9–11.

33. Shiner, *Diary*, 6–7, 9.

34. Thornton, "Diary," 179; Smith, *First Forty Years*, 109; CM I, 56–57;
     Singleton, *Story of the White House*, 77; George McCue, *The Octagon*
     (Washington, DC: American Institute of Architects Foundation, 1976),
     59–60; CM II, 40; Shiner, *Diary*, 10; Dolley Madison to Mary Latrobe,
     3 December 1814, quoted in Talbot Hamlin, *Benjamin Henry Latrobe*
     (New York: Oxford University Press, 1955), 304.

35. Jennings, *Reminiscences,* 11; George Ticknor, *Life, Letters, and Journals of George Ticknor,* (Boston: James R. Osgood and Company, 1876), vol. 1: 29.

36. Frank A. Updyke, *The Diplomacy of the War of 1812* (Baltimore, MD: Johns Hopkins Press, 1915), 361–362. Updyke states that although Henry Carroll, another American secretary, and Anthony Baker, secretary of the British delegation, sailing together with the ratified copy of the treaty, landed in New York on 11 February, it was Hughes, whose ship landed at Annapolis, who reached Washington first and that Madison accepted Hughes's unratified copy of the treaty the evening it arrived, 14 February, and sent it on to the Senate the next day; Jennings, *Reminiscences,* 13–16, Jennings recalled that news of the peace treaty and of General Jackson's victory at New Orleans reached Washington about the same time, and they did, but news of the 8 January battle came first, on 4 February, followed by word of the treaty, which had been agreed to on 24 December, on 14 February; Ketcham, *Biography,* 596–597, 599; Dolley Madison to Hannah Gallatin, 26 December 1814, DMDE; Hamilton, *Men and Manners,* vol. 2: 14.

37. CM I, 42–43; Seale, *President's House,* vol. 1: 138; Benjamin Latrobe to Dolley Madison, 27 August 1813, DMDE; Benjamin Latrobe to Henry Doyhar, 4 September 1813, quoted in Talbot Hamlin, *Benjamin Henry Latrobe* (New York: Oxford University Press, 1955), 394, fn. 19; Henry Doyhar, 3 November 1813 and 3 January 1814 and 1 March 1814, RG 217, Miscellaneous Treasury Accounts, Account 29494, NARA; Henry Doyhar to James Madison, 19 May 1814 letter, Papers of James Madison, Manuscript Division, Library of Congress; John Freeman, 21 January 1817, Miscellaneous Treasury Accounts, NARA; Thomas Johnson Bill of Sale to John Shorter and John Freeman, 5 November 1816, Liber A.M. 334/243, No. 37, NARA; Stanton, "Well-Ordered Household," 9; for Shorter working for Madison, see James Madison to Dolley Madison, 23 August 1814, DMDE, and James Madison to Joseph Dougherty, 16 February 1819, *The Papers of James Madison, Retirement Series,* edited by David B. Mattern et al. (Charlottesville: University of Virginia Press, 2009), vol. 1: 418 (hereafter PJM-RS).

38. CM II, 78–79, Clay quoted in Ketcham, *Biography,* 601; Preston, *Reminiscences,* 10.

39. Jennings, *Reminiscences,* 12; Charles Hurd, *Washington Cavalcade* (New York: E. P. Dutton and Co., 1948), 53; Fearon, *Narrative of a Journey,* 286–288.

40. Hamilton, *Men and Manners,* vol. 2: 74; Jesse Torrey Jr., *A Portraiture of Domestic Slavery in the United States* (Philadelphia: Printed by John Bioren, 1817), 33, 40, 41, 42–43, 32.

41. Elijah H. Mills, "Letters of Hon. Elijah H. Mills," *Proceedings of the Massachusetts Historical Society* 19 (1881–1882): 16, 18; Allen C. Clark, *The Life and Letters of Dolly Madison* (Washington, DC: Press of W. F. Roberts Company, 1914), 194; Hunt, "Mrs. Madison's First Drawing Room," 143.

42. Jesse Torrey Jr. to James Madison, 3 March 1833 and 15 January 1822, James Madison to Jesse Torrey Jr., 30 January 1822, all JMP-LC; Mills, "Letters of Hon. Elijah H. Mills," 20.

43. "Letters of Hon. Elijah H. Mills," 22; James Madison to Charles Carroll, 4 April 1817, PJM-RS 1: 22; Robert L. Madison to James Madison, 21 January 1817, Founders Early Access: http://rotunda.upress.virginia .edu/founders/FOEA.html.

44. James K. Paulding, *Literary Life of J. K. Paulding,* compiled by William I. Paulding (New York: Charles Scribner and Company, 1867), 74.

CHAPTER THREE: "ENAMOURED WITH FREEDOM"

1. Account with Charles Taylor, 27 August 1818, PJM-RS 1: 352; Ralph Ketcham, *James Madison: A Biography* (Charlottesville: University of Virginia Press, 1990), 646; John Adams to Thomas Jefferson, 26 May 1817, Thomas Jefferson Papers, Library of Congress Web site: http://memory. loc.gov/ammem/mtjquery.html.

2. Mary Bagot, wife of the French minister, visiting in October 1817, "Exile in Yankeeland: The Journal of Mary Bagot 1816–1819," edited by David Hosford, *Records of the Columbia Historical Society of Washington, DC* 51 (1984): 47; unidentified visitor about 1833, "Mr. Madison," reprinted in *Baltimore Patriot,* 22 August 1834; Baron de Montlezun, "A Frenchman Visits Norfolk, Fredericksburg and Orange County, 1816, Part II: A Frenchman Visits President Madison, 1816," edited by L. G. Moffatt and J. M. Carriere, *Virginia Magazine of History and Biography* 53 (1945): 201; Drew R. McCoy, *The Last of the Fathers: James Madison and the Republican Legacy* (New York: Cambridge University Press, 1989), 282–284; James Madison, Memorandum on an African Colony for Freed Slaves, c. 20 October 1789, PJM-CS 12: 437–438. Madison referred to 600,000 in 1789, but by 1819 he was using the number 1.5 million.

3. Philip Alexander Bruce, *History of the University of Virginia, 1819–1919* (New York: Macmillan Company, 1820), vol. 1: 200–201; account with Charles Taylor, 27 August 1818, PJM-RS 1: 352.

4. CM II, 33, 37; Margaret Bayard Smith, *The First Forty Years of Washington Society,* edited by Gaillard Hunt (New York: Charles Scribner's Sons, 1906), 237; James K. Paulding, "An Unpublished Sketch of James Madison," edited by Ralph L. Ketcham, *Virginia Magazine of History and Biography* 67 (1959): 435.

5. CM II, 37–38.

6. John Latrobe visiting in 1832, John E. Semmes, *John H.B. Latrobe and His Times* (Baltimore, MD: Norman, Remington Co., 1917), 239; CM II, 38; Edward W. Johnston, "Madison," in *Homes of American Statesmen* (Hartford, CT: O.D. Case and Co., 1855), 188.

7. 1837 Insurance Map for Montpelier, Historical Society of Pennsylvania; Mark A. Trickett, "South Yard Excavation Report," August 2009, http://montpelier.org/explore/archaeology/reports/south_yard.pdf; John Finch, *Travels in the United States of America and* Canada (London: Longman, Rees, Orme, Brown, Green, and Longman, 1833), 239.

8. Thomas Allen, "Letters of a Convalescent, No. XIII, Montpelier—Residence of the Late President Madison," *Madisonian* (Washington, DC), 26 October 1839; CM II, 35.

9. Montlezun, "A Frenchman Visits," 213; Finch, *Travels,* 236.

10. Instructions for the Montpelier Overseer and Laborers, November 1790, PJM-CS 13: 304.

11. Paul Jennings, *A Colored Man's Reminiscences of James Madison* (Brooklyn: George C. Beadle, 1865), 16; James Madison to Richard Cutts, 13 July 1817, PJM-RS 1: 86; Henry Barnard, "The South Atlantic States in 1833 as Seen by a New Englander," edited by Bernard C. Steiner, *Maryland Historical Magazine* 13 (1918): part 3, 381; Semmes, *John H. B. Latrobe and His Times,* 239; Montlezun, "A Frenchman Visits," 199; unidentified visitor about August 1820, "Montpelier, the Seat of Mr. Madison," *Daily National Intelligencer* (Washington, DC), 9 August 1820; Paulding, "Sketch of James Madison," 435–436.

12. Montlezun, "A Frenchman Visits," 199; Allen, "Letters of a Convalescent."

13. CM II, 40, 45; Jennings, *Reminiscences,* 17.

14. CM I, 43; Jennings, *Reminiscences,* 18; "Mrs. Madison's Slaves," article filed 19 February for *Albany Patriot,* reprinted in the *Liberator* (Boston, MA), 31 March 1848; "Mrs. Madison's Slaves Again," *Albany Patriot,* 15 March 1848.

15. CM II, 66; Gaillard Hunt, *The Life of James Madison* (New York: Doubleday, Page and Co., 1902), 381.

16. Jennings, *Reminiscences,* 17; Robert Roberts, *The House Servant's Directory, An African American Butler's 1827 Guide* (republished Mineola, NY: Dover Publications, 2006), 35.

17. Benjamin Ogle Tayloe, *Our Neighbors on La Fayette Square* (Washington, DC: Junior League of Washington reprinted 1982, first published 1872), 14; Smith, *First Forty Years,* 236; CM II, 66.

18. Hunt, *Life of James Madison,* 381; James A. Bear Jr. and Lucia Stanton, *Jefferson's Memorandum Books: Accounts, with Legal Records and Miscellany, 1767–1826* (Princeton, NJ: Princeton University Press, 1997), vol. 2: 815, fn.

19. Ralph Ketcham, *The Madisons at Montpelier: Reflections on the Founding Couple* (Charlottesville: University of Virginia Press, 2009), 95. James Madison to Dolley Madison, 4 December 1826, DMDE; Dolley Madison to James Madison, 5 December 1826, DMDE; James Madison to Dolley Madison, 17 July 1827, DMDE.

20. Jennings, *Reminiscences,* 18; Lucia Stanton, *Free Some Day: The African-American Families of Monticello* (Charlottesville, VA: Thomas Jefferson Memorial Foundation, 2000), 120–125, 129; Thomas Jefferson to James Madison, 11 April 1820, in *The Republic of Letters: The Correspondence between Thomas Jefferson and James Madison,* edited by James Morton Smith (New York: W. W. Norton and Company, 1995), 1824.

21. "Once the Slave of Thomas Jefferson," *New York World,* 30 January 1898.

22. James A. Bear Jr., ed., *Jefferson at Monticello: Recollections of a Monticello Slave and a Monticello Overseer* (Charlottesville: University of Virginia Press, 1967), 102–103; Thomas Jefferson to John Barnes, 14 June 1817, quoted in Stanton, *Free Some Day,* 64; Thruston Hern was, in Edmund Bacon's words, "never recovered."

23. Sylvia Jennings Alexander interviews, 2008–2009, on file with the Montpelier Foundation; CM I, 43; on the same page Cutts claims that Jennings's yearning for freedom took him to New York and that "when his funds were exhausted he remembered his home of ease, and wrote imploringly his master to receive him again, which he did, and believing in his repentance, his journey to New York was never mentioned," but no support for this unlikely scenario is known. Ellen Randolph to Martha Jefferson Randolph, 28 January 1818, Ellen Wayles Randolph Coolidge Correspondence, University of Virginia.

24. John H. B. Latrobe to William C. Rives, 9 May 1866, William C. Rives Papers, Manuscript Division, Library of Congress; Henry Gilpin, "A Tour of Virginia in 1827: Letters of Henry D. Gilpin to His Father," edited by Ralph D. Gray, *Virginia Magazine of History and Biography* 76 (1968): 470; Smith, *First Forty Years,* 235.

25. Semmes, *John H. B. Latrobe,* 243; CM II, 41; List of Articles in Dining Room at Montpelier, 1 July 1836, DMDE. The image that Mary Cutts described as an "African king" is apparently the same one referred to in the dining room inventory as "likeness of a Negroes Head." Will of James Madison Sr., 17 September 1787, James Madison Papers, Manuscript Division, Library of Congress; Smith, *First Forty Years,* 234–235.

26. James Brooks, Washington correspondent of the *Portland Advertiser,* visiting in May 1833, "Visit to Mr. Madison," *Niles Register* (Baltimore), 17 August 1833; George C. Shattuck Jr. to Dr. George C. Shattuck, 24 January 1835, George Shattuck Papers, Massachusetts Historical Society; Semmes, *John H. B. Latrobe,* 239–240; Roberts, *House Servant's Directory.*

27. Barnard, "South Atlantic States in 1833," 319, recalling Shirley, the Carter estate; Hunt, *Life of Madison,* 382; CM I, 34; Jennings, *Reminiscences,* 17–18; Memoirs of Thomas Jefferson Randolph, 1874, Edgehill-Randolph Papers, University of Virginia.

28. William C. Rives Papers, Box 132, Manuscript Division, Library of Congress; Madison told Charles Ingersoll that of his one hundred slaves, nearly two-thirds were too young or too old to work much, and to Harriet Martineau he mentioned that one-third of his slaves were children under five.

29. "Madison's Servant," *Decatur Republican,* 14 June 1886; "Old Ailsey Payne at Montpelier," clipping from an unidentified c. 1907 newspaper, found in Marion duPont Scott's scrapbook, of an article based on an interview conducted "a few years ago," Montpelier archives.

30. CM II, 35; James Madison to Nelly Conway Madison, 20 October 1809, PJM-PS 2: 22; Paul Jennings in Orange to Sukey in Washington, 13 May 1844, Dolley Madison Papers, Manuscript Division, Library of Congress; Sylvia Jennings Alexander interviews, 2008–2009.

31. CM II, 36–37, 39.

32. Paulding, "Sketch of James Madison," 435; "The Autobiography of Mrs. William Cabell Rives," William C. Rives Papers, Manuscript Division, Library of Congress, 67; "Madison's Servant."

33. Montlezun, "A Frenchman Visits," 199; CM II, 78–79; Allen C. Clark, *The Life and Letters of Dolly Madison* (Washington, DC: Press of W. F. Roberts Company, 1914), 208; Ketcham, *Biography,* 616.

34. Maud Wilder Goodwin, *Dolly Madison* (New York: Charles Scribner's Sons, 1896), 235; Ketcham, *Biography,* 616–618; for Chapman and Jennings in Washington, see chapter 6; Roberts, *House Servant's Directory,* 56.

35. Dolley Madison to Anna Payne Cutts, 5 July 1816, DMDE; Sarah Conway as reported by Hunt, *Life of Madison,* 381; Anne Mercer Slaughter, "Personal Reminiscences of a Daughter of the Revolution," edited by Jacob Lychenheim, *New Peterson Magazine* 3 (1894): 566; the phrase "a bit of faery in the prosaic world" was given as "fairyland in this prosaic world" when this article was reprinted with numerous changes in *Tyler's Quarterly Magazine* in 1937; Matthew Reeves, "A Brief History of the Montpelier Landscape," August 2009, http://montpelier.org/explore /archaeology/media/pdf/Brief_Landscape_History.pdf; George C. Shattuck Jr. to Dr. George C. Shattuck; Montlezun, "A Frenchman Visits," 202.

36. George C. Shattuck Jr. to Dr. George C. Shattuck; Slaughter, "Personal Reminiscences," 566; Sarah Worthington King Peter, mid-August 1835 letter to her mother, in Anna Shannon McAllister, *In Winter We Flourish: Life and Letters of Sarah Worthington King Peter* (New York: Longman, Green and Co., 1939), 107; James Monroe to James Madison, 25 July 1810, PJM-PS 2: 437; CM II, 38–39, 43–44.

37. Slaughter, "Personal Reminiscences," 566; CM II, 44; Jennings, *Reminiscences,* 13–14; Finch, *Travels,* 237–238.

38. Ann L. Miller, *Antebellum Orange: The Pre–Civil War Homes, Public Buildings and Historic Sites of Orange County, Virginia* (Orange, VA: Orange County Historical Society, 1988), 119–120; Bishop William Meade, *Old Churches, Ministers, and Families of Virginia* (Philadelphia: J. B. Lippincott and Co., 1857), vol. 2: 96–97; Ralph Dornfeld Owen, "Howard, an Early Philadelphia Family," *Pennsylvania Genealogical Magazine* 21 (1959): 209–213.

39. 1795 inventory of the estate of Erasmus Taylor, Will Book 3: 332, and 1800 division of the slaves of Erasmus Taylor, Deed Book 22: 59, Orange County Courthouse Records, Orange, VA.

40. 1789 will of Erasmus Taylor, Will Book 3: 321, Orange County Courthouse Records, Orange, VA; that Fanny was lady's maid to a mistress of the Taylor family is based on Franklin Jennings's c. 1901 interview with Assistant Librarian of Congress Daniel Murray, although Franklin erroneously described her as a sister of President Zachary Taylor. Daniel Murray, *Paul Jennings and His Times, President Madison's Biographer and Valet,* Miscellaneous Manuscripts Collection 1970, Library of Congress;

Dolley Madison to Anna Payne Cutts, c. 23 July 1818, DMDE; CM I, 17.

41. Charles P. Howard to James Madison, 8 March 1818, PJM-RS 1: 235–236; *Franklin Jennings v. Elizabeth Webb*, 1896, case file #470, Records of the United States Court of Appeals, District of Columbia, Record Group 276, National Archives and Records Administration (NARA); 1800 division of the slaves of Erasmus Taylor, Deed Book 22: 59, and 1856 inventory of the estate of Charles P. Howard, Will Book 12: 245, Orange County Courthouse Records, Orange, VA; Dolley Madison to Anna Payne Cutts, c. 23 July 1818, DMDE; *The Duties of a Lady's Maid with Directions for Conduct, and Numerous Receipts for the Toilette* (London: Printed for James Bulcock, 1825), table of contents.

42. Murray, *Paul Jennings and His Times;* deposition of Edmund Spotsey, *Franklin Jennings v. Elizabeth Webb*, 1896, case file #470; Stanton, *Free Some Day,* 61; Diary of Francis Taylor, 1786–1799, Virginia State Library, Richmond, VA.

43. John Henshaw to James Madison, 10 October 1824, Founders Early Access: http://rotunda.upress.virginia.edu/founders/FOEA.html.

44. James Madison to Jedidiah Morse, 28 March 1823, JMP-LC; James Madison to Robert J. Evans, 15 June 1819, PJM-RS 1: 471.

45. CM I, 36; Edward Coles to Hugh Blair Grigsby, 23 December 1854, quoted in Ralph L. Ketcham, "The Dictates of Conscience: Edward Coles and Slavery," *Virginia Quarterly Review* 36 (1960): 59; Kurt E. Leichtie and Bruce Carveth, *Crusade against Slavery: Edward Coles, Pioneer of Freedom* (Carbondale: Southern Illinois University Press, 2011), 61; also see Edward Coles to James Madison, 20 July 1819, PJM-RS 1: 487–488.

46. James Madison to Robert J. Evans, 15 June 1819, PJM-RS 1: 468–473; James Madison to Thomas R. Dew, 23 February 1833, JMP-LC.

47. James Madison to Robert J. Evans, 15 June 1819, PJM-RS 1: 469; James Madison to Thomas R. Dew, 23 February 1833, JMP-LC; McCoy, *Last of the Fathers,* 277–286; James Madison to Robert Walsh, Jr., 27 November 1819 and 11 January 1820, PJM-RS 1: 553–558, 584.

48. James Madison to Francis Corbin, 26 November 1820, in *The Writings of James Madison,* edited by Gaillard Hunt (New York: G. P. Putnam's Sons, 1908), 40; James Madison to Jedidiah Morse, 28 March 1823, JMP-LC.

49. National Museum of American History exhibit, 2009; Frederick Douglass, *My Bondage and My Freedom* (New York: Miller, Orton and Mulligan, 1855), 11.

50. CM I, 35; Jennings, *Reminiscences,* 15; Brooks, "Visit to Mr. Madison"; Hunt, *Life of Madison,* 380–381; Charles J. Ingersoll, "A Visit to Mr. Madison at Montpelier," *Washington Globe,* 6 August 1836; John Payne Todd, Private Correspondence and Journal, 1816–1825, Manuscript Division, Library of Congress.

51. Dolley Madison to Anna Payne Cutts, c. 23 July 1818, DMDE; Dolley Madison to Richard Cutts, 11 August 1833, DMDE; Dolley Madison to Mary Cutts, October 1835, DMDE.

52. Finch, *Travels,* 243–244; Gilpin, "Tour of Virginia," 469–470; Basil Hall, *Travels in North America, in the Years 1827 and 1828* (Edinburgh: Cadell and Company, 1829), vol. 3: 201.

53. Finch, *Travels,* 244, 239; Harriet Martineau, *Retrospect of Western Travel* (London: Saunders and Otley, 1838), 193; James Madison to Jedidiah Morse, 28 March 1823, JMP-LC; Richard Beale Davis, ed., *Jeffersonian America: Notes on the United States of America Collected in the Years 1805– 6–7 and 11–12 by Sir Augustus John Foster* (San Mateo, CA: Huntington Library, 1954), 136.

54. Finch, *Travels,* 244, 247–248; Jennings, *Reminiscences,* 17; deposition of Edmund Spotsey.

55. James Madison to Dolley Madison, 5 November 1824, DMDE; James Madison to Thomas Jefferson, 17 October 1784, PJM-CS 8: 121; Joseph J. Ellis, *Founding Brothers: The Revolutionary Generation* (New York: Alfred A. Knopf, 2004), 263; James Madison to the Marquis de Lafayette, 1 February 1830, JMP-LC.

56. "Old Ailsey Payne at Montpelier," clipping from an unidentified c. 1907 newspaper; Roberts, *House Servant's Directory,* 41; CM II, 41; Slaughter, "Personal Reminiscences," 566; Cudden Davis shop ledger, Orange, VA, September 1824.

57. Montlezun, "A Frenchman Visits," 199–200, 204; Evelyn Bence, ed., *James Madison's Montpelier* (Orange, VA: Montpelier Foundation, 2008), 103–104; CM II, 44–45; Jennings, *Reminiscences,* 15.

58. Auguste Levasseur, *Lafayette in America in 1824 and 1825,* translated by Alan R. Hoffman (Manchester, NH: Lafayette Press, 2006), 243, 239; Finch, *Travels,* 235–236.

59. CM II, 35–36; Montlezun, "A Frenchman Visits," 213.

60. M. Jules Cloquet, *Recollections of the Private Life of General Lafayette* (New York: Leavitt, Lord and Company, 1836), 65–66, 282.

61. For background on Frances Wright, see Celia Morris Eckhardt, *Fanny Wright: Rebel in America* (Cambridge, MA: Harvard University Press, 1984); Frances Wright to Julia Garnett, 12 November 1824, *Harvard*

Library Bulletin 23 (1975): 229; James Madison to Frances Wright, 1 September 1825, JMP-LC.

62. Martineau, *Retrospect of Western Travel,* 195–196.

63. George Ticknor quoted in George T. Curtis, *Life of Daniel Webster* (New York: Appleton and Company, 1870), vol. 1: 223.

64. George Ticknor, *Life, Letters, and Journals of George Ticknor* (Boston: James R. Osgood and Company, 1876), vol. 1: 346–347; Daniel Webster to Jeremiah Mason, 29 December 1824, *The Papers of Daniel Webster, Correspondence,* edited by Charles M. Wiltse (Hanover, NH: University Press of New England, 1974), vol. 1: 379; Curtis, *Life of Webster,* vol. 1: 427, 220–221, 223–224.

65. "Further Excerpts from the Correspondence of Christopher Hughes of Maryland," edited by Jesse S. Reeves, *Michigan Alumnus Quarterly Review* 42 (1936): 175–176.

CHAPTER FOUR: "NOT EVEN PAUL"

1. Hugh Blair Grigsby, *The Virginia Convention of 1829–30, A Discourse Delivered before the Virginia Historical Society on 15 September 1853* (Richmond, VA: Macfarlane and Fergusson, 1854), 8; Joanne L. Gatewood, "Richmond during the Virginia Constitutional Convention of 1829-30, An Extract from the Diary of Thomas Green," *Virginia Magazine of History and Biography* 84 (1976): 307; Hugh Blair Grigsby, "Sketches of Members of the Constitutional Convention of 1829–1830," *Virginia Magazine of History and Biography* 61 (1953): 52; Dolley Madison to John C. Payne, 4 December 1829, DMDE; Diary of Robert Scott, quoted in Ralph Ketcham, *James Madison: A Biography* (Charlottesville: University of Virginia Press, 1990), 637.

2. James Monroe to James Madison, 4 October 1829, Founders Early Access: http://rotunda.upress.virginia.edu/founders/FOEA.html. *Niles Register,* 14 November 1829; this Baltimore newspaper referred to the occasion being "the Saturday before," but it was two Saturdays before 14 November, namely 31 October; see Gatewood, "Richmond during the Virginia Constitutional Convention," 304. Grigsby, *The Virginia Convention of 1829–30,* 8.

3. Dolley Madison to John C. Payne, 4 December 1829, DMDE; Deborah Logan to Sarah Logan, 22 November 1824, quoted in Ketcham, *Biography,* 623; Samuel Whitcomb Jr., visiting in June 1824, typescript memorandum, Special Collections, University of Virginia; Paul Jennings, *A*

Colored Man's Reminiscences of James Madison (Brooklyn: George C. Beadle, 1865), 18.

4. Account of Nelly Conway Madison Estate, Orange County Chancery Causes, 1833-023, *Chapman, Administrator v. Madison et al*, Library of Virginia, Richmond, VA; Samuel L. Knapp, "Literary and Intellectual Statistics," *New England Magazine* 1 (1831): 421.

5. Account of Nelly Conway Madison Estate; Advertisement, *Virginia Herald* (Fredericksburg, VA), 18 July 1829.

6. James Madison to Edward Coles, quoted in Ketcham, *Biography,* 615; Dolley Madison to Anna Payne Cutts, 6 June 1829, DMDE; CM II, 69.

7. CM II, 68; Dolley Madison to John C. Payne, 4 December 1829, DMDE.

8. Ralph Ketcham, ed., *Selected Writings of James Madison* (Indianapolis, IN: Hackett Publishing Company, 2006), 356–357; Drew R. McCoy, *The Last of the Fathers: James Madison and the Republican Legacy* (New York: Cambridge University Press, 1989), 240–250; Lance Banning, *The Sacred Fire of Liberty: James Madison and the Founding of the Federal Republic* (Ithaca, NY: Cornell University Press, 1995), 183.

9. Proceedings and Debates of the Virginia State Convention, quoted in Gaillard Hunt, *The Life of James Madison* (New York: Doubleday, Page and Co., 1902), 365–366; Grigsby, *Virginia Convention,* 8.

10. Dolley Madison to John C. Payne, 4 December 1829, DMDE; Robert S. Starobin, ed., *Blacks in Bondage: Letters of American Slaves* (New York: New Viewpoints, 1974), 72; notes on Paul Jennings, Daniel Murray Papers, Reel Five, Library of Congress.

11. David Walker, *Appeal to the Coloured Citizens of the World,* edited and with an introduction and annotations by Peter P. Hinks (University Park: Pennsylvania University Press, 2002), 67, 92.

12. Charles L. Perdue Jr. et al, *Weevils in the Wheat: Interviews with Virginia Ex-Slaves* (Charlottesville: University of Virginia Press, 1976), 49; James Madison to James Monroe, 21 January 1830, JMP-LC; Dolley Madison reported to niece Dolley Cutts, "I had, indeed, my 'quantum sufficit' of gayety in Richmond," 10 March 1830, DMDE.

13. CM II, 41–42; Henry Barnard, "The South Atlantic States in 1833 as Seen by a New Englander," edited by Bernard C. Steiner, *Maryland Historical Magazine* 13 (1918): part 3, 381; Dolley Madison to Dolley Cutts, December 1831, DMDE; Dolley Madison to Frances Lear, 14 February 1832, DMDE; James Madison to Nicholas Trist, 10 December 1831, Founders Early Access: http://rotunda.upress.virginia.edu/founders/FOEA.html.

14. CM II, 69; Dolley Madison described Paul Jennings as five foot three and one-half inches tall in the document she drafted setting his purchase price in 8 July 1845: Dolley Madison Papers, Manuscript Division, Library of Congress; Maud Wilder Goodwin, *Dolly Madison* (New York: Charles Scribner's Sons,1896), 235–236.

15. George Tucker quoted in Evert A. Duyckinck, *National Portrait Gallery of Eminent Americans* (New York: Johnson, Fry and Company, 1862), vol. 1: 392.

16. That husband and wife indeed shared a bedchamber is confirmed in Dolley Madison to James Madison, 5 December 1826, DMDE; Dolley Madison to Dolley Cutts, May 1835, DMDE.

17. James Dinsmore to James Madison, 29 October 1809, PJM-PS 2: 44–45; CM II, 86. Though many visitors to Montpelier during Madison's nineteen-year retirement described the first floor, none referred to the wing addition as a library.

18. CM II, 42. Mary Cutts's statement that the library remained upstairs is consistent with an 1840 visitor's notation that a window in the library "commands the most distant view of the road," Kate Nickleby to Louisa Nourse, October 1840, Dumbarton House Library; "Madison's Servant," *Decatur Republican,* 14 June 1886; Woody Holton, *Abigail Adams* (New York: Free Press, 2009), 115; Abigail Adams's description of her "pretty closet" with a window and a number of book shelves matches precisely the comparable second-floor space at Montpelier; Douglass Adair, ed., "James Madison's Autobiography," *William and Mary Quarterly* 2 (1945): 203.

19. Dolley Madison to Dolley Cutts, 11 May 1835, DMDE; Septimia Randolph, n.d., "Montpelier Quiet Home Life of Mr. and Mrs. Madison," Randolph-Meikleham Family Papers, University of Virginia; "Madison's Body-Servant," *Milwaukee Sentinel,* 18 May 1884.

20. "Further Excerpts from the Correspondence of Christopher Hughes of Maryland," edited by Jesse S. Reeves, *Michigan Alumnus Quarterly Review* 42 (1936): 175–176; Dolley Madison to Christopher Hughes, 2 December 1833, DMDE; George C. Shattuck Jr. to Dr. George C. Shattuck, 24 January 1835, George Shattuck Papers, Massachusetts Historical Society; unidentified visitor, "Mr. Madison," *Salem Gazette* (Massachusetts), 20 November 1835.

21. Margaret Bayard Smith, *The First Forty Years of Washington Society,* edited by Gaillard Hunt (New York: Charles Scribner's Sons, 1906), 236; M. T., "Days of My Youth," *Lippincott's Magazine of Popular Literature and Science* (December 1877): 713.

22. *Franklin Jennings v. Elizabeth Webb,* 1896, case file #470, Records of the United States Court of Appeals, District of Columbia, Record Group 276, National Archives and Records Administration (NARA); 1800 division of the slaves of Erasmus Taylor, Deed Book 22: 59, and 1856 inventory of the estate of Charles P. Howard, Will Book 12: 245, Orange County Courthouse Records, Orange, VA.

23. Henry Gilpin, "A Tour of Virginia in 1827: Letters of Henry D. Gilpin to His Father," edited by Ralph D. Gray, *Virginia Magazine of History and Biography* 76 (1968): 469; Margaret Bayard Smith, "Mrs. Madison," in Sarah Josepha Hale, *Sketches of All Distinguished Women from 'the Beginning' to 1850* (New York: Harper and Brothers, 1853), 397; unidentified visitor about 1833, "Mr. Madison," reprinted in *Baltimore Patriot,* 22 August 1834; James Brooks, Washington correspondent of the *Portland Advertiser,* visiting in May 1833, "Visit to Mr. Madison," *Niles Register* (Baltimore, MD), 17 August 1833; Charles J. Ingersoll, "A Visit to Mr. Madison at Montpelier," *Washington Globe,* 6 August 1836.

24. Susan Dunn, *Dominion of Memories: Jefferson, Madison, and the Decline of Virginia* (New York: Basic Books, 2007); Brooks, "Visit to Madison"; Christopher Hughes to Dolley Madison, 8 November 1827, DMDE.

25. James Madison to Horatio Gates, 10 March 1802, PJM-SS 3: 19; according to John Quincy Adams, quoted in Ketcham, *Biography,* 621; James Madison to James Madison Hite, 25 November 1835, JMP-LC; Ingersoll, "Visit to Madison at Montpelier."

26. Francis Corbin to James Madison, 24 September 1818, PJM-RS 1: 357; Thomas Jefferson to Stephens T. Mason, 27 October 1799, *Papers of Thomas Jefferson,* edited by Julian P. Boyd (Princeton, NJ: Princeton University Press, 1954), vol. 31: 222; Ingersoll, "Visit to Madison at Montpelier."

27. Dolley Madison to Mary Cutts, 22 January 1825, DMDE; James Madison to Edward Coles, 3 October 1834, JMP-LC; on hiring enslaved laborers, see, for example, James Madison to Isaac Winston, 18 August 1818 and 3 December 1818, PJM-RS 1: 348, 385–386.

28. Dolley Madison to Mary Cutts, October 1834, DMDE; James Madison to Edward Coles, 3 October 1834, JMP-LC; Irving Brant, *James Madison, Volume Six: Commander in Chief* (Indianapolis, IN: Bobbs-Merrill Company, 1961), 511; James Madison to William Taylor, April 1835, JMP-LC; McCoy, *Last of the Fathers,* 254–256, including quotes from John Willis to Edward Coles, 19 December 1855.

29. Brooks, "Visit to Madison"; James Madison to Edward Coles, 15 October 1834, JMP-LC; Ingersoll, "Visit to Madison at Montpelier"; Barnard,

"South Atlantic States in 1833," 379; George C. Shattuck Jr. to Dr. George C. Shattuck, 24 January 1835; CM II, 67; John C. Payne to James Madison Cutts, 20 June 1836, published in the *National Intelligencer*, Washington, DC, 2 July 1836 (also see John C. Payne to Edward Coles, 18 July 1836, DMDE).

30. Brooks, "Visit to Madison"; unidentified visitor, "Mr. Madison," *Salem Gazette* (Massachusetts), 20 November 1835; Jennings, *Reminiscences*, 18; John E. Semmes, *John H. B. Latrobe and His Times* (Baltimore, MD: Norman, Remington Co., 1917), 242; John C. Payne to James Madison Cutts, 20 June 1836.

31. Harriet Martineau, *Retrospect of Western Travel* (London: Saunders and Otley, 1838), 190–192; Mary Weston Chapman, ed., *Harriet Martineau's Autobiography* (London: Elder, Smith and Company, 1877), vol. 3: 275.

32. W. W. Scott, *A History of Orange County, Virginia* (Richmond, VA: Everett Waddey Co., 1907), 177; McCoy, *Last of the Fathers*, 307, quoting Harriet Martineau from "The Brewing of the American Storm," *Macmillan's Magazine* 6 (1862): 98–99; Martineau, *Retrospect of Western Travel*, 192–193.

33. Edward Coles to James Madison, 8 January 1832, Founders Early Access: http://rotunda.upress.virginia.edu/founders/FOEA.html.

34. Ibid.; Edward Coles to Thomas Jefferson Randolph, 29 December 1831, "Letters of Edward Coles," *William and Mary Quarterly* 7 (1927): 106; James Madison Will, April 1835, Will Book 8: 134–135, Orange County Courthouse Records, Orange County, VA.

35. James Madison to Jared Sparks, 1 June 1831, JMP-LC; CM II, 69.

36. Unidentified visitor, "Mr. Madison"; Jennings, *Reminiscences*, 18; Ralph Ketcham, ed., *Selected Writings of James Madison* (Indianapolis, IN: Hackett Publishing Company, 2006), 356; Hunt, *Life of Madison*, 384–385.

37. Jennings, *Reminiscences*, 19; James Barbour, *Eulogium upon the Life and Character of James Madison* (Washington, DC: Gales and Seaton, 1836), 28; Barbour described the June funeral of Madison at an August memorial in Orange. Edward Coles to Sally Coles Stevenson, 12 November 1836; also see Edward Coles to Sally Coles Stevenson, 28 July 1836, both available at DMDE.

38. John Willis to Edward Coles, 19 December 1855, Edward Coles Papers, Princeton University, Princeton, NJ; McCoy, *Last of the Fathers*, 320–321, including quote from Edward Coles, Memorandum, September 1849 (in this same memorandum Coles claimed that Henry Clay stated

that Dolley Madison told him "that her Husband expected her to free his slaves at her death"); "Mrs. Madison's Slaves Again," *Albany Patriot,* 15 March 1848.

39. James Madison Will, April 1835; Edward Coles to Sally Coles Stevenson, 12 November 1836, referring back to sale he witnessed in August, available at DMDE.

40. James Madison, speech at the Virginia Ratifying Convention, 17 June 1788, PJM-CS 11: 151; Gilpin, "Tour of Virginia," 469; Kurt E. Leichtie and Bruce Carveth, *Crusade against Slavery: Edward Coles, Pioneer of Freedom* (Carbondale: Southern Illinois University Press, 2011), 153; Fanny Wright wrote "Emancipation without expatriation seems impossible" to Julia Garnett, 12 November 1824, *Harvard Library Bulletin* 23 (1975): 230.

41. Quoted in David B. Cheseborough, *Frederick Douglass: Oratory from Slavery* (Westport, CT: Greenwood Press, 1998), 79.

CHAPTER FIVE: "CHANGE OF MIND"

1. Judith Walker Rives to Dolley Madison, 23 February 1837, DMDE. Payne Todd was in Washington at this time, at least by April, when George Featherstonhaugh wrote to Judith Rives's husband (Featherstonhaugh to William Cabell Rives, 10 April 1837, available at DMDE) that it is "well known that [Payne Todd's] intimates are the Blacklegs and Gamblers of Washington. Their Gigs and Flasks stand at his door, and he appears to be in their hands."

2. Frances F. Donaldson, *The President's Square* (New York: Vantage Press, 1968), 13; Talbot Hamlin, *Benjamin Henry Latrobe* (New York: Oxford University Press, 1955), 301; CM I, 53; Jacob Barker, *Incidents in the Life of Jacob Barker* (originally published in Washington, 1855, reprinted Ann Arbor: University of Michigan Library, 2006), 110.

3. CM II, 15–16, 55, 87, 77; Dolley Madison to John G. Jackson, 29 November 1822, DMDE; Dolley Madison to Margaret Bayard Smith, 10 September 1838, DMDE.

4. John H. McCormick, "The First Master of Ceremonies of the White House," *Records of the Columbia Historical Society of Washington, DC* 7 (1904): 192–194; Dolley Madison to Martha Jefferson Randolph, 6 January 1836, DMDE.

5. CM II, 89, 75–77; Dolley Madison to John Payne Todd, 23 March 1837, DMDE; Dolley Madison to Anthony Morris, 2 September 1837, DMDE; John Finch, *Travels in the United States of America and Canada*

(London: Longman, Rees, Orme, Brown, Green, and Longman, 1833), 239.

6. Dolley Madison to Mary Cutts, 16 September 1831, DMDE; James Hugo Johnston, *Race Relations in Virginia and Miscegenation in the South, 1776–1860* (Amherst: University of Massachusetts Press, 1970), 153–154; William Lloyd Garrison to George Benson, 28 September 1836, Boston Public Library.

7. CM II, 87.

8. Dolley Madison to Mary Cutts, undated (approximately 1840), Cutts Family Collection of Papers of James and Dolley Madison, Manuscript Division, Library of Congress. The phrase "sent to Coventry" means shunned or ostracized.

9. Dolley Madison to Margaret Bayard Smith, 10 September 1838, DMDE; Julia Tayloe to Dolley Madison, undated notes, Dolley Madison Papers, Special Collections, University of Virginia; "Madison's Servant," *Decatur Republican* (Michigan), 14 June 1886; Ralph Ketcham, *James Madison: A Biography* (Charlottesville: University of Virginia Press, 1990), 660; Dolley Madison to Anna Payne Cutts, 2 August 1832, DMDE.

10. Harold Donaldson Eberlein and Cortlandt Van Dyke Hubbard, *Historic Houses of Georgetown and Washington City* (Richmond, VA: Dietz Press, 1958), 272; Sarah E. Vedder, *Reminiscences of the District of Columbia* (St. Louis, MO: A. R. Fleming Printing Company, 1909), 66. For other references to Gadsby's slave trading, see Charles Hurd, *Washington Cavalcade* (New York: E. P. Dutton and Company, 1948), 102, and George Featherstonhaugh, *Excursion through the Slave States* (New York: Harper and Brothers, 1844), 37–38, fn; John Gadsby's will excerpted at www.decaturhouse.org/history_african-american-residents.html; www.syphaxfamilyreunion.com/tree.html.

11. Thomas Hamilton, *Men and Manners in America* (Philadelphia: Carey, Lea & Blanchard, 1833), vol. 2: 6; Lucia Stanton, "'A Well-Ordered Household': Domestic Servants in Jefferson's White House," *White House History* 17 (2006): 19; Solomon Northup, *Twelve Years a Slave,* edited by Sue Eakin and Joseph Logsdon (Baton Rouge: Louisiana State University Press, 1968), 15–19; Frances Anne Butler, aka Fanny Kemble, *Journal of Frances Anne Butler* (London: John Murray, 1835), 117.

12. Vedder, *Reminiscences,* 16, also see "Reminiscences of Washington, Part VII, the Tyler Administration," *Atlantic Monthly* 46 (1880): 531. Vedder's word "burying" was well chosen since those celebrating the defeat of this measure were "escorting a catafalque on which was a coffin labeled,

'The Sub-Treasury.'" Jefferson Morley, "The 'Snow' Riot," *Washington Post Magazine,* 6 February 2005; Henry Robinson, "Some Aspects of the Free Negro Population of Washington, DC, 1800–1862," *Maryland Historical Magazine* 64 (1969): 49–50; Barbara Carson, Ellen Donald, and Kym Rice, "Household Encounters: Servants, Slaves, and Mistresses in Early Washington," in *The American Home: Material Culture, Domestic Space, and Family Life,* edited by Eleanor Thompson (Winterthur, DE: Henry Francis du Pont Winterthur Museum, 1998), 89–90; Michael Shiner, *The Diary of Michael Shiner Relating to the History of the Washington Navy Yard 1813–1869,* edited by John G. Sharp (Navy Department Library online, 2007), 61, http://www.history.navy.mil/library/online /shinerdiary.html.

13. Constance Green, *The Secret City: A History of Race Relations in the Nation's Capital* (Princeton, NJ: Princeton University Press, 1967), 33; Henry Fearon, *Narrative of a Journey of Five Thousand Miles through the Eastern and Western States of America* (London: Longman, Hurst, Rees, Orme, and Brown, 1818), 286–288; Charles Dickens, *American Notes* (London: Chapman and Hall, 1842), vol. 1: 281–282; Hurd, *Washington Cavalcade,* 78; Wilhelmus Bryan, *A History of the National Capital* (New York: Macmillan Company, 1914), vol. 2: 497; Butler, aka Fanny Kemble, *Journal,* 187–188.

14. Esther Singleton, *The Story of the White House* (New York: McClure Company, 1907), vol. 1: xx–xi; George Townsend, *Washington Outside and Inside* (Hartford, CT: James Betts and Company, 1874), 198; "The Last Presidential Drawing Room," *Pennsylvanian* 28 (March 1833); Hurd, *Washington Cavalcade,* 84–85; Maud Wilder Goodwin, *Dolly Madison* (New York: Charles Scribner's Sons, 1896), 261–263; Bryan, *History of the Capital,* vol. 2: 449; Merrill Peterson, *The Great Triumvirate: Webster, Clay, and Calhoun* (New York: Oxford University Press, 1987), 324–325; Samuel Busey, *Pictures of the City of Washington in the Past* (Washington, DC: Ballantyne and Sons, 1898), 366–367; Anne Hollingsworth Wharton, *Social Life in the Early Republic* (Philadelphia: J. B. Lippincott and Company, 1902), 306.

15. Eberlein and Hubbard, *Historic Houses of Georgetown and Washington City,* 266; Benjamin Perley Poore, *Perley's Reminiscences of Sixty Years in the National Metropolis* (Philadelphia: Hubbard Brothers, 1886), 206, 221; Busey, *Pictures of the City of Washington,* 366–367.

16. CM II, 80–81; "Reminiscences of Washington, Part VII, the Tyler Administration," *Atlantic Monthly* 46 (1880): 534–535, 537, 542; Robert V. Remini, *Daniel Webster: The Man and His Time* (New York: W. W.

Norton and Company, 1997), 660; George T. Curtis, *Life of Daniel Webster* (New York: Appleton and Company, 1870), vol. 2: 231.

17. Mary Clemmer Ames, *Ten Years in Washington: Life and Scenes in the National Capital, as a Woman Sees Them* (Hartford, CT: A. D. Worthington & Company, 1874), 568; Vedder, *Reminiscences,* 22; "Madison's Servant."

18. Edward Coles to Sally Coles Stevenson, 12 November 1836, DMDE; John Payne Todd to Dolley Payne Madison, 31 January 1844, Papers of Dolley Madison, Manuscript Division, Library of Congress; George Waggaman to Dolley Madison, 6 October 1839, and Dolley Madison to George Waggaman, 10 October 1839, in David Mattern and Holly Shulman, *Selected Letters of Dolley Payne Madison* (Charlottesville: University of Virginia Press, 2003), 348–349; Dolley Madison to John Payne Todd, c. 1 September 1842, in Mattern and Shulman, *Selected Letters,* 359–360.

19. Sylvia Jennings Alexander interviews, 2008–2009, on file with the Montpelier Foundation; Will of Dolley Madison, 1 February 1841, in Mattern and Shulman, *Selected Letters,* 355–356.

20. "Humanity, Pity, Fraternity," *Albany Patriot,* 24 May 1848; "Madison's Servant"; "Madison's Body Servant," *Milwaukee Sentinel,* 18 May 1884.

21. Sarah Stewart to Dolley Madison, 19 December 1843, and John Payne Todd to Dolley Madison, 31 January 1844, both in Papers of Dolley Madison, Manuscript Division, Library of Congress; John Payne Todd to Dolley Madison, November 1844, in Mattern and Shulman, *Selected Letters,* 379 (note: full wording determined by examination of original letter at the Manuscript Division of the Library of Congress); Sarah Stewart to Dolley Madison, 28 April 1847, Papers of Dolley Madison, Manuscript Division, Library of Congress. That Rebecca/Becca is the same individual is clear from the 11 May 1844 letter Peter Walker sent to "Rebecca" in Washington, which Mistress Dolley docketed as to "Becca"; William Dixon to Dolley Madison, 9 July 1844, Papers of Dolley Madison, Manuscript Division, Library of Congress; Depositions of John Willis and Thomas Slaughter, 1847, Orange County Courthouse Records, Orange, VA.

22. John Payne Todd to Dolley Madison, 6 April 1844, Papers of Dolley Madison, Manuscript Division, Library of Congress; Paul Jennings to Dolley Madison, 23 April 1844, in Mattern and Shulman, *Selected Letters,* 369–370.

23. Peter Walker to Rebecca Walker, 11 May 1844, and Paul Jennings to Sukey, 13 May 1844, both Papers of Dolley Madison, Manuscript Divi-

sion, Library of Congress. For more on use of "brother" and "sister" for fictive kin, see Susan Dabney Smedes, *Memorials of a Southern Planter* (Baltimore, MD: Cushings & Bailey, 1887), 86: "[Colored people] called each other 'brer' or 'sis,' referring not to the natural relationship, but to their relationship to the church," and Green, *Secret City,* 40: "The appellation 'Brother' or 'Sis' was reserved for members of the same church as a mark of Christian fellowship."

24. Testimony of Franklin Jennings and deposition of Edmund Spotsey, *Franklin Jennings v. Elizabeth Webb,* 1896, case file #470, Records of the United States Court of Appeals, District of Columbia, Record Group 276, National Archives and Records Administration (NARA); John Payne Todd to Dolley Madison, 5 August 1844, and Paul Jennings to Dolley Madison, 6 August 1844, both Papers of Dolley Madison, Manuscripts Division, Library of Congress. The 6 August letter to Dolley Madison was dated 1845 by oversight; that it was written for Jennings by Charles Howard is based on comparison of the handwriting in Charles Howard letters to James Madison. (Of the four letters of Jennings's that can be examined, this is the only one not in his hand.)

25. Articles of Agreement between Dolley Payne Madison, John Payne Todd, and Henry W. Moncure, 8 August 1844, in Mattern and Shulman, *Selected Letters,* 373–374; Dolley Madison to George Waggaman, 10 October 1839, DMDE; two July 1844 deeds of slaves to Payne Todd: the 16 July deed is in Mattern and Shulman, *Selected Letters,* 372, and the 17 July deed is in Papers of Notable Virginia Families, Special Collections, University of Virginia. "June" rather than July was written on the first deed apparently in error, as it is clear from internal wording that the deeds were prepared a day apart (also, correcting footnote on p. 372 in *Selected Letters,* it is Raif Senr listed in the second deed); together these deeds reference forty-three men, women, and children, but sales over the next two years reduced the number of slaves held by Payne Todd and his mother to about twenty-five persons.

26. John Payne Todd to Dolley Madison, undated but c. 21 November 1844, Papers of Dolley Madison, Manuscript Division, Library of Congress; for discussion of July 1844 deeds to Payne Todd of slaves, see note 25; indenture of sale from Henry Moncure to Benjamin Thornton, Deed Book 41: 42, Orange County Courthouse Records, Orange, VA; CM II, 86; Ketcham, *James Madison,* 616; Gilberta S. Whittle (possibly a pseudonym for Willa Cather), "Smiled Amid Sorrow: Dolly Madison's Life Clouded by Scapegrace Son," *Washington Post,* 26 January 1902; on Dolley being dunned, there are many such notes from the 1840s in the

Dolley Madison Papers at the Library of Congress, including a dozen or more from the same long-standing creditor who repeatedly implores, 'Madam, will you please have the goodness to let me have something upon your sons account?'

27. CM II, 83; Dolley Madison to John Payne Todd, 17 July 1845, in Mattern and Shulman, *Selected Letters,* 381; Bryan, *History of the Capital,* vol. 2: 449; Anson and Fanny Nelson, *Memorials of Sarah Childress Polk* (New York: Anson D. F. Randolph and Company), 93.

28. William Dusinberre, *Slavemaster President: The Double Career of James Polk* (New York: Oxford University Press, 2003), 126, 25, 8; William Seale, *The President's House* (Washington, DC: White House Historical Association, 1986), vol. 1: 255–259.

29. Visitors quoted in Singleton, *Story of the White House,* vol. 1: 313–315; Seale, *President's House,* vol. 1: 268, 196; White House Curator William Allman, e-mail communication, 28 December 2009; "Scenes of the Last War—Mrs. Madison's Flight from Washington," *Cleveland Herald* (Cleveland, OH), 22 May 1849; *New York Herald* article, reprinted in the Middletown, CT, *Sentinel and Witness,* 7 May 1845.

30. Deposition of Edmund Spotsey, *Franklin Jennings v. Elizabeth Webb,* 1896; undated letter from Paul Jennings to Dolley, transcription from Holly C. Shulman, Papers of Dolley Madison Project, University of Virginia; Dolley Madison to John P. Todd, 14 June 1845, in Mattern and Shulman, *Selected Letters,* 379–380.

31. Dolley Madison to David Hume (Orange postmaster), 9 July 1845, quoted in Allen Clark, *The Life and Letters of Dolly Madison* (Washington, DC: W. F. Roberts Company, 1914), 361; drafts of documents emancipating Jennings and selling Jennings, 8 July 1845, Dolley Madison Papers, Manuscript Division, Library of Congress.

32. Dolley Madison to John P. Todd, 17 July 1845, in Mattern and Shulman, *Selected Letters,* 381; "Mrs. Madison's Slaves Again," *Albany Patriot,* 15 March 1848.

33. Payne Todd Journal, November 1845, Peter Force Collection, Manuscript Division, Library of Congress; "Mrs. Madison's Slaves Again."

34. Remini, *Daniel Webster,* 608; also see 307 on Charlotte Goodbrick, a slave purchased and freed by Webster who worked as a housemaid in Webster's Boston home and by whom he possibly fathered a son; Poore, *Perley's Reminiscences,* 282; Peter Harvey, *Reminiscences and Anecdotes of Daniel Webster* (Boston: Little, Brown, and Company, 1877), 368–369.

35. Harvey, *Reminiscences of Daniel Webster,* 310–313; 1850 federal census, Washington 4th ward (Monica McCarty listed as Monica Carter and

in the same household as another Webster servant, William Johnson); Peterson, *Great Triumvirate,* 388; Poore, *Perley's Reminiscences,* 282.

36. Curtis, *Life of Webster,* vol. 2: 329; for reasons unknown but perhaps related to Webster not wanting to advertise his act, Henry Pleasants's registration in the District of Columbia Free Negro Register makes no mention of Webster; 1850 federal census.

37. Ann Bean's age derived from her listing in Webster's own Massachusetts household in 1850 Federal Census; Harvey, *Reminiscences of Daniel Webster,* 313–315.

38. "Mrs. Madison's Slaves," article filed 19 February for *Albany Patriot,* reprinted in the *Liberator* (Boston, MA), 31 March 1848; sale of Paul Jennings to Pollard Webb, 28 September 1846, recorded 4 March 1846, Record Group 351, Records of the Government of the District of Columbia, WB 130: 281, Jennings's sale to Webb was first discovered by Michael R. Winston, who chanced upon a document relating to the sale in a private collection (personal communication, 30 August 2007); this author's locating the recordation of this transaction at NARA confirms Dr. Winston's finding; for Webster document, see note 41, below; Jennings, *Reminiscences,* iii, 15; CM I, 43.

39. Paul Jennings to Dolley Madison, 16 October 1846, and Dolley Madison to John Payne Todd, 23 April 1846, Papers of Dolley Madison, Manuscript Division, Library of Congress.

40. Adele Cutts quoted in Goodwin, *Dolly Madison,* 262; Mary Cutts to Dolley Madison, undated but approximately 1846 to 1849, Papers of Dolley Madison, Manuscript Division, Library of Congress.

41. The Webster document is known through the surviving copies of the facsimiles that were inlaid in *A Colored Man's Reminiscences of James Madison* (see chapter 7); the original document is unlocated. (It is not at Howard University's Moorland Spingarn Research Center, as is sometimes cited in error; e-mail communication with Curator of Manuscripts Joellen Elbashir, 11 January 2008). Since no entry on Jennings is included in Washington's Free Negro Register, Webster apparently never followed through on his intention to file a record. "Mrs. Madison's Slaves."

CHAPTER SIX: "HIS OWN FREE HANDS"

1. Mary Kay Ricks, *Escape on the* Pearl: *The Heroic Bid for Freedom on the Underground Railroad* (New York: William Morrow, 2007), 40; Daniel Drayton, *Personal Memoir of Daniel Drayton* (Boston: Bela Marsh, 1855), 29–30.

2. Ricks, *Escape,* 40; "Mrs. Madison's Slaves," article filed 19 February for *Albany Patriot,* reprinted in the *Liberator* (Boston, MA), 31 March 1848; "Mrs. Madison's Slaves Again," *Albany Patriot,* 15 March 1848.

3. Mary Cable, *The Avenue of the Presidents* (Boston: Houghton Mifflin Company, 1969), 88; *National Intelligencer,* Washington, DC, 27 February 1849; Sarah E. Vedder, *Reminiscences of the District of Columbia* (St. Louis, MO: A. R. Fleming Printing Company, 1909), 24.

4. Webster's house on D Street faced Louisiana Avenue, which has since been rerouted; George T. Curtis, *Life of Daniel Webster* (New York: Appleton and Company, 1870), vol. 2: 308, 310; 1850 federal census, 1853 city directory; for Sarah Smith as Webster servant, see Curtis, vol. 2: 664, and Robert V. Remini, *Daniel Webster, the Man and His Time* (New York: W. W. Norton and Company, 1997), 759.

5. While Webster occupied the house, a one-story addition was built on the western side and the entrance moved to the center; afterward an additional story was added to the structure, which about 1874 became an office building and was named the Webster Building: "Old Residences and Family History in the City Hall Neighborhood," *Records of the Columbia Historical Society of Washington, DC* 7 (1904): 155; Daniel Webster to George Ticknor, 24 January 1846, quoted in Curtis, *Life of Daniel Webster,* vol. 2: 296.

6. Frances Anne Butler, aka Fanny Kemble, *Journal of Frances Anne Butler* (London: John Murray, 1835), 120–121; Merrill Peterson, *The Great Triumverate: Webster, Clay, and Calhoun* (New York: Oxford University Press, 1987), 401, 394 for quote; Remini, *Daniel Webster,* 125, 517; Philip Hone, *The Diary of Philip Hone,* edited by Allan Nevins (New York: Dodd, Mead and Company, 1936), 728.

7. Peter Harvey, *Reminiscences and Anecdotes of Daniel Webster* (Boston: Little, Brown, and Company, 1877), 278; Benjamin Perley Poore, *Perley's Reminiscences of Sixty Years in the National Metropolis* (Philadelphia: Hubbard Brothers, 1886), 382–383, 265 quoting Poore; Hone, *Diary,* 767, 689, 737; Daniel Webster to Mr. Blatchford, 12 March 1851, in *The Private Correspondence of Daniel Webster,* edited by Fletcher Webster (Boston: Little, Brown and Company, 1857), vol. 2: 422; Cable, *Avenue,* 89.

8. Paul Jennings, *A Colored Man's Reminiscences of James Madison* (Brooklyn: George C. Beadle, 1865), 14; CM I, 7.

9. "Mrs. Madison's Slaves"; Dolley Madison to John Payne Todd, 24 April 1848, David Mattern and Holly Shulman, *Selected Letters of Dolley Payne Madison* (Charlottesville: University of Virginia Press, 2003), 387;

George Townsend, *Washington Outside and Inside* (Hartford, CT: James Betts and Company, 1874), 470–471; Smithsonian Anacostia Museum and Center for African American History and Culture, *The Black Washingtonians* (Hoboken, NJ: John Wiley & Sons, 2005), 36; Keith Melder, *City of Magnificent Intentions: A History of Washington, District of Columbia* (Washington, DC: Intac, Inc., 1983), 79; James Oliver Horton, "The Genesis of Washington's African American Community," in *Urban Odyssey: A Multicultural History of Washington, DC,* edited by Francine Curro Cary (Washington, DC: Smithsonian Institution Press, 1996), 36–37.

10. Ricks, *Escape,* 106, 9–12, 18–19; federal census and city directories data; John H. Painter [*sic*], "The Fugitives of the *Pearl,*" *Journal of Negro History* 1 (1916): 251 and fn. 9; Paul Jennings married at the John Wesley A.M.E. Zion Church in 1870, see chapter 7; G. Franklin Edwards and Michael R. Winston, "Commentary: The Washington of Paul Jennings—White House Slave, Free Man, and Conspirator for Freedom," *White House History* 1 (1983): 59.

11. Horton, "Genesis of Washington's African American Community," 37–38; Drayton, *Personal Memoir,* 28; Ricks, *Escape,* 39, 23, 25; William L. Chaplin to Gerrit Smith, 25 March 1848, Papers of Gerrit Smith, Syracuse University Library.

12. Stanley Harrold, *Subversives: Antislavery Community in Washington, D.C., 1828–1865* (Baton Rouge: Louisiana State University Press, 2003), 129, 96; federal census and city directories data show that John H. Paynter lived with his parents at 1733 L Street in 1880 when he was about eighteen, while his grandfather John Brent and great-uncle Samuel Edmonson and others with knowledge of the escape event lived in the same neighborhood; for his *Journal of Negro History* article, Paynter stated that he was limiting the article's content to the participation of the "Edmonson children"; Painter [*sic*], "The Fugitives of the *Pearl,*" 243 and fn. 3 and 13; John H. Paynter, *Fugitives of the* Pearl (Washington, DC: Associated Publishers, 1930), 2, 17.

13. The first historians in modern scholarship to connect Paul Jennings to the *Pearl* incident by citing Paynter's book were David Levering Lewis—*District of Columbia: A Bicentennial History* (New York: W. W. Norton & Company, 1976), 50–53—and G. Franklin Edwards and Michael R. Winston—"Commentary: The Washington of Paul Jennings—White House Slave, Free Man, and Conspirator for Freedom," *White House History* 1 (1983). In her 2005 book, *The* Pearl, *a Failed Slave Escape on the Potomac* (Chapel Hill: University of North Carolina Press), Josephine

Pacheco states (p. 70), without citation, that Paynter labeled his book a novel and did not intend it to be read as serious history. Evidence to the contrary, the book was published by the press Carter Woodson established for publication of African-American history, contains a scholarly introduction, and covers the same material as Paynter's earlier *Journal of Negro History* article, expanded and dramatized. While the latter element is certainly problematic, it does not cancel the book's value as historical narrative. Accounts of black activism counter the false historical impression that African Americans of the period waited on the largesse and intercession of white people and were not actively engaged as agents of change themselves. Ricks, *Escape,* 40; "Mrs. Madison's Slaves"; "Mrs. Madison's Slaves Again" (Chaplin sometimes used pseudonyms including "Hampden"); Harrold, *Subversives,* 96, 99, 154, also p. 84, fn. 37 Harrold points out that names were not mentioned as a matter of policy in Underground Railroad activities.

14. Drayton, *Personal Memoir,* 25, 26–27 quoting Foote; Paynter, *Fugitives of the* Pearl, 20–22; Painter [*sic*], "The Fugitives of the *Pearl*," 245–246; Ricks, *Escape,* 74–75; James Madison on property, 29 March 1792, PJM-CS 14: 267.

15. Paynter, *Fugitives of the* Pearl, 25–26, 34, 51–52; Pacheco, *Pearl,* 66–69; Ricks, *Escape,* 23–24, 84.

16. Stanley Harrold, "The *Pearl* Affair," *Records of the Columbia Historical Society of Washington, DC,* 50 (1980): 32; Ricks, *Escape,* 61–62, 75-76; Painter [*sic*], "The Fugitives of the *Pearl*," 247.

17. Drayton, *Personal Memoir,* 32; Paynter, *Fugitives of the* Pearl, 89; Painter [*sic*], "The Fugitives of the *Pearl*," 248–250; Harriet Beecher Stowe, *The Key to Uncle Tom's Cabin* (Boston: John P. Jewett and Company,1854), 313; Ricks, *Escape,* 102, 91.

18. Ricks, *Escape,* 86, 23–24; Pacheco, *Pearl,* 207, quotes Foote stating that the *Pearl* incident was "one of the most enormous outrages ever perpetrated on the rights of property . . . one of the most unblushing, high-handed, fiendish, outrageous attacks upon the rights of property ever existing in the District"; for more on the rioting, see Stanley Harrold, "The *Pearl* Affair: The Washington Riot of 1848," *Records of the Columbia Historical Society of Washington, DC* 50 (1980); Drayton, *Personal Memoir,* 40–41.

19. Ricks, *Escape,* chapter 5, also 183, 195; Painter [*sic*], "The Fugitives of the *Pearl*," 252, 255; Paynter, *Fugitives of the* Pearl, 178. As one of the fundraisers, Jennings may well have been present at the home of John and Elizabeth Brent where the sisters were taken by carriage

upon their release for a neighborhood celebration that went on far
into the night.

20. Ricks, *Escape,* 106, 244; Drayton, *Personal Memoir,* 121; Ricks (164,
    273) points out that Drayton's altruistic motives are exaggerated in his
    memoir, in the writing of which he was assisted by Richard Hildreth,
    a lawyer who appreciated the role Drayton's memoir could play in the
    abolitionist cause.

21. "Mrs. Madison's Slaves"; John Payne Todd to Dolley Madison, 18 Sep-
    tember 1847, in David B. Mattern and Holly C. Shulman, ed., *Selected
    Letters of Dolley Payne Madison* (Charlottesville: University of Virginia
    Press, 2003), 384.

22. *New York Tribune* Washington correspondent, article reprinted in the
    New York Evangelist, 20 April 1848; article on owners asked to come for-
    ward is dateline Washington, 19 April 1848, *New York Herald,* 21 April
    1848; Ricks, *Escape,* 132–133; Drayton, *Personal Memoir,* 58–59.

23. Dolley Madison to John Payne Todd, 24 April 1848, in Mattern and
    Shulman, *Selected Letters,* 387; William Chaplin, "Humanity, Frater-
    nity, Pity," *Albany Patriot,* 24 May 1848; Pacheco, *Pearl,* 114; Joseph
    E. Snodgrass, "Doings in Maryland," dateline Baltimore, 20 June 1848,
    North Star (Rochester, NY), 14 July 1848 (also see Ricks, *Escape,*145,
    and note that Pacheco, 109, incorrectly identifies John Slingerland as the
    person who received Ellen Stewart into freedom in Baltimore); William
    Chaplin, "Grace Russell and Ellen Madison [*sic*] Redeemed," *Emanci-
    pator* (New York, NY), 16 August 1848; Benjamin Stewart to Dolley
    Madison, 13 July 1848, Papers of Dolley Madison, Manuscript Divi-
    sion, Library of Congress.

24. Sarah Ridg, 1809 Diary, Sarah Ridg Papers, Manuscript Division, Li-
    brary of Congress; Arlington County marriage records (Alexandria
    County was renamed Arlington County in 1920); Leticia Woods Brown,
    Free Negroes in the District of Columbia, 1790–1846 (New York: Ox-
    ford University Press, 1972), fn. 84; Dorothy S. Provine, ed., *Alexandria
    County, Virginia Free Negro Registers, 1797–1861* (Bowie, MD: Heritage
    Books, 1990), 67. Also named in the Alexandria Free Negro Register
    are daughters Ann Elizabeth, Ellen, Sarah Jane, and Mary Georgiana.
    Desdemona's son Gouvenour is named in the 1850 federal census. The
    source of the Brooks surname, whether Desdemona's parent or an ear-
    lier husband, has not been determined; Sylvia Jennings Alexander inter-
    views, 2008–2009, on file with the Montpelier Foundation.

25. Daniel Webster, memorandum, 12 June 1849, and Daniel Webster
    to Caroline LeRoy Webster, 13 June 1849, in Charles M. Wiltse, ed.,

Papers of Daniel Webster, Correspondence (Hanover, NH: University Press of New England, 1984), vol. 6: 341 and 462.

26. Peterson, *Great Triumvirate,* 386–388; Curtis, *Life of Webster,* vol. 2: 664.

27. Curtis, *Life of Webster,* vol. 2: 329–331 (including Ticknor quote); also see Remini, *Daniel Webster,* 627, 642, 644.

28. CM II, 90; "Funeral of Mrs. D.P. Madison," *Weekly Herald* (New York), 21 July 1849; Charles Hurd, *Washington Cavalcade* (New York: E. P. Dutton and Company, 1948), 84; Dolley Madison's remains eventually were transported to the Madison family cemetery at Montpelier; Jennings, *Reminiscences,* 14; Sylvia Jennings Alexander interviews, 2008–2009.

29. CM II, 87; Catherine Allgor, *A Perfect Union: Dolley Madison and the Creation of the American Nation* (New York: Henry Holt and Company, 2006), 400–402; for a review of Dolley Madison's wills, see William Cabell Rives to James C. McGuire, undated but post-1849, Papers of Notable Virginia Families, Special Collections, University of Virginia; Ralph Taylor to John Payne Todd, 5 November 1849 and 4 April 1850, Dolley Madison Papers, Manuscript Division, Library of Congress; indenture for sale of Lafayette Square house from John Payne Todd to Charles Wilkes, JAS 31, Recorder of Deeds, District of Columbia, 3 April 1851.

30. CM II, 94 (including Payne Todd's last words); Clara Payne to husband John C. Payne, 15 February 1852, Sue Kort, personal collection; Townsend, *Washington Outside and Inside,* 472–473 (also see 224 for more of Townsend's take on this "class of native-born errants").

31. Gilberta S. Whittle, "Smiled Amid Sorrow: Dolly Madison's Life Clouded by Scapegrace Son," *Washington Post,* 26 January 1902; Will of John Payne Todd, 31 December 1851, Record Group 2, Superior Court, National Archives and Records Administration (NARA); Clara Payne to husband John C. Payne, 15 February 1852; summons for James C. McGuire in Petition for Freedom of Ralph Taylor and wife Catherine and their children Henry, Sarah, John, and Ellen, 12 November 1852, Record Group 21, Case Papers, 1802–1863, Civil Trials, NARA.

32. Federal censuses for 1850 and 1860, Washington City directory for 1853, compiled and published by Alfred Hunter and printed by Kirkwood and McGill, Washington, DC.

33. Alfred Chapman Papers, Southern Historical Collection, Manuscripts Department, University of North Carolina, Chapel Hill.

34. The full title for the U.S. Official Register published every second year by the Government Printing Office is *Register of Officers and Agents, Civil, Military, and Naval in the Service of the United States;* Washington

City directories; Alfred Chapman to wife Mary Chapman, 25 December 1850, Alfred Chapman Papers; *Georgia Telegraph,* 15 May 1849.

35. Stephen Forman, *A Guide to Civil War Washington* (Washington, DC: Elliot and Clark Publishing, 1995), 20; this is the same William Winder who was commanding general in the War of 1812. Mrs. John A Logan, *Thirty Years in Washington* (Hartford, CT: A. D. Worthington and Company, 1901), 468; U.S. Official Register for 1847 and 1853; Cable, *Avenue,* 84; "Principal Buildings at Washington, D.C.," *Gleason's Pictorial Drawing Room Companion,* 11 March 1854, 152.

36. Charles J. Robertson, *Temple of Invention: History of a National Landmark* (London: Scala Publishers Ltd., 2006), 39–40, 43; *Weekly Raleigh Register* (Raleigh, NC), 4 April 1855; Isabella Strange Trotter, *First Impressions of the New World on Two Travellers from the Old* (London: Longman, Brown Green, Longmans, and Roberts, 1859), 134.

37. The other three measures provided for California to be admitted to the Union as a free state, allowed the question of slavery to be determined by popular sovereignty in Utah and New Mexico territories, and stipulated that the Republic of Texas relinquish lands it claimed in present-day New Mexico while receiving $10 million to satisfy its debt to Mexico.

38. Curtis, *Life of Webster,* vol. 2: 397; Philip Hone, *Diary,* 904; Bessie Rowland James, *Annie Royall's USA* (New Brunswick, NJ: Rutgers University Press, 1972), 372.

39. Curtis, *Life of Webster,* vol. 1: 527–529; Townsend, *Washington Outside and Inside,* 470; Judge Morrel quoted in Walter C. Clephane, "The Local Aspects of Slavery in the District of Columbia," *Records of the Columbia Historical Society of Washington, DC* 3 (1900): 243; Poore, *Perley's Reminiscences,* 384–385; Peterson, *Great Triumvirate,* 395.

40. Peterson, *Great Triumvirate,* 389; Curtis, *Life of Webster,* vol. 2: 674, 677 (quoting George Ticknor), 698–699, 700–701; Remini, *Daniel Webster,* 756–757, 759. Note: Webster biographer Peter Harvey seems to conflate Ann Bean's husband, first name unknown, and William Johnson: They are two different men, and there is no evidence that Ann Bean's husband worked for Webster.

CHAPTER SEVEN: FIRST FAMILIES OF COLOR

1. Deed of indenture between Paul Jennings and John S. James and wife, 28 September 1854, recorded 15 May 1856, Liber JAS 116: 287–289, Recorder of Deeds, Washington, DC; deed of trust between Paul and

Desdemona Jennings and George McGlue, 31 October 1854, recorded 9 November 1854, Liber JAS 89: 160–163, Recorder of Deeds, Washington, DC. Although Desdemona Jennings was a party to the agreement wherein she and her husband borrowed money from George McGlue, described as trustee to John James, she was not listed as co-owner of the house itself in the deed of indenture. Charles Hurd, *Washington Cavalcade* (New York: E. P. Dutton and Company, 1948), 102.

2. City directories; Lucia Stanton, "'A Well-Ordered Household': Domestic Servants in Jefferson's White House," *White House History* 17 (2006): 19; Hurd, *Washington Cavalcade,* 98, 101; Sarah E. Vedder, *Reminiscences of the District of Columbia* (St. Louis, MO: A. R. Fleming Printing Company, 1909), 20, 62.

3. Deed of emancipation for William Jennings, Deed Book 43: 29, Orange County Courthouse Records, Orange County, VA; W. W. Scott, *A History of Orange County* (Richmond, VA: Everett Waddey Company, 1907), 172; Evelyn Bence, ed., *James Madison's Montpelier* (Orange, VA: Montpelier Foundation, 2008), 53; James Taylor to Dolley Madison, 23 June 1844, Dolley Madison Papers, Manuscript Division, Library of Congress.

4. Federal census and slave schedule data; notes on Paul Jennings, Daniel Murray Papers, Reel Five, Library of Congress; *Franklin Jennings v. Elizabeth Webb,* 1896, case file #470, Records of the United States Court of Appeal, District of Columbia, Record Group 276, National Archives and Records Administration (NARA); interviews with Sylvia Jennings Alexander, 2008–2009, on file with the Montpelier Foundation; Quintus Barber to Charles Howard, 6 September 1840, in Robert S. Starobin, ed., *Blacks in Bondage: Letters of American Slaves* (New York: New Viewpoints, 1974), 88; papers of the Grinnan and related Bryan and Tucker families of Virginia, Special Collections, University of Virginia. The three men in addition to Quintus Barber were William, Robert, and Lucian (surnames unknown).

5. Deed of emancipation for Franklin Jennings, Deed Book 44: 6, Orange County Courthouse Records, Orange County, VA. One of the slaves freed by Howard was an Ann Gordon, the same surname as Paul Jennings's wife Fanny.

6. 1854 Will of Charles P. Howard, Will Book 12: 211, and 1856 inventory of the estate of Charles P. Howard, Will Book 12: 245, Orange County Courthouse Records, Orange County, VA. While there are both a "John" and a "Jack Willis" in the inventory of slaves, the latter is most likely the John/Jack Jennings who was Paul's son, given that his middle initial was

W.; last names of individuals who migrated to Ohio include McNeal, Spotsey, Webb, Teara (?); those to Pennsylvania include Dangerfield and Barber. Hayward Jennings's birth date of August 1856 and birthplace of Virginia is from the 1900 federal census.

7. That William Jennings could read and write while his siblings could not is derived from census, military, and legal records. The 1870 census has a listing for literacy, and while Paul Jennings and son William had no check marks under "cannot read" and "cannot write," daughter Frances and son John did (Franklin is missing from the 1870 census); Frances and Franklin gave only their marks on documents (Franklin's military service records in 1864 and his 1924 will both display an "X" in place of a signature), although John provided his signature for his Freedman's Bank account in 1873; deed of release between Paul and Desdemona Jennings and George McGlue (trustee to John James), 6 May 1856, recorded 15 May 1856, Liber JAS 116: 285–287, Recorder of Deeds, Washington, DC; deed of indenture between Paul Jennings and his daughter Frances Jennings and John James and his wife, 23 November 1856, recorded 5 May 1857, Liber JAS 133: 103–105, Recorder of Deeds, Washington, DC; deed of trust between Paul and Frances Jennings and George Mc-Clue, 26 November 1856, recorded 1 January 1857, Liber 126, folio 1, Recorder of Deeds, Washington, DC; additional information on the three houses built and sold by John James is revealed in a 1858 suit that Francis Wheatley brought against James (also naming Jennings, as current owner of two of the houses, as a party), claiming he had never been fully paid for supplying lumber and other materials to the carpenter, see Chancery Case # 1403, Rules 5, Box 231, NARA.

8. Henry S. Robinson, "Some Aspects of the Free Negro Population of Washington, DC, 1800–1862," *Maryland Historical Magazine* 64 (1969): 62–63; Mary Cable, *The Avenue of Presidents* (Boston: Houghton Mifflin Company,1969), 115–116; Dorothy Provine, "The Economic Position of the Free Blacks in the District of Columbia, 1800–1860," *Journal of Negro History* 58 (1973): 63; quote from Thomas Hamilton, *Men and Manners in America* (London: Carey, Lea & Blanchard, 1833), vol. 2: 17; Constance Green, *The Secret City: A History of Race Relations in the Nation's Capital* (Princeton, NJ: Princeton University Press, 1967), 43.

9. Robinson, "Free Negro Population," 44; Stanton, "Well-Ordered Household," 19; federal census and city directories data; John H. Painter [*sic*], "The Fugitives of the *Pearl*," *Journal of Negro History* 1 (1916): 251, fn. 9, and family genealogy, 261–264; U.S. Official Register; Dorothy

Provine, *District of Columbia Free Negro Registers, 1821–1861* (Bowie, MD: Heritage Books, 1996) 430, 495; Harold T. Pinkett, *A History of John Wesley A.M.E. Zion Church* (Baltimore, MD: Gateway Press, 1989), 8.

10. "A Citizen" to Levi Woodbury, 27 August 1831, quoted at http://genealogytrails.com/washdc/bio_muse_l.html; Journal of the Senate of the U.S., 14 August 1856, accessed at Library of Congress "American Memory" Web site (http://memory.loc.gov); U.S. Official Register; Provine, "Economic Position of Free Blacks," 69–70.

11. Cable, *Avenue,* 115–116; Provine, "Economic Position of Free Blacks," 69; 1860 federal census.

12. For background, see John W. Cromwell, "The First Negro Churches in the District of Columbia," *Journal of Negro History* 7 (1922) and "Schools of the Colored Population" in *Special Report of the Commissioner of Education of the Condition and Improvement of Public Schools in the District of Columbia* (Washington, DC: Government Printing Office, 1871); 1889 Will of Catharine Taylor, District of Columbia Archives; James Oliver Horton, "The Genesis of Washington's African American Community," in *Urban Odyssey: A Multicultural History of Washington, DC,* edited by Francine Curro Cary (Washington, DC: Smithsonian Institution Press, 1996), 36; Cable, *Avenue,* 115–116; Provine, "Economic Position of Free Blacks," 72; "News from the Capital," *Philadelphia Christian Recorder,* 20 May 1861.

13. Michael Shiner, *The Diary of Michael Shiner Relating to the History of the Washington Navy Yard 1813–1869,* edited by John G. Sharp (Navy Department Library online, 2007), http://www.history.navy.mil/library/online/shinerdiary.html, 151–152; Kenneth Stampp, *America in 1857: A Nation on the Brink* (New York: Oxford University Press, 1990), 93–94.

14. Franklin Jennings testimony and Edmund Spotsey deposition, *Franklin Jennings v. Elizabeth Webb,* 1896; federal census data. A new street numbering system went into effect in Washington in 1869; before that Jennings's address was 237 L Street.

15. 1857 Will of Melinda Colbert Freeman, District of Columbia Archives. Charles Syphax and Edward M. Thomas are first listed in the neighborhood in the 1858 Boyd city directory; both (along with Jennings) are identified as laborers in the pension office, an occupation confirmed by the U.S. Official Register; E. Delorus Preston Jr., "William Syphax: A Pioneer in Negro Education in the District of Columbia," *Journal of Negro History* 20 (1935): 449–450; www.syphaxfamilyreunion.com/tree .html.

16. Federal census and city directories data; C. Peter Riley, ed., *The Black Abolitionist Papers, Volume V, 1859–1865* (Chapel Hill: University of North Carolina Press, 1991), 141, fn. 2; for Thomas and Freemasonry, see http://unitedsupremecouncilnjpha.org/page2.html.

17. Mary Jane Windle, *Life in Washington* (Philadelphia: J. B. Lippincott, 1859), 158–159; Charles Hurd, *Washington Cavalcade* (New York: E. P. Dutton and Company, 1948), 98–101; Wilhelmus Bryan, *A History of the National Capital* (New York: Macmillan Company, 1914), vol. 2: 529.

18. Hurd, *Washington Cavalcade,* 100 Cable, *Avenue,* 107, 103–104, 131; Sylvia Jennings Alexander interviews, 2008–2009; Shiner, *Diary,* 160.

19. *Franklin Jennings v. Elizabeth Webb,* 1896; Daniel Murray, *Paul Jennings and His Times: President Madison's Biographer and Valet,* Miscellaneous Manuscripts Collection 1970, Library of Congress. There is a hint of Jennings's renting his house on L Street in a quit claim deed on the property filed by Samuel Platt and wife in June 1862; see Liber JAS 218: 303–304, Recorder of Deeds, Washington, DC.

20. This author's research led to identification of the "J.B.R." of the preface of *A Colored Man's Reminiscences of James Madison,* as well as recognition of the memoir's original 1863 publication in the *Historical Magazine and Notes and Queries Concerning the Antiquities, History and Biography of America.* John Brooks Russell's birth name was John Russell Estabrook; in 1820 he legally changed his name for family reasons. Russell was a contributor to the *Historical Magazine* both before and after the Jennings's memoir; usually he used only his initials but at least once (December 1868) he provided his full name. He worked in the pension office until he transferred to the newly formed Department of Agriculture in 1868, where he became the departmental librarian; U.S. Official Register for 1861 and subsequent editions; federal census and city directory data.

21. Paul Jennings, *A Colored Man's Reminiscences of James Madison* (Brooklyn: George C. Beadle, 1865), 12; Cable, *Avenue,* 121; Stephen Forman, *A Guide to Civil War Washington* (Washington, DC: Elliot and Clark Publishing, 1995), 18–19; Charles J. Robertson, *Temple of Invention: History of a National Landmark* (London: Scala Publishers Ltd., 2006), 50.

22. Henry Louis Gates Jr., *Lincoln on Race and Slavery* (Princeton, NJ: Princeton University Press, 2009), 243, 235–241; Thomas wrote a letter to the President two days after the White House meeting and agreed to present Lincoln's colonization plan to "leading colored men" in the North (Abraham Lincoln Papers at the Library of Congress, transcribed

and annotated by the Lincoln Studies Center, Knox College, Galesburg, IL); Green, *Secret City,* 33; Shiner, *Diary,* 178.

23. Cable, *Avenue,* 132–133; Turner quoted in Letitia Woods Brown and Elise M. Lewis, *Washington from Banneker to Douglass* (Washington, DC: National Portrait Gallery, 1971), 30–31.

24. Frederick Douglass, *The Life and Times of Frederick Douglass* (Mineola, NY: Courier Dover Publications, 2003), 245; Versalle F. Washington, *Eagles on Their Buttons* (Columbia: University of Missouri Press, 1999), xii.

25. John Jennings's military service records, Record Group 94 (U.S. Colored Troops Military Service Records, 1861–1865), NARA; for training and movement of the 5th USCT, see Washington, *Eagles on Their Buttons,* and for that of the 5th Massachusetts Colored Cavalry, see John Dwight Warner Jr., "Crossed Sabres: A History of the Fifth Massachusetts Volunteer Cavalry, an African American Regiment in the Civil War," Ph.D. diss., Boston College, 1997.

26. Warner, "Crossed Sabres," 240–242; Washington, DC, enlistments were credited to Massachusetts, as all the men recruited for this cavalry regiment were, in order to reach that state's federal service quota; Franklin Jennings's and John S. Brent's military service records, Record Group 94, NARA.

27. "Siege of Petersburg," *Frank Leslie's Illustrated Newspaper,* 9 July 1864; Warner, "Crossed Sabres," 287–288; Washington, *Eagles on Their Buttons,* 41–43; Pauli Murray, *Proud Shoes: The Story of an American Family* (New York: Harper and Brothers, 1956), 143, 150–152 (Murray's grandfather fought in the 5th Massachusetts Colored Cavalry and kept a diary with many telling insights).

28. Franklin Jennings's military service records, Record Group 94, NARA; Sylvia Jennings Alexander interviews, 2008–2009; Washington, *Eagles on Their Buttons,* xii, 56.

29. John and William Jennings's military service records, Record Group 94, NARA; Samuel P. Bates, *History of Pennsylvania Volunteers, 1861–1865* (Harrisburg, PA: B. Singerly, State Printer, 1869–1871), 1010.

30. Cable, *Avenue,* 132–133; Robertson, *Temple,* 53; Forman, *Civil War Washington,* 21.

31. That the 5th Massachusetts Colored Cavalry was the first regiment into Richmond is from Dudley Cornish, *The Sable Arm: Negro Troops in the Union Army 1861–1865* (New York: W. W. Norton and Company, 1966), 282, 320, while Warner in "Crossed Sabres," 406–407, amends that slightly, stating that only General Weitzel's escort preceded the 5th

Massachusetts Colored Cavalry, which still gives the 5th the distinction of being the first regiment to enter Richmond; see Warner, "Crossed Sabres," 400, for Grant ordering the 5th to the front, 407 for quote from copying clerk, 406–407 for quote from trooper's letter; interviews with Sylvia Jennings Alexander, 2008–2009. (Many a war story has been embellished, as was Franklin's—in his telling it was General Grant himself whom Franklin set on the right road to Richmond.)

32. Cable, *Avenue,* 132–133; Noah Brooks, *Washington in Lincoln's Time: A Memoir of the Civil War Era by the Newspaperman who Knew Him Best* (New York: Century Company, 1895), 234–235.

33. John, William, and Franklin Jennings's military service records, Record Group 94, NARA; Warner, "Crossed Sabres," 420; Sylvia Jennings Alexander interviews, 2008–2009.

34. *Christian Recorder* (Philadelphia, PA), 14 March 1863, 21 March 1863, and 18 April 1863; *Daily National Intelligencer* (Washington, DC), 7 January 1865.

35. "Sale of Autographs," *Historical Magazine and Notes and Queries Concerning the Antiquities, History and Biography of America* 9 (April 1865): 136.

36. For background on Shea, see Peter Guilday, *John Gilmary Shea: Father of American Catholic History* (New York: United States Catholic Historical Society, 1926), and on Munsell, see David S. Edelstein, *Joel Munsell: Printer and Antiquarian* (New York: Columbia University Press, 1950); Joseph Sabin, *A Dictionary of Books Relating to America, from Its Discovery to the Present* (New York: J. Sabin and Sons, 1877), vol. 9: 261; "The Bladensburg Races," *Historical Magazine and Notes and Queries Concerning the Antiquities, History and Biography of America* 9 (March 1865): 104; A. Growell, *American Book Clubs* (New York: Dodd, Mead and Company, 1897), 157–161, in keeping with Growell's assertion, a copy of *A Colored Man's Reminiscences of James Madison* owned by Vassar College Library examined by this author bore the handwritten words "Presented by G.J. Shea" on the title page.

37. Jennings and Thomas are first listed as the two laborers in the pension office under the Interior Department in the 1853 edition of the U.S. Official Register.

38. U.S. Official Register; *Daily National Intelligencer* (Washington, DC), 1 January 1865; federal census and city directories data; Wesley E. Pippenger, ed., *District of Columbia Marriage Licenses, Register 2, 1858–1870* (Lovettsville, VA: Willow Bend Books, 1996); Sylvia Jennings Alexander interviews, 2008–2009.

39. Federal census and city directories data.

40. Ibid.; "Madison's Servant," *Decatur Republican* (Michigan), 14 June 1886; "Madison's Body Servant," *Milwaukee Sentinel,* 18 May 1884; "Ben Stewart Is Made to Walk the Plank by Boss Mahone," *Daily Enquirer Sun* (Columbus, GA), 23 January 1884: this article and Stewart's editorial in response, which ran in the newspaper's 29 January 1884 edition, reveal that Stewart was a porter or guide in the Senate wing of the Capitol from 1878 to 1884. Given that he held that position when he was featured in the "Madison's Servant" article, the piece must be based on an interview that was conducted two years or more before it ran in the *Decatur Republican.* In the "Madison's Body Servant" article, Stewart, as the title indicates, claims more than his due, giving his age as eighty (when he was closer to sixty) in order to place himself on the scene of the burning White House in 1814.

41. Federal census and city directories data; 1889 Will of Catharine Taylor, District of Columbia Archives; Preston, "William Syphax," 456–458; www.syphaxfamilyreunion.com/tree.html; Report of the Board of Trustees of Colored Schools of Washington and Georgetown, DC (Washington, DC: M'Gill and Witherow, 1871), accessed at Library of Congress "American Memory" Web site (http://memory.loc.gov); "The Amateur Authors" [Washington, DC public school students who applied for membership in the *Washington Post*'s Amateur Authors' Association], *Washington Post,* 9 June 1889,16. Hayward Taylor Jennings and his brother Ralph L. Jennings, both particularly light-skinned, moved to New York City as young men and "passed" for white: personal communication with Elsie Styles Harrison, and census and military records listing these individuals as white.

42. Mary Clemmer Ames, *Ten Years in Washington: Life and Scenes in the National Capital, as a Woman Sees Them* (Hartford, CT: A. D. Worthington & Company, 1874), 568; John H. McCormick, "The First Master of Ceremonies of the White House," *Records of the Columbia Historical Society of Washington, DC* 7 (1904): 181, 183; Sylvia Jennings Alexander interviews, 2008–2009; "Madison's Servant"; "Madison's Body Servant." The first-named article reports that Stewart claimed it was "my mother that cut Martha Washington's picture out of the frame with a carving knife," with "Martha" instead of "George" an apparent slip of the pen as the second-named article refers to the *George* Washington portrait (besides, there was no companion portrait of Martha Washington in the White House in 1814); Betty C. Monkman, "Reminders of 1814," *White House History* 1 (1983): see p. 225 on conservation study.

43. 1870 Will of Paul Jennings, District of Columbia Archives; Dorothy Provine, ed., *District of Columbia Marriage Records, 1870–1877* (Lovettsville, VA: Willow Bend Books, 1997), 105.

44. Ibid. federal census and city directories data (Boyd city directories for 1871 and 1872 have Jennings as bookbinder); notes on Paul Jennings, Daniel Murray Papers, Reel Five, Library of Congress; F*ranklin Jennings v. Elizabeth Webb,* 1896; Murray has 1873 as Jennings's death year, but it is repeatedly given as 1874 in the *Jennings v. Webb* court case documents; Paul Jennings's ten grandchildren and their ages at his death would be: Frances's sons Taylor, twenty-nine, and Hayward, eighteen; William's daughters Avena, seven, Sarah Matilda, four, and Anna, two; Franklin's children William, five, Hugh, three, and Ella, one; and John's children Fannie, two, and John, one.

EPILOGUE: THE RIGHT TO RISE

1. Rachel Swarns, "Madison and the White House, through the Memoir of a Slave," *New York Times,* 16 August 2009; David Montgomery, "For DC Family, a Distinguished, if Little-Known Ancestor," *Washington Post,* 25 August 2009; William Allman, White House Curator, e-mail communication, 28 December 2009.

2. James Madison to Jedidiah Morse, 28 March 1823, JMP-LC; James Madison to the Marquis de Lafayette, November 1826, JMP-LC.

3. See G. S. Boritt, *Lincoln and the Economics of the American Dream* (Memphis: Memphis State University Press, 1978).

4. James Madison to W. T. Barry, 4 August 1822, JMP-LC.

5. Unidentified1842 visitor to Montpelier, "Visit to Montpelier," *New Hampshire Patriot and State Gazette* (Concord, NH), 11 March 1850; notes on Paul Jennings, Daniel Murray Papers, Reel Five, Library of Congress; *Franklin Jennings v. Elizabeth Webb,* 1896, case file #470, Records of the United States Court of Appeals, District of Columbia, Record Group 276, National Archives and Records Administration (NARA); Sylvia Jennings Alexander interviews, 2008–2009, on file with the Montpelier Foundation; Montpelier, a National Trust site, has been administered by the Montpelier Foundation since 2000.

6. Amelia Jennings relinquishing her interest in the estate of Paul Jennings, 28 April 1879, Record Group 21, NARA; Register of Cases, p. 31, Government Hospital for the Insane, Record Group 418, NARA; St. Elizabeths Hospital was originally intended to care for the insane of the U.S. Army and Navy and indigent residents of the District of Columbia; Ste-

phen Forman, *A Guide to Civil War Washington* (Washington, DC: Elliot and Clark Publishing, 1995), 110–112.

7. *Franklin Jennings v. Elizabeth Webb,* case file #470.

8. Ibid.; "Proof of Marriage Essential: Judge Bradley Passes on the Titles to Property Formerly Owned by Slaves," *Washington Post,* 19 January 1895; "Born in Slave Wedlock," *Washington Post,* 5 February 1896.

9. Wills of Franklin Jennings (1924) and Mary Logan Jennings (1941), District of Columbia Archives; federal census and city directories data. One of Paul Jennings's direct descendants, Ellen Early Hayes, was a long-time teacher at Stevens School.

10. Solomon Northup, *Twelve Years a Slave,* edited by Sue Eakin and Joseph Logsdon (Baton Rouge: Louisiana State University Press, 1968), xii–xiv; George Forbes, "The Negro behind President Madison," *Colored American* 15–17 (1909): 217.

11. Kathleen M. Lesko, Valerie Babb, and Carroll R. Gibbs, *Black Georgetown Remembered* (Washington, DC: Georgetown University Press, 1991), 52–53, 57–59, 65, 127, 166; Raleigh Marshall interviews, 2008–2009, on file with the Montpelier Foundation.

BIBLIOGRAPHY

For manuscript sources, see Notes.

Adams, Lois Bryan. *Letter from Washington, 1863–1865.* Edited and with an introduction by Evelyn Leasher. Detroit, MI: Wayne State University Press, 1999.

Allgor, Catherine. *Parlor Politics.* Charlottesville: University Press of Virginia, 2000.

Allgor, Catherine. *A Perfect Union: Dolley Madison and the Creation of the American Nation.* New York: Henry Holt and Company, 2006.

Ames, Mary Clemmer. *Ten Years in Washington: Life and Scenes in the National Capital, as a Woman Sees Them.* Hartford, CT: A.D. Worthington and Company, 1874.

Anthony, Katharine. *Dolley Madison: Her Life and Times.* Garden City, NY: Doubleday and Company, 1949.

Austin, James T. *The Life of Elbridge Gerry.* Boston: Wells and Lilly, 1829.

Ball, Charles. *Slavery in the United States: A Narrative of the Life and Adventures of Charles Ball, a Black Man.* New York: John S. Taylor, Brick Church Chapel, 1837.

Barker, Jacob. *Incidents in the Life of Jacob Barker.* Originally published in Washington, 1855; reprinted Ann Arbor: University of Michigan Library, 2006.

Bear, James A. Jr. *Jefferson at Monticello, Recollections of a Monticello Slave and a Monticello Overseer.* Charlottesville: University of Virginia Press, 1967.

Berkeley, Edmund Jr. "Prophet without Honor: Christopher McPherson, Free Person of Color." *Virginia Magazine of History and Biography* 77 (1969).

Boritt, G. S. *Lincoln and the Economics of the American Dream.* Memphis, TN: Memphis State University Press, 1978.

Brown, Leticia Woods. *Free Negroes in the District of Columbia, 1790–1846.* New York: Oxford University Press, 1972.

Bruce, Philip Alexander. *History of the University of Virginia, 1819–1919,* Vol. 1. New York: Macmillan Company, 1920.

Bryan, Wilhelmus. *A History of the National Capital,* Vol. 1 (1790–1814) and Vol. 2 (1815–1878). New York: Macmillan Company, 1914.

Butler, Frances Anne. *Journal of Frances Anne Butler* (better known as Fanny Kemble). London: John Murray, 1835.

Burstein, Andrew, and Nancy Isenberg. *Madison and Jefferson.* New York: Random House, 2010.

Busey, Samuel. *Pictures of the City of Washington in the Past.* Washington, DC: Ballantyne and Sons, 1898.

Cable, Mary. *The Avenue of the Presidents.* Boston: Houghton Mifflin Company, 1969.

Carson, Barbara, Ellen Donald, and Kym Rice. "Household Encounters: Servants, Slaves, and Mistresses in Early Washington." In Eleanor McD. Thompson, ed., *The American Home: Material Culture, Domestic Space, and Family Life.* Winterthur, DE: Henry Francis du Pont Winterthur Museum, 1998.

Cary, Francine Curro, ed. *Urban Odyssey: A Multicultural History of Washington, D.C.* Washington: Smithsonian Institution Press, 1996.

Chambers, Douglas B. *Murder at Montpelier: Igbo Africans in Virginia.* Jackson: University Press of Mississippi, 2005.

Chester, Thomas Morris. *Thomas Morris Chester, Black Civil War Correspondent: His Dispatches from the Virginia Front.* Edited by R. J. M. Blackett. Baton Rouge: Louisiana State University Press, 1989.

Clark, Allen C. *The Life and Letters of Dolly Madison.* Washington, DC: Press of W.F. Roberts Company, 1914.

Clark-Lewis, Elizabeth. *First Freed: Washington, D.C. in the Emancipation Era.* Washington, DC: Howard University Press, 2002.

Cloquet, M. Jules. *Recollections of the Private Life of General Lafayette.* New York: Leavitt, Lord and Company, 1836.

Cornish, Dudley. *The Sable Arm: Negro Troops in the Union Army, 1861–1865.* New York: W. W. Norton and Company, 1966.

Crowninshield, Frances, ed. *Letters of Mary Boardman Crowninshield, 1815–1816.* Cambridge, MA: Riverside Press, 1905.

Curtis, George T. *Life of Daniel Webster* (2 vols.). New York: Appleton and Company, 1870.

Davis, Richard Beale, ed. *Jeffersonian America: Notes on the United States of America Collected in the Years 1805–6–7 and 11–12 by Sir Augustus John Foster, Bart.* San Marion, CA: Huntington Library, 1954.

Dixon, Joan M. *National Intelligencer Newspaper Abstracts, 1849.* Westminster, MD: Heritage Books, 2007.

Donaldson, Frances F. *The President's Square.* New York: Vantage Press, 1968.

Drayton, Daniel. *Personal Memoir of Daniel Drayton.* Boston: Bela Marsh, 1855.

Dunn, Susan. *Dominion of Memories: Jefferson, Madison, & the Decline of Virginia.* New York: Basic Books, 2007.

Dusinberre, William. *Slavemaster President: The Double Career of James Polk.* New York: Oxford University Press, 2003.

Eberlein, Harold Donaldson, and Cortlandt Van Dyke Hubbard. *Historic Houses of George-town and Washington City.* Richmond, VA: The Dietz Press, 1958.

Eckhardt, Celia Morris. *Fanny Wright: Rebel in America.* Cambridge, MA: Harvard University Press, 1984.

Edwards, G. Franklin, and Michael R. Winston. "Commentary: The Washington of Paul Jennings—White House Slave, Free Man, and Conspirator for Freedom." *White House History* 1 (1983).

Ellis, John B. *The Sights and Secrets of the National Capital.* Chicago: Jones, Junkin and Company, 1869.

Ellis, Joseph J. *Founding Brothers: The Revolutionary Generation.* New York: Alfred A. Knopf, 2004.

Fearon, Henry. *Narrative of a Journey of Five Thousand Miles through the Eastern and Western States of America.* London: Longman, Hurst, Rees, Orme, and Brown, 1818.

Featherstonhaugh, George. *Excursion through the Slave States.* New York: Harper and Brothers, 1844.

Fieser, James, ed. *The Life and Philosophy of George Tucker. Vol. 1: Tucker's Life and Writings.* Bristol, UK: Thoemmes Continuum, 2004.

Finch, John. *Travels in the United States of America and Canada.* London: Longman, Rees, Orme, Brown, Green, and Longman, 1833.

Fogle, Jeanne. *Proximity to Power.* Washington, DC: Tour De Force Publications, c. 2000.

Forbes, George. "The Negro Behind President Madison." *Colored American Magazine* 15–17 (1909).

Forman, Stephen. *A Guide to Civil War Washington.* Washington, DC: Elliot and Clark Publishing, 1995.

Gates, Henry Louis Gates Jr., ed. *Lincoln on Race and Slavery.* Princeton, NJ: Princeton University Press, 2009.

Gatewood, Willard. *Aristocrats of Color: The Black Elite.* Bloomington: Indiana University Press, 1990.

Gerry, Elbridge Jr. *The Diary of Elbridge Gerry, Jr.* Preface and footnotes by Claude G. Bowers. New York: Brentano's, 1927.

Gilpin, Henry. "A Tour of Virginia in 1827: Letters of Henry D. Gilpin to his Father." Edited by Ralph D. Gray. *Virginia Magazine of History and Biography* 76 (1968).

Goodwin, Maud Wilder. *Dolly Madison.* New York: Charles Scribner's Sons, 1896.

Gordon-Reed, Annette. *The Hemingses of Monticello: An American Family.* New York: W. W. Norton and Company, 2008.

Green, Bryan Clark, and Ann L. Miller with Conover Hunt. *Building a President's House: The Construction of James Madison's Montpelier.* Orange, VA: Montpelier Foundation, 2007.

Green, Constance McLaughlin. *The Secret City: A History of Race Relations in the Nation's Capital.* Princeton, NJ: Princeton University Press, 1967.

Green, Constance McLaughlin. *Washington: Village and Capital, 1800–1878.* Princeton, NJ: Princeton University Press, 1962.

Grigsby, Hugh Blair. *The Virginia Convention of 1829–30: A Discourse Delivered before the Virginia Historical Society on 15 September 1853.* Richmond, VA: Macfarlane and Fergusson, 1854.

Grover, Kathryn. *The Fugitive's Gibraltar.* Amherst: University of Massachusetts Press, 2001.

Hamilton, Thomas. *Men and Manners in America* (2 vols.). Philadelphia: Carey, Lea & Blanchard, 1833.

Hamlin, Talbot. *Benjamin Henry Latrobe.* New York: Oxford University Press, 1955.

Harrold, Stanley. "The *Pearl* Affair: The Washington Riot of 1848." *Records of the Columbia Historical Society of Washington, D.C.* 50 (1980).

Harrold, Stanley. *Subversives: Antislavery Community in Washington, D.C., 1828–1865.* Baton Rouge: Louisiana State University Press, 2003.

Harvey, Peter. *Reminiscences and Anecdotes of Daniel Webster.* Boston: Little, Brown, and Company, 1877.

Hines, Christian. *Early Recollections of Washington City.* Washington, DC: Junior League of Washington, reprinted 1981; original 1866.

Holland, Jesse J. *Black Men Built the Capitol.* Guilford, CT: Globe Pequot Press, 2007.

Hone, Philip. *The Diary of Philip Hone.* Edited by Allan Nevins. New York: Dodd, Mead and Company, 1936.

Hunt, Gaillard. "The First Inauguration Ball." *Century Illustrated Magazine* 69 (1905).

Hunt, Gaillard. *The Life of James Madison.* New York: Doubleday, Page and Co., 1902.

Hunt, Gaillard. "Mrs. Madison's First Drawing Room." *Harpers Monthly Magazine* (June 1910).

Hunt-Jones, Conover. *Dolley and the Great Little Madison.* Washington, DC: American Institute of Architects Foundation, 1977.

Hurd, Charles. *Washington Cavalcade.* New York: E. P. Dutton & Co., 1948.

Hutchins, Stilson, and Joseph West Moore, *The National Capital Past and Present.* Washington, DC: Post Publishing Company, 1885.

James, Bessie Rowland. *Anne Royall's U.S.A.* New Brunswick, NJ: Rutgers University Press, 1972.

Janke, Lucinda Prout. "The President's Park (Give or Take a Few Acres)." *White House History* 27 (2010).

Jennings, Paul. *A Colored Man's Reminiscences of James Madison.* Brooklyn, NY: George C. Beadle, 1865.

Johnston, Edward W. "Madison." In *Homes of American Statesmen.* Hartford, CT: O.D. Case and Co., 1855.

Johnston, James Hugo. *Race Relations in Virginia & Miscegenation in the South, 1776–1860.* Amherst: University of Massachusetts Press, 1970.

Ketcham, Ralph. "The Dictates of Conscience: Edward Coles and Slavery." *Virginia Quarterly Review* 36 (1960).

Ketcham, Ralph. *James Madison: A Biography.* Charlottesville: University of Virginia Press, 1990.

Ketcham, Ralph. *The Madisons at Montpelier: Reflections on the Founding Couple.* Charlottesville: University of Virginia Press, 2009.

Ketcham, Ralph. "Uncle James Madison and Dickinson College." In *Early Dickinsoniana: The Boyd Lee Spahr Lectures.* Carlisle, PA: Library of Dickinson College, 1961.

Klaptor, Margaret. "Benjamin Latrobe and Dolley Madison Decorate the White House." *Contributions from the Museum of History and Technology* 49 (1965).

Kolchin, Peter. *American Slavery, 1619–1877.* New York: Hill and Wang, 1993.

Knight, Henry Cogswell (published under the pseudonym of Arthur Singleton). *Letters from the South and West.* Boston: Richardson and Lord, 1824.

Leichtie, Kurt E., and Bruce Carveth. *Crusade Against Slavery: Edward Cole, Pioneer of Freedom.* Carbondale: Southern Illinois University Press, 2011.

Lesko, Kathleen M., Valerie Babb, and Carroll R. Gibbs. *Black Georgetown Remembered.* Washington, DC: Georgetown University Press, 1999.

Levasseur, Auguste. *Lafayette in America in 1824 and 1825.* Translated by Alan R. Hoffman. Manchester, NH: Lafayette Press, 2006.

Lewis, David L. *District of Columbia: A Bicentennial History.* New York: W. W. Norton & Company, 1976.

Logan, Mrs. John. *Thirty Years in Washington.* Hartford, CT: A.D. Worthington and Company, 1901.

Love, Matilda Lee. "Recollections of Matilda Lee Love." In *Lee Chronicle: Studies of the Early Generations of the Lees of Virginia* by Cazenove Gardner Lee Jr., edited by Dorothy Mills Parker. New York: New York University Press, 1957.

Lusane, Clarence. *The Black History of the White House.* San Francisco: City Lights Books, 2011.

Maguire, J. Robert, ed. *The Tour to the Northern Lakes of James Madison & Thomas Jefferson, May–June 1791.* Ticonderoga, NY: Fort Ticonderoga, 1995.

Major, Gerri, with Doris E. Saunders. *Black Society.* Chicago: Johnson Publishing Company, 1976.

Mann, Mary Lee, ed. *A Yankee Jeffersonian, Selections from the Diary and Letters of William Lee of Massachusetts Written from 1796 to 1840.* Cambridge, MA: Belknap Press of Harvard University Press, 1958.

Martin, Joseph. *New and Comprehensive Gazetteer for Virginia, and the District of Columbia.* Charlottesville, VA: Joseph Martin, 1835.

Martineau, Harriet. *Retrospect of Western Travel.* London: Saunders and Otley, 1838.

Mason, Matthew. *Slavery and Politics in the Early American Republic.* Chapel Hill: University of North Carolina Press, 2006.

Mattern, David B., and Holly C. Shulman. *Selected Letters of Dolley Payne Madison.* Charlottesville: University of Virginia Press, 2003.

McCormick, John H. "The First Master of Ceremonies of the White House." *Records of the Columbia Historical Society of Washington, DC* 7 (1904).

McCoy, Drew R. *The Last of the Fathers: James Madison and the Republican Legacy.* New York: Cambridge University Press, 1989.

McCue, George. *The Octagon.* Washington, DC: American Institute of Architects Foundation, 1976.

Melder, Keith E. *City of Magnificent Intentions: A History of Washington, D.C.* Washington, DC: Intac, Inc., 1997.

Miller, Ann L. *The Short Life and Strange Death of Ambrose Madison.* Orange, VA: Orange County Historical Society, 2001.

Murray, Pauli. *Proud Shoes: The Story of an American Family.* New York: Harper & Brothers, 1956.

Nelson, Anson and Fanny. *Memorials of Sarah Childress Polk.* New York: Anson D.F. Randolph & Company, 1892.

Northup, Solomon. *Twelve Years a Slave.* Edited by Sue Eakin and Joseph Logsdon. Baton Rouge: Louisiana State University Press, 1968.

Owen, Ralph Dornfeld. "Howard, an Early Philadelphia Family." *Pennsylvania Genealogical Magazine* 12 (1959).

Pacheco, Josephine F. *The* Pearl: *A Failed Slave Escape on the Potomac.* Chapel Hill: University of North Carolina Press, 2005.

Passonneau, Joseph R. *Washington through Two Centuries: A History in Maps and Images.* New York: Monacelli Press, 2004.

Paulding, William I. *Literary Life of J. K. Paulding,* New York: Charles Scribner and Company, 1867.

Paynter, John H. *Fugitives of the Pearl.* Washington, DC: Associated Publishers, 1930.

Painter [*sic*], John H. "The Fugitives of the Pearl." *Journal of Negro History* 1, No. 3 (June 1916).

Peterson, Merrill. *The Great Triumverate: Webster, Clay, and Calhoun.* New York: Oxford University Press, 1987.

Poore, Benjamin Perley. *Perley's Reminiscences of Sixty Years in the National Metropolis.* Philadelphia: Hubbard Brothers, 1886.

Preston, E. Delorus Jr. *William Syphax: A Pioneer in Negro Education in the District of Columbia. Journal of Negro History* 20, No. 4 (October, 1935).

Preston, William C. *The Reminiscences of William C. Preston.* Edited by Minnie Clare Yarborough. Chapel Hill: University of North Carolina Press, 1933.

Provine, Dorothy. "The Economic Position of the Free Blacks in the District of Columbia, 1800–1860." *Journal of Negro History* 58 (1973).

Provine, Dorothy S., ed. *Alexandria County Virginia Free Negro Registers, 1797–1861.* Bowie, MD: Heritage Books, 1990.

Provine, Dorothy S., ed. *District of Columbia Free Negro Registers, 1821–1861.* Bowie, MD: Heritage Books, 1996.

Qunicy, Edmund. *Life of Josiah Quincy of Massachusetts.* Boston: Fields, Osgood & Company, 1869.

Remini, Robert V. *Daniel Webster, the Man and His Time.* New York: W. W. Norton and Company, 1997.

Ricks, Mary Kay. *Escape on the* Pearl: *The Heroic Bid for Freedom on the Underground Railroad.* New York: William Morrow, 2007.

Ridg, Sarah. 1809 Diary, Sarah Ridg Papers, Manuscript Division, Library of Congress.

Riley, C. Peter, ed. *The Black Abolitionist Papers, Volumes IV (1847–1858) and V (1859–1865).* Chapel Hill: University of North Carolina Press, 1991.

Roberts, Robert. *The House Servant's Directory: An African American Butler's 1827 Guide.* Originally published in 1827. Mineola, NY: Dover Publications, 2006.

Robertson, Charles J. *Temple of Invention, History of a National Landmark.* London: Scala Publishers, 2006.

Robinson, Henry. "Some Aspects of the Free Negro Population of Washington, DC, 1800–1862." *Maryland Historical Magazine* 64 (1969).

Rutland, Robert. *James Madison, the Founding Father.* Columbia: University of Missouri Press, 1986.

Rutland, Robert, ed. *James Madison and the American Nation: An Encyclopedia.* New York: Simon and Schuster, 1994.

Scott, W. W. A *History of Orange County, Virginia.* Richmond, VA: Everett Waddey Co., 1907.

Seale, William. *The President's House,* Volumes 1 and 2. Washington, DC: White House Historical Association, 1986.

Seaton, Josephine. *William Winston Seaton of the "National Intelligencer," a Biographical Sketch.* Boston: J. R. Osgood and Company, 1871.

Shiner, Michael. *The Diary of Michael Shiner Relating to the History of the Washington Navy Yard 1813–1869.* Edited by John G. Sharp. Navy Department Library online, 2007, www.history.navy.mil/library/online /shinerdiary.html.

Singleton, Esther. *The Story of the White House.* Vol. 1. New York: McClure Company, 1907.

Smedes, Susan Dabney. *Memorials of a Southern Planter.* Baltimore, MD: Cushings & Bailey, 1887.

Smith, James Morton, ed. *The Republic of Letters: The Correspondence between Thomas Jefferson and James Madison.* New York: W. W. Norton and Company, 1995.

Smith, Margaret Bayard. *The First Forty Years of Washington Society.* Edited by Gaillard Hunt. New York: Charles Scribner's Sons, 1906.

Smithsonian Anacostia Museum and Center for African American History and Culture. *The Black Washingtonians: The Anacostia Illustrated Chronology.* Hoboken, NJ: John Wiley & Sons, 2005.

Stampp, Kenneth M. *America in 1857: A Nation on the Brink.* New York: Oxford University Press, 1990.

Stanton, Lucia. *Free Some Day: The African-American Families of Monticello.* Charlottesville, VA: Thomas Jefferson Foundation, 2000.

Stanton, Lucia. *Slavery at Monticello.* Charlottesville, VA: Thomas Jefferson Foundation, 1996.

Stanton, Lucia. "'A Well-Ordered Household': Domestic Servants in Jefferson's White House." *White House History* 17 (2006).

Starobin, Robert S., ed. *Blacks in Bondage: Letters of American Slaves.* New York: New Viewpoints, 1974.

Stowe, Harriet Beecher. *The Key to Uncle Tom's Cabin.* Boston: John P. Jewett and Company, 1854.

Tayloe, Benjamin Ogle. *Our Neighbors on La Fayette Square.* Washington, DC: Junior League of Washington reprint 1982; first published 1872.

Taylor, Francis. Diary 1786–1799. Virginia State Library, Richmond, VA.

Thornton, Anna. "Diary of Mrs. William Thornton, Capture of Washington by the British." Edited by W. B. Bryan. *Records of the Columbia Historical Society of Washington, DC* 19 (1916).

Ticknor, George. *Life, Letters, and Journals of George Ticknor, Vols. 1 and 2.* Boston: James R. Osgood and Company, 1876.

Torrey, Jesse Jr. *A Portraiture of Domestic Slavery in the United States.* Philadelphia: John Bioren, 1817.

Townsend, George. *Washington Outside and Inside.* Hartford, CT: James Betts and Company, 1874.

Trotter, Isabella Strange. *First Impressions of the New World on Two Travellers from the Old.* London: Longman, Brown Green, Longman, and Roberts, 1859.

Tyler-McGraw, Marie. *An African Republic: Black and White Virginians in the Making of Liberia.* Chapel Hill: University of North Carolina Press, 2007.

Updyke, Frank A. *The Diplomacy of the War of 1812* (2 vols.). Baltimore, MD: Johns Hopkins Press, 1915.

Vedder, Sarah E. *Reminiscences of the District of Columbia.* St. Louis, MO: A. R. Fleming Printing Company, 1909.

Walker, David. *Appeal to the Coloured Citizens of the World.* Edited and with an introduction and annotations by Peter P. Hinks. University Park: Pennsylvania University Press, 2002.

Walker, Frank S. Jr. *Remembering: A History of Orange County, Virginia.* Orange, VA: Orange County Historical Society, 2004.

Warner, John Dwight Jr. "Crossed Sabres: A History of the Fifth Massachusetts Volunteer Cavalry, an African American Regiment in the Civil War." Ph.D. diss., Boston College, 1997.

Washington, Versalle F. *Eagles on their Buttons: A Black Infantry Regiment in the Civil War.* Columbia: University of Missouri Press, 1999.

Wharton, Anne Hollingsworth. *Social Life in the Early Republic.* Philadephia: J. B. Lippincott and Company, 1902.

Windle, Mary Jane. *Life in Washington.* Philadelphia: J. B. Lippincott and Company, 1859.

INDEX

and James Madison, xvi, xix–xxiii, 65, 70,
    72–5, 78, 92, 98, 111–30, 230–6
and Daniel Webster, xxi, 106–9, 156–60,
    162–5, 176–83, 186, 214
republicanism, 7, 16, 39, 43, 67, 95, 99
Richmond, 109–17
Ricks, Mary Kay, 168
Rives, Judith, 135, 138
Russell, John Brooks ("J.B.R."), 204–5, 226

Sawney (Montpelier slave), 4–5, 21, 23, 28,
    81, 112–13
Sayres, Edward, 169, 172–4
Seaton, Sarah, 39, 47
Seaton, William, 39
Shea, John Gilmary, 214, 226
Shiner, Michael, 41–2, 52, 142, 199, 206
Shorter, John, 55
Sioussat, John, 37–8, 52–3, 55, 79, 137,
    218–19
slave insurrections, 50, 92, 138–9, 142
slave narratives, xix–xxiii
slave trade, xv–xvi, xix, 4–5, 17, 42–4, 57, 88,
    90–4, 103, 112–15, 124–5, 132–3,
    140–1, 147–60, 162–3, 167, 172–5,
    187, 192–4
Slavemaster President: The Double Career of
    James Polk (Dusinberre), 153
Smith, Gerrit, 167–8, 173
Smith, Robert, 230
Smith, Samuel H., 45
Smith, Sarah, 163, 182, 188–9
Smith, James, 51, 231
Smith, John Cotton, 8–9
Smith, Margaret Bayard, 45, 50, 66, 74,
    77–8, 81, 121–2, 140
Smithsonian American Art Museum, 185
Snodgrass, Joseph E., 176
Snow Riot, 142, 166
Spotsey, Edmund, 89, 122, 151, 225
Spotswood, Alexander, 2
St. Mary's College, 24
Stevens School, 218, 226
Stevenson, Andrew, 110, 234
Stevenson, Sally Coles, 54, 109–10, 234
Stewart, Benjamin, 7, 81–2, 119–21, 146,
    148–9, 152, 216–17
Stewart, Ellen, 148–50, 161–3, 165, 168–9,
    172, 174–6
Stewart, Juno, 216
Stewart, Sarah, 149–50
Stowe, Harriet Beecher, 173

Stuart, Gilbert, 35, 98
Sukey/Susan (Dolley's maid), 7, 28–9, 32, 36,
    45, 47, 50–1, 81, 97–8, 119–20, 125,
    128, 130–1, 139–40, 147–52, 161,
    174–6, 219, 231–3, 236
"Summer White House," 16–18
Syphax, Charles, 201–2, 217
Syphax Sr., Charles S., 201
Syphax, Colbert, 217
Syphax, Nancy, 141, 145, 201
Syphax, William, 217–18

24th United States Colored Troops (USCT),
    210
Tayloe, Benjamin Ogle, 73, 140
Tayloe, John B., 52, 233
Taylor, Catharine ("Caty"), 91, 152, 182
Taylor, Dr. Charles, 63
Taylor, Erasmus (Madison's great uncle), 3,
    13, 87–8
Taylor, Francis, 12, 63, 90
Taylor, Jane Moore (Madison's great aunt),
    12–13
Taylor, James (Madison's maternal great-
    grandfather), 2, 13
Taylor, Ralph, 91, 152, 160, 182
Taylor, Robert, 12–13, 132
Taylor, William, 124–5
Taylor, Zachary, 143, 180
Ten Years in Washington (Ames), 146
"term slavery," 42
Texas annexation, 146
Third Division (Army of the James), 208–9
Thirteenth Amendment, 215
Thomas, Edward M., 201–2, 213, 229
Thornton, Anna, 34–5, 45, 51–2, 142
Thornton, William, 34
Ticknor, Anna, 106
Ticknor, George, 53, 106–8, 163, 179, 188–9
Todd, John, 9
Todd, Payne (Madison's stepson), 24–5, 35,
    48, 55–6, 82–3, 97, 102, 111–13, 135,
    137, 155, 181–2, 213
Toddsberth, 152
Torrey, Jesse, 57–60, 105–6
Townsend, George, 181
Treaty of Ghent (1814), 53–4
Tripoli wars, 140
Trotter, William Monroe, 226
Tucker, George, 119
Turner, Henry McNeal, 206–7
Turner, Nat, 138–9, 142, 223